THE ANTHROPOLOGY OF LABOR UNIONS

THE ANTHROPOLOGY OF LABOR UNIONS

EDITED BY E. Paul Durrenberger and Karaleah S. Reichart

UNIVERSITY PRESS OF COLORADO

Published by the University Press of Colorado
5589 Arapahoe Avenue, Suite 206C
Boulder, Colorado 80303

Printed in the United States of America

The University Press of Colorado is a proud member of
the Association of American University Presses.

The University Press of Colorado is a cooperative publishing enterprise supported, in part, by Adams State College, Colorado State University, Fort Lewis College, Mesa State College, Metropolitan State College of Denver, University of Colorado, University of Northern Colorado, and Western State College of Colorado.

∞ The paper used in this publication meets the minimum requirements of the American National Standard for Information Sciences—Permanence of Paper for Printed Library Materials. ANSI Z39.48-1992

Library of Congress Cataloging-in-Publication Data

The anthropology of labor unions / E. Paul Durrenberger and Karaleah S. Reichart, editors.
p. cm.
Includes bibliographical references and index.
ISBN 978-0-87081-965-0 (hardcover : alk. paper) 1. Labor unions—History. 2. Labor unions—Political activity—History. 3. Labor unions—United States—History. I. Durrenberger, E. Paul, 1943– II. Reichart, Karaleah S.
HD6451.A58 2010
331.880973—dc22

2009047987

Design by Daniel Pratt

18 17 16 15 14 13 12 11 10 09 10 9 8 7 6 5 4 3 2 1

Contents

THE ANTHROPOLOGY OF LABOR UNIONS

ONE

Introduction

E. Paul Durrenberger and Karaleah Reichart

The Anthropology of Labor Unions in a Global Political Economy

This collection is a move toward a definition of an anthropology of unions. Questions about unions can only arise in complex social orders with class structures that define incompatible interests between owners of capital and workers. Unions only come into existence when those with privileged access to resources hire others to create value the owners can appropriate for their own use. When those without privileged access to resources organize to identify, promote, and protect their interests, labor unions are born.

Most studies of unions are developed from historical perspectives or are based on national data sets collected by government agencies. Few use the defining method of socio-cultural anthropology: ethnography, which has much to teach us about the nature of unions. The studies in this book bring ethnographic methods to bear on unions. Anthropology is also comparative. The authors in this volume situate their individual ethnographies within a broader comparative framework that tells us what the ethnography of unions can contribute to a broader anthropology of contemporary states.

While most of the works in this collection address labor unions inside the United States and look outward from that perspective toward its global supply and production lines, the picture would look quite different through a view from the South (such as Zlolniski sketches), from Africa (as Otañez develops), or from Europe. In Northern Europe, for instance, jobs are more stable than they are in the United States; although "structural" unemployment is high in countries such as Germany, the state is more supportive of working-class organizations than the North American state has ever been. We cannot go into the details of such a comparison here, but we hope to lay the groundwork for comparative studies of unions within a larger global framework.

The postindustrial United States is the site of six of the book's eight studies, inviting regional comparisons as well as suggesting national trends. The other two chapters describe working life among people in two countries that provide some of the lowest wages in the global labor market: Mexico and Malawi. The globalization of manufacturing as well as agricultural products such as vegetables from Mexico and tobacco from Malawi is a component of a larger global process of integration promoted by the Bretton Woods agreements that were intended to provide stability after World War II. These international agreements have resulted in the normalization of neo-liberal economic policies of free trade and a race to reduce labor costs by exporting manufacturing and production of raw materials. These processes have resulted in the exportation of manufacturing jobs to low-wage markets and the immigration of people from low-wage lands to Europe and North America. Both processes pose challenges for the American labor movement.

Ethnography is local, so each study in this book discusses a local response to these issues of globalization. Although we do not explicitly develop them, regional comparisons within the United States could develop the themes the local ethnographies discuss—for instance, the place of rugged individualism and the American myth in the "right-to-work" states of the West that Smith discusses in her ethnographic treatment of miners in Wyoming versus eastern states with longer traditions of unionism such as Reichart discusses in her ethnography of West Virginia miners. The question of regional differences in the role of religion in U.S. politics and culture comes to the fore in Smith-Nonini's treatment of farmworkers in North Carolina. Likewise, the comparison of agricultural workers in North Carolina with those on the California border arises from Zlolniski's description of agricultural production in Baja California. The mutual dependency of transnational corporations and state-sponsored unions that Otañez and Zlolniski discuss illustrates the power of global political and economic forces when national elites give them free reign to keep their citizens living and working in serf-like conditions. Matters of place are the central focus of Savage's discussion of how a union is but one dimension of the complex lives of its members. Zlolniski points to similar gender issues of the timing of agricultural and domestic work that Savage discusses in connection with healthcare work and domestic duties.

In addition to the insight these studies provide into processes of globalization, they offer a privileged window through which to study the processes of class as they unfold over time and across space. Unions are perforce a phenomenon of class. The study of unions therefore helps elucidate the operation of classes in stratified social orders.

Collective Action

Unions are a form of collective action to achieve shared goals. These chapters focus on unions as such rather than on collective action. The topic of collective action is important in anthropology because it has played such a large role in both our biological and our cultural evolution (Goldschmidt 2005) and poses significant questions for academic reflection as well as practical action (Acheson 2003). Several questions resonate through the studies in this volume, including:

- What happens to unions that are denied a collective goal? How can they organize members for collective action when collective action is not available to them?
- How do organizations pursue collective goals in the face of strong opposition?
- How do members whose individual interests are not being directly served but who are financing collective action conceive of such collective action, and to what extent should they support it to achieve longer-term, more abstract goals?

All these questions are important from the standpoint of theory as well as practice. Anthropologists agree that culture is collective, although they may question what groups of people share it, as Ulf Hannerz (1996) does. But there is quite a leap from collective thought to collective action.

Economic theorists distinguish categories of goods according to two continuous criteria: (1) excludability—how easy it is to deprive others from using the resource, and (2) subtractability—the extent to which one person's use of a resource precludes someone else from using it (Ostrom 1998). The intersection of these two criteria defines a four-by-four table of possibilities:

		Subtractability	
		high	low
Excludability	difficult	common pool	public
	easy	private	toll

Those goods from which it is difficult to exclude others' use and that are highly subtractable are common-pool resources. The classic example is fisheries resources (Acheson 2003). If one person takes fish from the sea, there are fewer for the next; further, it is difficult to police the seas. Goods with low subtractability and that are difficult to exclude others from using (excludability) are public goods. Police protection and education are examples Elinor Ostrom (1998) develops. If everyone enjoys the good and it is not possible to exclude anyone from its enjoyment, there must be some form of organization to produce the good. The typical "solution" is institutional structures to tax those who benefit from that good. The other two categories of goods are private property (high subtractability, easy excludability) and toll goods (low subtractability, easy excludability).

Cultural usage and public policy define subtractability and excludability, so different polities or cultural usages may define the same goods in different ways. For instance, in medieval Iceland there was no institutionalized state to easily exclude others from using the land one claimed. Claims to exclusivity could only be enforced by whatever force one could muster through coalitions of armed fighters. Thus land could not be considered private property and, according to this scheme, was more like a common-pool resource with a private boundary defense, as James Acheson (2003) has described for lobstermen in Maine.

Until Iceland's contemporary government enacted a system of Individual Transferable Quotas (ITQs) in 1990 that redefined fish as private property, fish were a common-pool resource. The ITQ policy, however, transformed them into private property. After September 11, 2001, the Bush administration and the U.S. Congress agreed that airport security should be a public good, provided by the government to benefit all citizens, rather than a private or toll good provided by airline companies for the benefit of their passengers.

Bonnie McCay (1998:193) has observed that the conclusions of Ostrom and similar theorists are limited by the "high and sometimes misleading levels of abstraction from empirical cases" that often omit significant details of how political and economic factors are embedded in social relations and cultural constructs. She further believes their perspective is narrowly focused on institutions as constraints that define rules of the game rather than on how institutions both restrain and empower people and establish values that create sense and meaning. The works in this volume contribute empirical ethnographic work on unions to provide more adequate data upon which to base such theories of collective action.

None of the collective action theorists contemplates a scenario in which people successfully organize to achieve collective class goals against a different class that responds by changing laws and culture to undo those achievements and thwart further collective action. None of these theorists contemplates class warfare on behalf of the capitalist class.

The contributions to this book are more concerned with how, and under what circumstances, unions do or do not achieve their goals. Rather than defining the topic as an economic or a political abstraction, we have examined it using the traditional method of ethnography: participant observation. Several of the chapters are self-consciously first-person accounts (Smith, Smith-Nonini, Durrenberger and Erem), while others, although equally based on firsthand observation, take a more distanced view (Richardson, Zlolniski, Otanez, Reichart). These are not romantic or nostalgic celebrations of great victories of the working class (although we would like to edit that book someday); that is not what we and our colleagues have been seeing in our ethnographic work. We instead see successful corporate co-optation of issues such as international child labor (Otanez), wages, benefits and safety (Smith), and even the epistemological definition of what jobs are (Richardson). But we also see union organizers building personal relationships with members to build strength in the workplace based on a community of common interests (Savage).

The Role of State Policy

We have mentioned the works of Zlolniski and Otañez that depict the role of corporate-friendly state policies in the formation of conditions of work and in the emasculation of unions in Mexico and Malawi. In the United States, the 1947 Taft-Hartley amendments to the Wagner Act of 1935 inhibited union organization by focusing on the servicing functions of negotiating contracts and handling grievances (Bronfenbrenner et al. 1998). Employers' political and workplace actions introduce other institutional impediments (Wells 1996). In short, any union faces massive opposition because the rules at all levels are designed to oppose them. In some jurisdictions, the arenas of action such as labor boards are equally arraigned against effective union action (Wells 1996).

The academic literature does not discuss the consequences of the capture of public apparatus for the benefit of private interests—for example, the use of armed forces to suppress labor action (Saitta 2007; Reichart, this volume)—or the outsourcing of functions such as police, education, and military or government bailouts of irresponsible lending agencies to preserve their grasp on wealth at the public's expense. Collective action theorists seem to see these matters as parts of natural processes rather than as historically given cultural or political matters as those who act for collective interests, whether on behalf of the capitalist or the working class, struggle for control of the apparatus of the state—the power to make and enforce law and regulations.

The characteristics of goods, excludability and subtractability, do not occur in nature; they are not given by the nature of things but are culturally defined. Where states shape usage through policy and enforcement, policy determines the nature of goods. Thus policy defines whether union representation is a collective good.

Policy may require all workers in a place to belong to a union and to pay dues to support its operation. This is familiar in the corporatist states of Scandinavia, but in the United States it is called a "closed shop." The Taft-Hartley amendments forbade the practice unless a majority of workers in a place voted in favor of it. Even that was too strong for business interests, however, and the law was changed in 1951 so they could support "right-to-work" legislation in their states. In the one-third of states that have passed such legislation, unions can represent workers, but workers are not required to pay for union services (including any increased wages, benefits, and leaves they receive through the union-negotiated contract). So these laws do not prohibit collective action but instead prohibit those who organize such action from forcing its beneficiaries to pay for it, unlike the way a state can force its citizens to pay through taxation. Thus, those workers who are union members pay for the services the union provides for all their non–dues-paying fellow workers.

Other states require that workers pay at least their fair share of the costs, usually defined as a large portion of union dues. Still other states require that if workers at a site elect a union to represent them, all workers must be members and must pay dues, as in a closed shop. Thus states within the United States define different collective action rules for unions.

An argument for closed shops is that everyone should pay for the benefits they receive. An argument against them is that requiring such payment is an infringement of individual rights. The analogue for airport security might be that searching any individual passenger is an infringement of that person's individual rights. The counterargument would be that the individual must waive that right to ensure security for all. The right-to-work legislation is analogous to asking only those passengers who elect to be searched to pay for the privilege or asking those on the ground who feel directly threatened by the possibility of being blown up by a hijacked airplane to pay for the protection they receive.

For unions, the financial issue includes the institutional wherewithal to pay people to negotiate and enforce contracts. Thus unions in right-to-work states face a dilemma—whether to expend resources to bargain on behalf of all workers in a worksite in which only some of the members pay for the benefits or to represent no workers in that bargaining unit. Many opt for the former, in the hope that in the long term the majority will pay their way and the union will grow strong enough and have enough political influence to change the right-to-work law. Clearly this approach imposes costs on members in return for very long-term and often abstract goals. This is a problem unions representing agricultural workers in Mexico also face, as Zlolniski discusses.

Organizers in right-to-work states appeal to the morality of the people they represent and show them the differences the union makes in their work lives in terms of pay, benefits, and working conditions. As a final recourse, organizers mention that while unions are required by law to represent all workers who have grievances, regardless of whether they pay for that representation, unions are not required to represent them in bargaining contracts that give them those benefits. Thus if larger portions of the workers in other divisions are dues-paying members, the union will bargain more aggressively for their interests. Finally, only dues-paying members may vote on whether to ratify and accept the contract union representatives reach with management.

Unions represent workers in such situations to gain some influence in those workplaces while pushing for long-term legislative changes that would more greatly favor unions. When the legislation does change, either because of lobbying or the replacement of legislators, the union will be in place to reap the benefits. Like community police and school functions (Ostrom 1998), unions rely on co-production among members for the public good—the people who benefit from the service must help produce it. Members must provide negotiating teams to assist in negotiating contracts and provide stewards to help enforce them once they are in place.

Dilemmas

One of the dilemmas of the contemporary union movement is that the ability to negotiate and enforce contracts depends largely on the power of unions to control certain segments of the labor market. This has been a traditional element of the skilled-trades unions such as carpenters and plumbers, who now see their ability to maintain good wages eroded by an influx of non-union competition. But it is also a factor in organizing less-skilled workers. This was a major issue when mining operations began to open in Wyoming, the topic of Smith's chapter in this book.

The urban service industry provides another example. If all in-house and contracted janitors in an area belong to a union, that union has the power to negotiate good contracts for all. But if only some janitors belong to the union, employers have the option of using nonunion workers or contractors. This was the difference between the very favorable pay and benefits downtown Chicago janitors enjoyed in the late 1990s compared with the unhappy working conditions of suburban janitors. Thus one of the goals of Chicago's SEIU Local 1, which E. Paul Durrenberger (2002) studied in the late 1990s, was to organize all suburban janitors in an effort to protect the downtown janitors' higher wages and benefits.

Some, such as the workers Smith discusses, may believe their skill isolates them from the threat of easy replacement. Historically, though, capital replaces labor; examples include the containerization of freight (Erem and Durrenberger 2008), the automation of butchering and meat packing that replaced skilled butchers with unskilled labor (Stull, Boradway, and Griffith 1995), and the automation of automobile manufacturing, as Richardson discusses in this book.

Organizing all workers in an industry or industrial sector requires resources that might otherwise be used to provide services to current members. This poses one collective action dilemma because it imposes costs on current members for the long-term future benefit of the collective. With their dues, current members underwrite the organization of future members. It was the dues of the United Mine Workers of America in West Virginia that Reichart discusses that paid for the organizers who tried to organize the miners in Wyoming that Smith describes. Why would West Virginia miners pay to organize miners in Wyoming?

Leaders recognize this dilemma in their discussions of the benefits and costs of what they call the "servicing model," which concentrates on negotiating and policing contracts, versus the "organizing model," which shifts resources from such services to organizing—a longer-term and more abstract goal (Durrenberger 2002). Ethnographic work suggests that while leaders are aware of these dilemmas and favor longer-term goals, members favor the servicing model (Durrenberger and Erem 1999a, 1999b, 2005).

Chicago union stewards' knowledge of available actions and outcomes is determined by the day-to-day realities at their worksites, not by the programs of their unions. Members judge actions to be more or less reasonable insofar as they affect conditions at their workplaces. Thus they hold that such actions as registering people to vote or using union resources for political action are not as reasonable as resolving grievances (Durrenberger 2002), even though their unions are making more resources available for organizing and political action (Durrenberger and Erem 1999a, 1999b).

Anthropology and the Union Movement Today

Where is the union movement today, after more than a hundred years? In the summer of 2005 the venerable American Federation of Labor–Congress of Industrial Organization (AFL-CIO) split into the successor AFL-CIO and the Change to Win Federation. This ineffectiveness stems from the alliance of unions with capital that Samuel Gompers (1850–1924) and his successors in the labor movement developed. This alliance disguised and denied both the existence of classes and the necessity of class struggle and also curtailed traditions of direct action (Fletcher and Gapasin 2008). The Taft-Hartley amendments defined collective bargaining agreements as enforceable contracts between the unions and management. Unions became responsible for seeing that their members adhered to the contracts, especially not striking during the term of the contract. Corporate America had bought labor peace, and unions became bureaucracies for resolving grievances that arose between workers and management. From the workers' point of view, unions were like insurance companies to protect them against arbitrary management actions (Durrenberger and Erem 2005).

These policies reoriented unions from constantly organizing workers to maintain strength in worksites and to develop a nationwide and worldwide workers' movement to negotiating and enforcing contracts and handling grievances. Unions became professionalized bureaucracies whose leaders were hard to distinguish from their counterparts in the corporate world—management bosses.

Another policy change undid even the pretense of the power of labor. Starting with Ronald Reagan's busting of the air traffic controllers' union in 1981, there has been an organized attack on unions in the United States. Having become as complacent as C. Wright Mills (1951) suggested they would, unions have failed to respond effectively to the assault, and corporate interests have organized even more virulent collective action for attacking unions (Brodkin and Strathmann 2004). A multimillion-dollar industry of anti-union consulting has grown in the United States since the 1990s. John Logan (2002, 2006) has shown that two of every three organizing efforts will face the opposition of such firms, and unions have yet to develop a successful response beyond collusion with management in so-called top-down organizing.

Although unions can be vehicles for industrial democracy (Smith, Savage), the chapters in this book document failures of democracy (Durrenberger and Erem) as well as failures of unions (Smith, Richardson, Otañez, Zlolniski, Reichart). Some are co-opted by corrupt states (Zlolniski) or by corporate strategies (Otañez, Smith). In her chronicle of a successful union campaign, Smith-Nonini holds out hope to gain popular community support. That hope was blunted, however, by an e-mail message she sent on April 14, 2007, as we wrote these lines, carrying the news of the murder in Mexico of an organizer from the union with which she worked. But Savage's story of organizing a hospital shows the promise of grassroots organizing to build a community of interest and support among members.

As global warming becomes a daily topic of discussion, sustainability is present in college curricula, and American lives and treasures are squandered on an irrational war for oil in Iraq and a massive bailout of irresponsible and unregulated financiers, one need not accept adaptationist paradigms to understand some of Roy Rappaport's cautions about the relationships among truth, power, complexity, class, and sustainability. Rappaport (1979) argued that adaptation depends on accurate information. Differentials in power amplify the human ability to lie that communication-based symbolization confers. Because adaptation relies on truth, power undermines it with its potential for actions based on untruth. As societies become more differentiated, the more powerful are able to elevate their goals above those of all others. Symbolization brings consciousness and makes it possible to value reason, which is often self-serving. Economics, Rappaport pointed out, defines rationality as competitive activities that pit people against each other and is, by necessity, antisocial. These rational acts are "the application of scarce means to differentially graded ends to maximize the position of the actor vis-à-vis others" (Rappaport 1979:236).

Dimitra Doukas (2003) has shown that economics as a discipline is an important component of the corporate-sponsored cultural revolution that has been under way in the United States since the late nineteenth century. As the economist John Kenneth Galbraith (1992) has pointed out, economics carries an aura of sanctity, as it justifies corporate rapacity as natural and inventible. Thus is the relationship between sanctity and authority inverted. Authority is not contingent on sanctity, but sanctity has become an instrument of authority in defending the position of the privileged class. In complex systems, because authority distorts information, it is maladaptive.

Rappaport observed that power threatens truth and thus the cybernetics of adaptation. He (1979:237) observed that the theology of Buber's I-thou is not so much an ethical dictum as an ecological imperative. This puts democracy and its failures at the center of any meaningful research agenda for anthropology of complex societies.

Eric Wolf (1999, 2001) spent his life studying these questions and saw class and power as central to any understanding of culture. As Aram Yengoyan (2001:x) put it, "[C]ulture is fully embedded in power relations, nothing is neutral in modes of control, and, thus, social-structural relations are all marked by a differential defined by who controls what and who controls whom."

As anthropologists have studied these processes in complex societies, they have observed class and power. Some have focused on unions to understand not only the prospects for but also the failures of collective action.

The logic of unions is collective even if the practice is not. Individual workers in complex orders have virtually no agency or power apart from what the process of selling their labor confers. For any individual, that is insignificant. But the more individuals act for their common interests, the greater the power of the organization. Recognizing that power, corporations have successfully transformed law, practices (Smith), and appearances (Otañez) to counter it and manufactured the ideologies that justify, even sanctify their actions.

The anthropologists in this book have all seen these processes at work in industrial agriculture (Zlolniski, Otañez, Smith-Nonini), manufacturing (Richardson), mining (Smith, Reichart), transportation (Durrenberger and Erem), and healthcare (Savage).

We are not writing a manual for labor unions. We would if we could, but no anthropologist who has observed the hardworking and highly intelligent staff of today's labor movement thinks he or she has much to say to them that they don't already know. Even if we did, they wouldn't have time to read it. If perchance they did read it, it would just make them angry because we would be stating what to them is obvious. There is the other kind of union leader, the one who acts like Rappaport's holder of power in complex systems, who obfuscates realities and inhibits the collective action of his or her own members at the expense of the entire movement. Like their virtuous counterparts, these leaders wouldn't have the time or the inclination to hear any sermons from the holier-than-them.

But we have no compunction about speaking to our fellow anthropologists to call their attention to the importance of class, context, policy, law, power, and culture in understanding complex societies and the unions that strive to find a place within them. When we turn to understanding the constrictions on agency and thought these structures impose on workers, we have to understand their unions as one other context of power. It may be in Rappaport's sense virtuous, but it need not be. It may be obfuscatory, but it need not be. It may be collaborative with corporations, but it need not be. Such possibilities define the contexts for our research and the questions we ask.

To quote Rappaport (1979:243) again, "[T]he generation of the lie is continuously challenged by the living—by prophets, mystics, youth, revolutionaries, and reformers—who, in their search for wholeness, restore holiness ever again to the breaking world by re-establishing the adaptive connection of the timeless sacred and the immediate numinous to the continuing here and now." This, too, is our task in our study of anthropology and of unions.

Individually focused union practices have not inculcated in members the view that their own collective action creates the power to stand against the power of ownership and wealth. We will return to some of these questions in the Concluding Thoughts.

All but one of the chapters in this collection were originally presented as a session at the 2005 meeting of the American Anthropological Association. Lydia Savage's chapter was added later. The authors have since rewritten the chapters, and we have edited them for publication in this volume.

References Cited

Acheson, James M.

2003 *Capturing the Commons: Devising Institutions to Manage the Maine Lobster Industry*. Hanover, NH: University Press of New England.

Brodkin, Karen, and Cynthia Strathmann

2004 The Struggle for Hearts and Minds: Organization, Ideology, and Emotion. *Labor Studies Journal* 29(3): 1–24.

Bronfenbrenner, Kate, Sheldon Friedman, Richard W. Hurd, Rudolph A. Oswald, and Ronald L. Seeber

1998 Introduction. In *Organizing to Win: New Research on Union Strategies*, ed. Kate Bronfenbrenner, Sheldon Friedman, Richard W. Hurd, Rudolph A. Oswald, and Ronald L. Seeber, 1–15. Ithaca: Cornell University Press.

Doukas, Dimitra

2003 *Worked Over: The Corporate Sabotage of an American Community*. Ithaca: Cornell University Press.

Durrenberger, E. Paul

2002 Structure, Thought, and Action: Stewards in Chicago Union Locals. *American Anthropologist* 104(1): 93–105.

Durrenberger, E. Paul, and Suzan Erem

1999a The Weak Suffer What They Must: A Natural Experiment in Thought and Structure. *American Anthropologist* 101(4): 783–793.

1999b The Abstract, the Concrete, the Political, and the Academic: Anthropology and a Labor Union in the United States. *Human Organization* 58(3): 305–312.

2005 *Class Acts: An Anthropology of Urban Service Workers and Their Union*. Boulder: Paradigm.

Erem, Suzan, and E. Paul Durrenberger

2008 *On the Global Waterfront: The Fight to Free the Charleston 5*. New York: Monthly Review Press.

Fletcher, Bill, and Fernando Gapasin

2008 *Solidarity Divided: The Crisis in Organized Labor and a New Path toward Social Justice*. Berkeley: University of California Press.

Galbraith, John Kenneth
1992 *The Culture of Contentment.* New York: Houghton Mifflin.

Goldschmidt, Walter
2005 *The Bridge to Humanity: How Affect Hunger Trumps the Selfish Gene.* New York: Oxford University Press.

Hannerz, Ulf
1996 *Transnational Connections: Culture, People, Places.* New York: Routledge.

Logan, John
2002 Consultants, Lawyers, and the "Union Free Movement" in the US since the 1970s. *Industrial Relations Journal* 22(3): 197–214.
2006 The Union Avoidance Industry in the United States. *British Journal of Industrial Relations* 44(4): 651–675.

McCay, Bonnie
1998 *Oyster Wars and the Public Trust: Property, Law, and Ecology in New Jersey History.* Tucson: University of Arizona Press.

Mills, C. Wright
1951 *White Collar: The American Middle Classes.* New York: Oxford University Press.

Ostrom, Elinor
1998 The Comparative Study of Public Economies. Memphis, TN, Rhodes College, acceptance paper for the Frank E. Seidman Distinguished Award in Political Economy.

Rappaport, Roy
1979 *Ecology, Meaning, and Religion.* Berkeley: North Atlantic Books.

Saitta, Dean J.
2007 *The Archaeology of Collective Action.* Gainesville: University Press of Florida.

Stull, Donald, Michael J. Boradway, and David Griffith, editors
1995 *Any Way You Cut it: Meat Processing in Small-Town America.* Lawrence: University Press of Kansas.

Wells, Miriam
1996 *Strawberry Fields: Politics, Class, and Work in California Agriculture.* Ithaca: Cornell University Press.

Wolf, Eric R.
1999 *Envisioning Power: Ideologies of Dominance and Crisis.* Berkeley: University of California Press.

Wolf, Eric R., and Sydel Silverman, editors
2001 *Pathways of Power: Building an Anthropology of the Modern World.* Berkeley: University of California Press.

Yengoyan, Aram A.
2001 Forward: Culture and Power in the Writings of Eric. R. Wolf. In *Pathways of Power: Building an Anthropology of the Modern World*, ed. Eric R. Wolf and Sydel Silverman, vii–xvii. Berkeley: University of California Press.

TWO

Miners, Women, and Community Coalitions in the UMWA Pittston Strike

Karaleah Reichart

> I think if you really want to get something done, get a woman fired up and she'll do it for you. We've been followed, we've been harassed and different things. But we can stand there and take it and look back at them and just smile.
>
> —ELAINE PURKEY, JUNE 1989

The Pittston strike in the early 1990s marked miners' return to contract bargaining and the deliberate attempt of miners and their families to augment the power of the union to secure their economic and political goals. While neither side actually "won" the strike, women played important roles as they formed, dissolved, and re-formed a complex set of alliances and coalitions during the strike.

Women have been a critical organizing force in mining communities since the beginning of bituminous coal mining in the central Appalachian mountains in the 1800s. This chapter focuses mostly on women because social historians have often overlooked their contributions. This represents a trend among many academics to ignore women's collective action in highly gendered industries such as coal mining. At the same time, the region deserves an integrated ethnographic analysis of the multifarious ethnic and class differences that conflate gender distinctions and complicate social behaviors in the face of economic and political hardship. The contradictory interests of working-class men and women in coal communities have intermingled with ethnic and class differences to produce surprising outcomes. Such puzzling contradictions complicate historical depictions of the class conflict associated with labor organizing in the early twentieth century and raise interesting questions regarding gender and ethnicity in communities affected by extractive industries. The low ratio of blacks to whites in Logan, West Virginia, amplifies class differences in this highly stratified region. While whites are currently more politically visible in regional coal mining disputes, blacks were very influential in early union organizing efforts in coal communities (Trotter 1990).

Most conventional analyses of industrial relations focus on the terms and conditions of employment that workers, employers, and government agencies negotiate or otherwise develop (Dunlop 1958; Kochan, Katz, and McKersie 1986). These gender-neutral approaches separate work and employment relationships from other social institutions such as family and community networks.

Anthropologists know that changing gender roles influence the multiple social processes that converge at the intersections of these domains, but how should the study of industrial relations or other work and employment issues address and adapt to these changes in roles and the increasing interdependence of work, community, and gender relationships?

This chapter explores these intersections of gender and power through the voices of Appalachian women as they recounted their different roles in the 1989–1990 labor dispute between the Pittston Coal Company and the United Mine Workers of America (UMWA). By tracing the process by which these women shifted from their "domestic" roles as homemakers to build a community coalition that became an influential party to the conflict, the chapter shows how power relations and the dynamics of this dispute were affected and illustrates what conventional analyses of such events fail to detect.

The Conventional Strike Story

The 1970s and 1980s were decades of wildcat mining strikes, sporadic uprisings, and a sense of lingering unrest among miners and mining communities. During the Pittston strike, however, UMWA miners clearly held less power than management did. Because of the economic toll the strike would take on their families, miners faced the options of prolonging the strike to hold out for greater concessions or returning to work with reduced pensions and healthcare benefits. The roles of women in this process were diverse and critical for the successful resolution of the strike.

Since 1950, collective bargaining in the coal industry had taken place between the UMWA and the Bituminous Coal Operators Association (BCOA) (Miernyk 1980). In early 1987 the withdrawal of the Pittston Coal Group from the BCOA precipitated a prolonged labor dispute. Pittston argued that its forfeiture of BCOA membership was necessary to facilitate the development of a separate labor contract to meet the company's unique needs as a major coal exporter. Pittston was thus not a party to BCOA's new agreement with the UMWA in 1988.

On March 23, 1989, the United Mine Workers of America announced that Region 9 of the National Labor Relations Board (NLRB) had upheld its charge that the Pittston Company's Elkay Division in West Virginia had engaged in repeated unfair labor practices in violation of federal labor law. The agency cited twenty-five separate accounts of lawbreaking and upheld the union's contentions that Pittston was a single employer and that its coal operations constituted a single bargaining unit (Daykin 1989).

Among other complaints, the UMWA charged Pittston with improperly increasing the number of supervisors, unlawfully allowing supervisors to perform work properly belonging to UMWA members, illegally subcontracting work usually performed by UMWA-represented Pittston employees, improperly changing employees' work schedules and forcing miners to work overtime, and refusing to properly settle disputes, including the unqualified abandonment of arbitration.

Because of the depressed economic conditions in the central Appalachian coalfields, many believed a favorable decision by the NLRB meant the difference between a successful strike and one that resulted in the replacement of UMWA miners (Daykin 1989). In April 1989, just a few weeks after the NLRB ruling, the UMWA initiated a strike against the Pittston Coal Group and its subsidiaries throughout Kentucky, Virginia, and West Virginia. Pittston responded by announcing its intention to permanently replace picketing miners in violation of the NLRB ruling.

In the words of Michael Odom, president of the Pittston Coal Group, "[T]he company intends to keep its mines running and its customers supplied, while at the same time we continue to bargain with the union to reach an agreement" (quoted in Edwards 1989:2). The strike continued until October 1989, at which point U.S. secretary of labor Elizabeth Dole announced that she had asked UMWA president Rich Trumka and Pittston president Paul Douglas to meet with a special mediator, William J. Usery, to attempt to end the strike. The strike was soon officially ended.

While the initial NLRB ruling, the intervention of the secretary of labor, and the formal mediation process were all influential factors in the evolution of the Logan Pittston strike, many other factors also played a role. One of the most striking was the steady development of a community-based coalition between the Women's Auxiliary group "Logan Friends and Family" and the United Mine Workers of America. The group's central position was largely disregarded in both local and national media coverage of the dispute and in retrospective references to the strike throughout the academic literature (see, for example, *Daily Labor Report* 1990; Katz and Kochan 2000:216–217). These women altered critical power relationships and influenced the dynamics of the strike. By overlooking the group's vital role, analysts and reporters missed the complete story of the strike and its effects on workers, families, and the surrounding community.

The coalition-formation process had three primary phases. During the first phase, women attempted to garner support for the strike by soliciting donations from local businesses and organizations. When these efforts failed, women organized Logan Friends and Family and attempted to form an alliance with the United Mine Workers of America. When UMWA officials rejected this partnership, women continued to solicit support for their organization by meeting regularly and organizing community fund-raisers, sponsoring guest speakers, and staging rallies near the mine site. When those efforts were successful, the UMWA allowed the creation of a coalition between Logan Friends and Family and the UMWA and provided limited access to the organization's resources. In the final phase, Logan Friends and Family helped to prolong the strike in an effort to help the community gain as many concessions from management as possible.

Reinterpreting the 1989 Pittston Contract Strike

Because of the vast political and economic monopoly the coal industry has historically held in the area, displaced miners have had few employment opportunities. During the Pittston strike, the UMWA miners were clearly the subordinate group. Miners faced the options of prolonging the strike for greater concessions or returning to work and losing retirees' pensions and healthcare benefits. The roles of women in this process were diverse and critical.

Phase I: Pittston vs. the United Mine Workers of America

After calling a strike on April 5, 1989, the UMWA implemented a new tactic against Pittston Coal Group president Richard Trumka's corporate campaign. This involved withdrawing union deposits from a bank that made loans to Pittston, sending an UMWA stockholder to the annual meeting to question corporate officers, calling for the resignation of Pittston director Charles Haywood, and holding a proxy contest. The union hired a proxy solicitation firm to attempt to persuade Pittston shareholders to pass three resolutions: to allow a vote on an anti-takeover defense adopted by Pittston's board of directors, to give shareholders the right to secret ballot holding, and to recommend that a committee be appointed to examine the idea of selling some of Pittston's businesses.

Following the announcements of the strike and the proxy fight, members of the community in Logan were notified that the miners were going to be out of work for an undetermined time. Throughout the coalfields, women's sentiments toward Pittston were overwhelmingly negative. One account said that "with a median per capita income in 1984 of about $8,200 and little in the way of alternative employment, a perceived threat to the miners is a perceived threat to all" (Priest 1989:D1).

On April 30, 1989, nearly 10,000 people (including miners and their families) traveled to Wise County, Virginia, to attend a rally featuring Richard Trumka and Jesse Jackson. In Lebanon, Virginia, a group of miners' wives and women from the community occupied Pittston's coalfield headquarters for two days. In this act of civil disobedience, the group of wives, widows, daughters, and sisters of coal miners called themselves the Daughters of Mother Jones. The group's uniform consisted of white blouses, sneakers, blue jeans, and scarves fashioned from camouflage netting to complement the picket's camouflage outfits.

Local media representatives interviewed none of the women from the Daughters of Mother Jones. Journalists deemed the event "part of a new-look strike strategy being waged by the United Mine Workers of America in what it calls its most selective strike in this decade" (Baker 1989:B1). In a field study of the strike in Virginia, however, sociologist Virginia Seitz found that women's actions emerged from their own organizing efforts, not from an imposed "new-look" union strategy (Seitz 1995).

Back in Logan County, many women began to solicit funds from local supporters and garner resources for the striking miners and their families, but they were not yet organized into a coherent group. The newspaper accounts were unfavorable from the outset. In the *Charleston Daily Mail*, Philip Nussel reported that "members of a newly formed United Mine Workers ladies auxiliary say they are having problems convincing some businesses in Logan County to support the union in its month-old strike against the Pittston Coal Group, Inc." (Nussel 1989:B1).

Phase II: Logan Friends and Family and the UMWA Alliance

Two months into the strike, the group of women from Logan County had become a major force. Martha Conley, a prime organizer of the group, officially named the organization Friends and Family of the United Mine Workers. Although the group's membership had dwindled to seventy-five, the women were actively participating in strike activities.

The women of Friends and Family spent their time delivering food to the Slab Fork picket shack, sitting in court during injunction and contempt hearings against the union, begging the union to allow women to hold formal advocacy positions, and going to meetings to plan fund-raisers for the strikers and their families. Given the UMWA's reluctance to recognize and support the women's organization, why did they continue? One woman explained:

> It's because the UMW is not a social service organization. . . . They provide no money for people for mortgages to keep their homes. They don't provide money for electricity. They don't provide money to pay your water bill. The women were the ones that had to do that. And of course, they were as poor as their husbands, so they had to go out and raise money. (Life history interview, anonymous source, Logan, West Virginia, circa 1997)

Although this group was organized and led exclusively by women from Logan, media accounts continued to portray the organization as an offshoot of the United Mine Workers of America—a gross misconception according to all interview accounts. One woman explained to me how the Friends and Family was finally accepted by the United Mine Workers of America:

> They [the women] persisted, and as the strike went on, they kept going out and asking for more money. . . . They eventually got over $2,000, and at that point, when they had all this money, the men in the union finally accepted them and decided on the organization. At about $2,000 [the UMWA] thought, well, these women are really worth something. They're gonna help us. And at that time they were given . . . an office in the Logan UMW headquarters. They were never given a key to their own office. They used it, but if they left the men would come over then and lock it at lunchtime. And they would have to sit along the hall and wait . . . and they never complained about this. That's a very unusual thing, to have an office and not have a key to it. (Ibid.)

Several key events facilitated women's greater involvement in the strike effort. At a mass rally sponsored by the Coalition of Labor Union Women in June 1989, women union leaders argued that labor struggles, like those witnessed in Logan and surrounding states, would not be won without the dual support of men and women. Speaking to a crowd of 10,000 in Charleston, West Virginia, the national president of the coalition, Joyce Miller, stated that "we stand for aggressively organizing against the unorganized, so workers are not pitted against each other to provide for their families" (quoted in Avent 1989a:A1). Other women from the crowd agreed. One stated that "men and women are side by side in the work force, and we're also playing a leading role in solidarity action. I just think it's extremely important that women are coming forward in rank and file movements." Another woman stated, "It's easier for companies to divide people against each other. People always fall into that [trap] when they're hungry. Women are fighters. Mother Jones said that in the 1800s. I can't imagine men thinking that women are the weaker sex because we've always had to fight for everything we have" (quoted in Avent 1989a:A1).

In a newspaper article published during the strike, many women reported that changes in offices and factories facilitated greater acceptance of women's stake in labor issues. The president of the Charleston chapter of the National Organization for Women (NOW), Nahla Nimeh-Lewis, stated, "[W]e feel that we are at a point to strengthen the coalition between women, labor, other progressive forces. There is a strength in coalition. Plus, the labor force in this country is becoming more and more [made up of] women" (quoted in Avent 1989b:A1). The vice president of the national organization, who was also at the rally, said, "[W]hat has happened to us, I think, is that over much of this decade, our mutual opponents have planned and carried out a divide and conquer strategy. We all have to stand together if we hope to post that pendulum back from the right" (quoted in Avent 1989b:A1).

According to those who attended the 1989 NOW strike rally, women were a major part of the Pittston strike (and of what was deemed the "larger solidarity movement") because of several factors: (1) women were becoming a larger part of the workforce, which included 38 percent of the tri-state workforce in 1990; (2) women were joining unions and assuming work traditionally performed by men; (3) women were working harder to preserve the community and the family—as women found themselves threatened by big business, they banded together to support the community and the family, which depend on decent wages and working hours, benefits, and job security; and (4) women were realizing their strength and the need to join with other forces (Avent 1989b). According to Helen Rentch of the Charleston NOW chapter, "[T]he rally was an attempt to build a coalition to try to deal with what people see as the anti-people policies of the Reagan-Bush administration" (quoted in Avent 1989b:A1).

In June 1989, the weekly meeting of Logan Friends and Family was held to organize a rally two weeks hence and a carwash fund-raiser the following weekend. To coordinate the project, the group's leader called on "all the girls, captains and coordinators" in attendance to "get on your phone lines and find out how many kids would be interested in participating and make a list, and get it back to me as soon as possible. . . . If we want to get our kids involved, ages 9 to adult, we want the kids to handle this car wash. But we will need some of you beautiful ladies to supervise, and some of your husbands too if you can get them involved." Here is a quotation from the group's leader, Martha, taken from a transcript of the meeting made by an anonymous informant (speaker unknown; Logan, West Virginia, circa 1989):

> [A]s of right now, the ladies auxiliary does not have the funds or management support to feed the picket lines three times a day. . . . [I]n the near future we can get something worked out and we can handle it. Because girls we can do this. We can do a better job than what the men are doing. Now let's face that. The men just ain't getting it done. But we can do it.

Martha also read excerpts from the articles by Katie Avent, cited earlier, to the women at the meeting. "'Okay,' she said, 'and you all notice, here on this picture, now girls, we are finally getting some recognition. This is Cathy Justice, her husband James, and her son Gabriel. So there's one of ours that made the front page. So we are making a difference, ladies. We really are.' "

Members of Friends and Family were also in attendance at the NOW rally. Elaine Purkey, a miner's wife in Logan, attested to the work of the organization by commenting on its efforts, which included raising money, writing to members of Congress, learning about the disputed miners' contract, putting signs in stores, gaining public backing for their cause, cooking, making sandwiches, driving to nightly rallies, collecting food, entertaining the marchers, and taking care of strikers' homes. Purkey stated, "Force is another thing. You've got 297 men on strike over here—275 wives—some aren't married or their wives are dead. That almost doubles your numbers. You take an average of two children per family, and you've more than tripled your number" (quoted in Avent 1989b:A1).

Phase III: Violence and Alliance—Pittston and the UMWA–Logan Friends and Family Coalition

The UMWA had vigorously protested the inclusion of women in its ranks when they were first permitted to enter the mines in the late 1970s. The alliance formed among women community organizers during the Pittston strike was at times equally tenuous and strained. By late June 1989, however, Friends and Family was fully organized and actively engaged with the Pittston strike.

Miners' peaceful civil disobedience soon disintegrated into community violence and upheaval. Federal judge Dennis Knapp said, "I'm trying to figure out what kind of an animal they are. Do they look sinister, sir, like they might tear you up if you go in the mines? Like an animal that gets in the way, why not kick them out of the way" (quoted in Wessels 1989:1). That remark set the tone for the remainder of the Pittston strike. Citations for civil contempt were issued against miners for blocking the entrances to Pittston's mines and those of its subsidiaries, and Pittston Coal's initially tolerant strategy turned violent.

UMWA local president Bethel Purkey had stated before the onset of violence, "[T]he way they used to stop a truck in the old days was to turn it over and haul the driver out and give him a good thumping. I've seen people shot at, ours and theirs, and people thrown in the river, ours and theirs. Now we just stand there and ask the driver to honor our picket line. If he says no, we stand there anyhow. Or sit down. The trucks have been turning around" (quoted in Loh 1989:A1).

Women were also engaged in the violent activities that characterized this phase of the Pittston strike while continuing to organize rallies, maintain households, and seek political support for the union cause. Friends and Family organized a rally for the striking miners in early July 1989 at Logan High School and facilitated the integration of the Charleston chapter of the National Organization for Women into the activities. Along the picket line, the Logan "chow wagon" continued to operate.

In August 1989, striking miners simultaneously blocked multiple mine entrances in a coordinated effort, straining the resources of both the coal operators and the state police. The Rum Creek Sales Company hired nonunion workers to cross the community bridge and restart its strike-stalled coal plant. This spawned a new set of problems for the community. In one incident, eight women were sitting beneath a tarpaulin shelter near the bridge entrance with a sign that read "Please Mr. Holbrook, Save our bridge and let us go to school. The Children of Dehue." The bridge had steadily deteriorated as a result of the routine crossing of fully loaded coal trucks. School buses also used the bridge, and some women in the community feared that it was only a matter of time before the bridge collapsed. Holbrook was the vice president of Con-Serv, a nonunion company working the Rum Creek tipple during the strike. He arrived on the scene and struck three of the women with his truck. He was subsequently charged with two counts of attempted murder. One of the women, Linda Grimmett, received head and limb injuries, was hospitalized, and wore an arm brace for several weeks following the attack (Dale 1989).

Grimmett immersed herself gradually in the strike, first working with Friends and Family by bringing food to the picket lines, planning hot dog sales and sock hops, and keeping the other women company while their husbands worked strike duty in Virginia. Later, however, Grimmett took command of the "bridge brigade." She had her own picket shack on the bridge and was one of the only women to staff the shack twenty-four hours a day throughout the strike. Grimmett's husband initially opposed her involvement. She explained, "[H]e didn't want me away from home so much. The men, they're scared for the women." Her husband stated, "She surprised me, I'll tell you that. [The Holbrook incident] scared me, but it made me want her to do it [support the strike effort] even more." Of the women's actions at Dehue, Grimmett said, "our lives have changed. They'll never be the same" (quoted in Dale 1989:D1).

The violence perpetrated by management, picketing miners, and the scab workers continued well into the strike, including several incidents of shootings, vehicular attacks, firebombs, and overturned trucks. Throughout it all, women continued to play an important role in the strike effort and remained targets of the violence. By October 1989, coal miners' wives and their families had planned several rallies and meetings, including a demonstration at the Federal Courthouse in Charleston where UMWA picketers were called in before Judge Dennis Knapp. In a press release written for the demonstration by Friends and Family, member Cathy Justice said:

> We want to ask Judge Knapp why he continues to let Pittston Coal use his court to harass the miners, at taxpayers' expense. Pittston Coal has been found guilty by the NLRB of provoking this strike, yet nobody is hauling them into court time after time and heaping fine after fine on top of them. We want the judges in this state to stop playing on Pittston's team. It's time for them to stand up and say they are going to throw out all these trumped up charges and restore some dignity to the courts. (Justice 1989)

The Cultural Context of Coalitions

In October 1989, U.S. secretary of labor Elizabeth Dole announced that she had asked UMWA president Rich Trumka and Pittston president Paul Douglas to meet with her. A mediator was appointed, and an end to the strike was formally negotiated. In the minds of many miners, though, the 1990 settlement was not perfect. Months after the strike, miners were still laid off. The company won more flexibility regarding work rules, thus eroding previous union victories and shifting more control over the work process back to management. The terms of the agreement, however, were vastly more favorable than the union had dreamed possible before the strike (Sessions and Ansley 1993:222).

From the onset, although initially unorganized, women in the community actively supported the UMWA's efforts against Pittston. At the same time, the women fulfilled their "traditional" roles as supporters of the strike effort. When the UMWA refused to formally acknowledge their support, the organization was reinforcing its historical fraternal nature, a rejection that significantly disrupted the relationship between community organizers and the UMWA.

Recognizing the importance of protecting their interests in the negotiations, however, women continued to organize the community in an effort to draw together resources from neighboring businesses. But because it could hire replacement workers or shut down operations completely to subvert any union gains in negotiations and thereby weaken its power within the community structure, Pittston had more power than the community group or the union.

Even after the women in Logan had organized themselves into Logan Friends and Family and the group had established itself as a clearly supportive force in the conflict, the UMWA continued to reject them. When the officers of District 17 finally determined that women had attained enough power to make a difference in the negotiations, the UMWA offered to form a conditional alliance with Logan Friends and Family. This alliance eventually turned into a major coalition that endured both the strike and violence aimed against the miners and their families. The two parties drew strength and support from each other, although the officers of District 17 continued their attempts to exert authority over Logan Friends and Family. By controlling the group's access to UMWA resources, the union exercised authoritative power over the group, while Logan Friends and Family provided support for the strike effort.

Even though the UMWA attempted to exercise power over Logan Friends and Family, the coalition of the two groups gave them sufficient power to prolong the strike against Pittston and to "hold out" for greater wage and benefit concessions.

Conclusions and Implications

The Pittston strike and the participation of women in the community marked a turning point in relationships among the coal industry, the UMWA, and local families. By the late 1990s, the bulk of the local mining industry had shifted to mountaintop removal, whereby large sections of mountains are exploded to reach the rich coal seams below, so the Pittston strike was the last major underground coal mining strike in the region. A study of the changing gender roles and coalition formation in the Pittston strike provides a historical snapshot of gendered social relations of power. The relationships among mutually interested parties often converge in community alliances, which ultimately shape the outcomes of labor-management bargaining negotiations.

Although not formally employed by the coal mining industry, women in these communities operate within the cultural boundaries of the single-industry towns' social structures. During industrial conflicts, they disrupt norms of social interaction and resource flow to find common interests with one or more of the parties involved. The creation of community coalitions alters these parties' relative power and shifts the process from bilateral to multilateral. In so doing, additional parties enter the dispute with their own interests that extend well beyond the specific terms and conditions of a contract agreement.

By shifting attention away from dyadic union-management negotiation events, the holistic study of social structure and community relationships contributes to a more comprehensive understanding of labor disputes. This chapter provides one approach to exploring the nexus between the traditionally separated domains of the research and practice of work and employment on the one hand and of work and family on the other. Such ethnographic and historical methods will provide the thick descriptions needed to begin to build an empirically based understanding of the dynamic contexts of work, community, and family interactions.

A more complete understanding of these relationships also contributes to the multifarious strategies of labor disputes. Unions, for example, are becoming increasingly active in building coalitions with community groups in efforts to bolster their power both in collective bargaining and in local political affairs. Since the number of women in unions has grown considerably in recent years (women have accounted for two-thirds of new union members since the late 1990s) and women report a higher level of interest in joining unions than men do (Freeman and Rogers 1999; Kochan 1979), these trends will make a significant impact over time.

References Cited

Avent, Katie

1989a A Woman's Place Is in the Union, Organizers Say. *Herald-Dispatch* (Huntington, WV), June 12, A1.

1989b Women Standing Behind and Beside West Virginia Miners Striking at Pittston Coal. *Herald-Dispatch* (Huntington, WV), June 12, A1.

Baker, Donald

1989 Miners Use New Tactics in Virginia Strike. *The Washington Post,* April 20, B1, B10.

Daily Labor Report

1990 Washington, DC: Bureau of National Affairs, February 21.

Dale, Maryclaire

1989 Fear in the Hollow. *Sunday Gazette-Mail* (Charleston, WV), September 3, D1.

Daykin, Tom

1989 NLRB Cites Pittston Coal for Violations. *Lexington* [Kentucky] *Herald-Leader*, April 4, A6.

Dunlop, John T.

1958 *Industrial Relations Systems*. New York: Holt.

Edwards, Greg

1989 Miners' Strike Involves Entire Families. *Times-World News* (Roanoke, VA), April 21, 1–2.

Freeman, Richard B., and Joel Rogers

1999 *What Do Workers Want?* Ithaca: Cornell University Press.

Justice, Kathy

1989 Press release on behalf of Logan Friends and Family, September.

Katz, Harry C., and Thomas A. Kochan

2000 *An Introduction to Collective Bargaining and Industrial Relations,* 2nd ed. New York: McGraw-Hill.

Kochan, Thomas A.

1979 How American Workers View Unions. *Monthly Labor Review* 102 (April): 15–22.

Kochan, Thomas A., Harry C. Katz, and Robert B. McKersie

1986 *The Transformation of American Industrial Relations*. New York: Basic Books.

Loh, Jules

1989 Miners Use Tactics of Nonviolent Civil Disobedience. *Sunday Outlook* (*Gazette-Mail*) (Charleston, WV), July 23, A1.

Miernyk, William H.

1980 Coal. In *Collective Bargaining: Contemporary American Experience*, ed. Jack Barbash, 1–48. Madison, WI: Industrial Relations Research Association.

Nussel, Philip

1989 Women Lobbying for Strikers. *Charleston Daily Mail,* May 2, B1.

Priest, Dana

1989 Solidarity in the Coal Fields. *The Washington Post,* April 30, D1, D7.

Seitz, Virginia

1995 *Women, Development and Communities for Empowerment in Appalachia.* Albany: State University of New York Press.

Sessions, James, and Fran Ansley

1993 Singing across Dark Spaces: The Union/Community Takeover of Pittston's Moss 3 Plant. In *Fighting Back in Appalachia: Traditions of Resistance and Change*, ed. Stephen Fisher, 195–224. Philadelphia: Temple University Press.

Trotter, Joe W.

1990 *Coal, Class, and Color: Blacks in Southern West Virginia, 1915–32*. Urbana: University of Illinois Press.

Wessels, Andy

1989 Coal Miners Organizing March to Charleston. *Charleston Gazette,* June 8, 1.

THREE

Is This What Democracy Looks Like?

E. Paul Durrenberger and Suzan Erem

Questions of Democracy

Some see the outcomes of the 2000 and 2004 U.S. presidential elections as failures of democracy. One explanation is that people are widely deceived and tricked into voting against their interests (Frank 2005). George Soros (2008) locates the failure in the postmodern preference for the manipulation of reality over the pursuit of truth. He suggests that in addition to free elections, individual liberties, the rule of law, and the division of powers that define open societies, there should also be standards of honesty and truthfulness. Others call the purposeful manipulation of reality "mind control," or the control of culture (Durrenberger and Erem 2007). Still others see the failure of democracy as a consequence of a corporate-sponsored cultural revolution that started in the late nineteenth century with the rise of corporations in the United States (Doukas 2003; Fones-Wolf 1995).

The work upon which this study is based was funded by a grant from the National Science Foundation. We do not mention corporate names because Paul promised not to as a condition of entry to their facilities.

This chapter is about what we take to be a failure of democracy within the union movement—a free and open election in a democratic union that replaced progressive leadership with a self-interested clique. Suzan had worked as a union organizer and director of communications at a large Chicago local (see Erem 2001), and we had worked together on a study in Chicago in which we developed measures of union consciousness and participation (Durrenberger and Erem 2005). The unions we had worked with were highly centralized. They discouraged easy access to both the nomination and the by-laws process, discouraged horizontal communication among members and their representatives (stewards), and were personalistic.

Much of the ethnographic work on fisheries suggests that the more the fishers participate in management, the more effective it is and that the more centralized management is, the less effective it is (Durrenberger and King 2000). Other work on indigenous water management systems goes to the same point (Leaf 1998; Trawick 2002). We wanted to see whether more open and democratic unions would reveal the same contrast that was evident in fisheries and water management systems.

In 2003 the International Brotherhood of Teamsters Local 705 in Chicago was widely regarded as one of the most democratic and open union locals in the United States. Local 705 hired Suzan to edit its monthly newsletter shortly after she left her union job to freelance. She could see how the local worked from the inside—she would talk to members, officers, and stewards in the process of working on the newsletter. She already knew the local and its reputation from the outside, as it was an ally of her own local in a number of social justice struggles in Chicago during the seven years she had worked full-time.

We wanted to see whether being more democratic would make a difference in the way members participated in their union. Suzan approached the leaders of Local 705, and they agreed to permit us to interview staff and to observe and participate in their daily work. This is the story of the 2003 election in that local.

At 705 we saw democracy in membership meetings and stewards' meetings where anyone could speak up. Stewards met once a month for a meal and to talk to each other. They also met with others from their sectors—tank truck drivers, movers, delivery drivers, package service workers. Other unions we had studied did not encourage such horizontal communication among stewards and, in fact, actively discouraged it because no one knew what would happen if the most active members from different worksites met regularly. What would happen if they found out the details of each others' contracts? Nobody wanted to risk such openness. Local 705 saw these comparisons as an opportunity for increased participation rather than a threat to the leadership.

We saw democracy in the by-laws meeting where people debated and voted on the rules that govern the union, a meeting that was raucous but surely democratic by any measure. Given a toehold on the rule making, those members were not about to let anything happen without their input. This was a union with a history of making members "run the gauntlet" through threats and intimidation just to cast a ballot in a union election. The current leadership and staff regaled us with stories of "the good old days," which they did not consider so good for members like them who disagreed with the mob-like leaders of the time.

We saw democracy in the front lines of the class war. Shrouded in genteel accoutrements, management in suits sat at solid cherry bargaining tables in fancy legal offices opposite 705 negotiating teams composed of very articulate truck drivers. We saw it in the open nominations meeting where it took two people to get a slate on the ballot—one to nominate and one to second—rather than the impossible hurdles we saw at other locals. We saw it in the concern of reps and officers with representation and contract enforcement. "The way to get reelected is to provide excellent service," more than one person told us. And they were reelected twice.

Politics, Research Ethics, and the Fucking Feeder Drivers

Throughout, we heard about the "fucking feeder drivers" who drive big rigs between package delivery depots. The adjective always went before the noun, no matter who was speaking. Except for the feeder drivers. We met *them* at the picnic that launched the campaign to reelect Jerry Zero and his slate for a third term. They introduced themselves as "the opposition." We went to their depots and rode with their reps. When they put up an opposition candidate, we tried to get in with them, but they weren't having us. There's little trust in the labor movement, and guilt by association is the general M.O. We had been seen in the union's offices and introduced to members and stewards by the current leaders, therefore we were suspect.

We were interested in the politics of obligation we had seen in other locals (Durrenberger and Erem 2005), but our surveys of 705's stewards and staff showed us that something else was going on. No obligation went with saving a guy his job or getting a good contract or anything else. It's just what a union does. It's not a favor you need to think about repaying. In fact, many stewards became irate at the very suggestion that anyone owed anyone anything. In other unions, where the laws of reciprocity were held to be axiomatically true, this wasn't problematic and no one objected. With the union's cooperation, we had managed to get an excellent random sample of stewards, and everyone on the staff filled in our surveys. So there were no sampling issues with the survey.

As the election campaign heated up in midsummer we had no compunction about pitching in to help Jerry Zero and his slate. We discussed the ethics of the matter up one side and down the other. The long and short of it was that we liked these guys, owed our access to the union to their open-mindedness and their help, thought they were doing a great job, and wanted them to win. Besides, we wanted to learn more about the politics of the local, and the only way to do that was to get on the inside by helping with the campaign. So when it came down to brass tacks, we felt no ethical problem and saw every ethnographic justification for working with the campaign. This put us cheek by jowl with the folks we were trying to understand, on the front lines of democracy, getting out the vote.

Suzan went to Chicago for the vote count at Teamster City. I had to stay at Penn State and teach. I made it through my classes until Saturday, the day before Pearl Harbor Day. I could imagine the scene at the auditorium and tried to stay busy, but I called Suzan's cell phone four times asking for news. The phone was off. She didn't get the messages. She didn't call 'til early evening. She picks up the story from Teamster City, the complex of a parking garage, restaurant, auditorium, and two high-rise buildings at 300 South Ashland Avenue that house Local 705, the union's health center, other locals, and the union's joint council of locals for Chicago.

Counting the Ballots

The morning of December 6, 2003, all of us sat around the campaign room at the back of the auditorium to watch the vote count. Jerry Zero and the staff and supporters of the incumbents looked relaxed. Some were parked on the leather sofa, munching chips and drinking coffee. Someone always occupied the large leather office chair behind the desk, and a few were lined up along the paneled walls of the small, 1960s style office. They were settling in for a long day. We expected that we'd know the results by 6 p.m. The restaurant next door was reserved for the celebration that would cap off the six weeks of intensive campaigning with plenty of beer and the collective relief of having withstood another challenge. People were exhausted from the long hours they'd put in on top of their regular work and on their few vacation days, which they'd reserved for this use. Paul and I had been riding with them early in the mornings and late at night and working a phone bank in between. It was part of participant observation, Paul said, doing the ethnography.

People told jokes and stories. Veterans passed on the legends of the place and people to younger staff and visiting members who munched on chips or apples as they listened. Jerry came in and sat down to hold court and tell stories of the old days while admiring friends laughed or shrugged or joined in on the punch lines of narratives well rehearsed on similar occasions.

People said this was Louis Peick's old office from the days when Local 705 owned only the auditorium and not the modern seven-story glass building it later built next door. Little had changed in the office except for the padded indoor-outdoor carpeting that must have replaced what was probably dark green shag to match the decor of the time. The curved walnut and metal light fixtures over the matching desk were "retro," and the stuffed leather club chair was barely broken in.

The name Louis Peick brought back images of the old-time Teamster boss, a man who ruled Chicago in the 1950s and 60s with tough talk and strong arms. But among this crowd, Peick's name also carried with it the old way of doing things—a way that was out of sync with the new world. These new guys used the old reputation of the Teamsters, which men like Peick had built, to make innovations in union representation and organizing. They would never sell out, not once, but they did know that negotiating often got better results for members than "chest thumping," so they did that when they needed to, and they needed to almost every day.

The new way got results. They proved it. Week after week we'd watched these reps or business agents (BAs) state their case to six-member panels made up of half union and half management officials. Some panels were convened at the union hall and some at a suburban Holiday Inn. Business agents, stewards, and grievants would gather for breakfast and go over their cases, review their testimony, and tell stories. Always telling stories. Always mining those stories for the lessons they might offer.

The panel would convene in a meeting room and hear the case. Pacing union reps and supervisors filled the halls as they awaited their turn, both sides worried about what humiliation they might suffer in front of the panel. Often that pressure was sufficient to bring about a settlement and a handshake on the deal just moments before they headed into the room.

Grievances they couldn't resolve in the hallway went in to the panel. Inside the room, management and labor grilled lower-level staff from both sides who were making their cases under the watchful eye of the chairmen. When they were done with questions, one of the chairmen would proclaim "Parties," and all observers and principals would leave to pace the hallway as the panel went into "executive session."

This was where the higher-level settlements were made—ones that amazed us, where people who'd been "no-call, no-shows" for a month still returned to their jobs or a driver who hadn't signaled and had been in a serious accident was put back to work.

We'd all enter the room again after being called by the sergeant at arms, and we'd hear the decision. Most often, it was in the union's favor. The reps would smile proudly, knowing, as one rep said, they'd "caught lightning in a bottle."

But everyone was thinking about the election. One day Paul was at the union hall when a call came in. He picks up the story.

705 in Action

About 4 p.m. one day, Business Agent Dan Campbell (pronounced camp-BELL) and Reese McClain and Tony Gatson, vice president of the union, and I rushed to the parking lot, got in a car, and headed out to a suburban sorting station for a package delivery company. In a lot of places in Chicago, race matters. In 705 it mattered much less, and if the secretary-treasurer, the principle officer of the local, Jerry Zero, had his way, it wouldn't have mattered at all. Tony and Reese were black.

Long car rides through Chicago's traffic are congenial settings for long conversations and stories. In the car, the talk was about a fucking feeder driver who had been a 705 rep until he was fired. This guy was planning to run a slate against Jerry Zero. Campbell opined that all you have to do is mention his negatives—he didn't support the 1997 strike against the United Parcel Service (UPS). "That's what a rep does, is accumulate enemies of people for whom he hasn't been able to do what they wanted—and this wears off after a few years. So this guy can now try this [running the slate]—after being fired as a rep. Negative campaigning is bad, but there's no choice here and it's OK if it's true."

I hadn't seen such a concentration of union force for any other case. Campbell was the rep for the facility, but I didn't understand the heavy backup from union officers and staff. I asked what made this case so significant. They explained it was a big deal, an important case, because they had to show management as well as the union members their support for the steward and his witness. "The principle of equality is at stake," Campbell explained. Union stewards should be on a par with supervisors and be treated with equal respect.

The guys explained that a steward saw a person from management doing work reserved for the bargaining unit. This was a touchy issue I'd heard about many times as I rode with reps from the delivery service. Sorting packages, loading trucks, handling mail—that was work reserved for 705 people. The people on the line are always rushed. The sorting stations are buildings that cover city blocks, full of catwalks, moving conveyer belts, rushing people, and deafening noise. To the uninitiated, it feels like walking into a nightmare out of Fritz Lang's film *Metropolis* or that famous Lucy episode where she's working on the chocolate line.

Feeder drivers back their semi-trailers full of packages into loading bays with inches between them. Feeder drivers are elite. You have to work your way up to that status, and if you're driving one of those rigs, you've done everything else there is to do for a long, long time. After the feeder drivers position the trailers, other 705 members step into the trailers, take out the packages, and put them onto the belts that take them through the cavernous building where other 705 members put them onto other belts until they all get to the waiting open end of a package car, a delivery truck, where the driver sorts the packages into the truck's shelves in the way that best fits the route. Everyone carries a scanner. They scan the package when it comes off the truck and again when it goes onto the package car. The driver scans it again when it gets delivered and is out of the system.

Once, in a different facility with a different rep, I saw a guy high above the floor at a juncture of moving belts start to throw packages down and around, randomly, and shout incoherently, "going postal," as they say. One of his work mates left his station at a lower belt and talked to him soothingly, sorting the packages for him as they came up the belts, throwing them onto their proper belts as the packages piled up at his own station.

So workers don't mind too much if a supervisor lends a hand now and then. The problem is that if they make a habit of it, management staff winds up doing work that belongs to the bargaining unit, to 705 members. Even if individual workers don't mind, this erodes the power of the union. If management can take up the slack, they won't hire more workers, more union members.

To put a stop to the practice, 705 negotiated a contract clause that protected against it. If a worker saw a management person doing bargaining unit work, got a witness, and documented the time and location of the infraction on a form, the company would pay the worker time and a half for the amount of time the management person worked. But you had to be able to prove it. Management checked everything because lying is one of the cardinal infractions, something that gets you suspended or fired without the "innocent until proven guilty" provision of 705 contracts.

Now management at this suburban facility was firing two guys for lying. The workers said that they were at their workstations when they saw a management person working inside a trailer. Management checked. They said it wasn't possible to see into the trailer from those positions. The 705 guys in the car told me management was after one guy because he's a steward who stands up to management.

When we arrived, Campbell went up the ladders to the crow's nest offices high above the floor to meet with management. Tony, Reese, and I met with the steward and his witness, both white, in the break room on the main-floor level. In this room there was no race.

Reese tells a story from the days when he was a feeder driver and a steward for 705, the days before Jerry and his slate were elected from their various barns (705 talk for worksites) to run the local. "When a manager tells you something, you get someone else for your run and go in to defend the member. You gotta get in their face." He illustrates with "fucking this and fucking that," and his intensity is infective. "You gotta learn to talk to them like that." The steward looks amazed. "We can't talk to 'em like that," he says.

Campbell fetched us, and we went up the metal mesh stairs to a conference room. While we were downstairs, management had taken Campbell to the location of the alleged infraction to show him the lay of the land. At the meeting, management stated that the guys couldn't have witnessed the supervisor working for fifteen minutes if they were doing their jobs at the same time. The supervisor in question, a white woman, denied having worked. One worker had been suspended for seven days and the other for nine days. The hearing reached loggerheads. Tony, who had been silent throughout the proceedings, finally said, "Put an offer on the table." Campbell offered to drop the charge of management working and get the guys their wages. Management refused.

We caucused in another room. Tony said, "We gotta lock it up, put it on hold because we can't leave here without getting these guys their pay."

Management wasn't finished with its caucus, so I talked to the steward on a catwalk. He said the problem with this suburban facility was that management had no fear of the union.

When the meeting resumed, both sides agreed to put the case on "mutual hold" for the next panel.

We piled back into the car and the guys reiterated that in an election year they couldn't let this go, they had to get the pay for their steward and the witness.

Campbell explained that the steward had to be able to present his case, had to be able to investigate. Management's point was that he didn't investigate because he has two kids and works another job and has no time for investigations. The union's point, Campbell explained, was that he *should* be able to investigate on company time.

It was 7:30 when we pulled into the parking lot in front of the hall. (They call it "the hall," but it's the seventh floor of the second high-rise building behind the auditorium.) Suzan saw other cases. She picks it up here.

Representing Members

By law, the union is bound to represent its members. If a case has any credibility, it has to try. If it does not, the member can sue it for failure to represent. Thus, at the end of every case, the union side chair of the panel asks the member if he or she has had every opportunity to present information regarding the case and whether the local has properly represented the member. The two famous questions. And business agents or reps are supposed to warn their people about these questions so they know how to answer.

There was one troubling time when a less experienced agent was representing nineteen workers, all of whom had made themselves unavailable to work continuously when called in for a shift they didn't like. The company nailed them—discharged them. The resulting panel met in a meeting room at the hall. Each worker was called in, one by one. The others waited nervously outside.

I knew from my union organizing days that this was clearly some kind of concerted activity, but no one would say it, and I couldn't get anyone to tell me a convincing story about it.

The agent had prepared very little to represent the first of the workers in front of the panel, and the union official chairing his side was growing increasingly frustrated with the agent's lack of a case. To compensate, the chair and other members of the union side of the panel asked leading questions, pulling at the threads of the case the agent had presented to find something substantial to hang the case on without causing it to unravel by some unpredictable admission by the agent or grievant that would work in management's favor.

By now as many as a dozen agents and officers were in the room watching from chairs along the walls. Once in a while someone would pass a note to the chair, a panel member, or the agent. The agent's inability to present the case meant that when he and the defendant left, the chair would have to do a lot of fast talking and probably some cashing in of union political collateral in the executive session to get this grievant and the others back to work. Yet at the end of the first grievant's case, the chair asked the obligatory questions:

"Have you been able to present all the evidence and all the information that pertains to your case?"

"Yes," the grievant said.

"Have you been properly represented by your BA, your steward, and Local 705?"

This is where the grievant shocked the entire room.

"I think [my business agent] has done a good job. But I don't think Local 705's done anything for me."

The union chair stared at him while the management people tried not to notice. Later, the chair and others laughed about the comment, flabbergasted that anyone would think this agent had done his job and the union as a whole had not. More than a half dozen staff spent the better half of a day sitting in that grievance panel meeting, as panel members, support staff, or moral support for the agent and workers. The power of the union had created these panels to force settlement of issues with management before going to the much more expensive and lengthy arbitration process, in which an arbitrator picks one winner and one loser, without compromise. At the end of the day, fourteen of the nineteen workers received reduced levels of discipline and were returned to work.

The staff members involved patted themselves on the back and hoped that in the future this kind of situation wouldn't get as far as "panel."

Then there were the contracts 705 negotiated. This local, as part of the International Brotherhood of Teamsters, lived under nationwide master agreements in some sectors. But it also had a long tradition of negotiating extra "white paper" agreements that improved on the national-level master agreements. During the well-known 1997 UPS strike, for example, Local 705 stayed out on strike an extra two weeks to win additional improvements, some of which would come back to haunt it later. But the local's contracts, with or without the national agreements, were some of the best in the country. Most included the "innocent until proven guilty" language mentioned earlier, which means that a worker fired for an offense would remain on the job until the disposition of the grievance—even if it took months—unless the termination was for a cardinal infraction such as violence, theft, or lying.

In this industry, union negotiators had successfully won language that guaranteed "successor rights," or the requirement that any company that bought the current employer or any new name under which the employer operated still had to recognize the union and pay the same wages and benefits as the old company. This eliminated the industry's incentive to "double breast," or create shadow, nonunion companies. At one major package delivery company, Teamsters had negotiated such rock-solid job security language that business agents walked through a facility and checked supervisors' hands for dirt. If they looked like they had been working or if anyone witnessed them performing bargaining unit work, then the grievants named on the form would receive time and a half pay under the agreement. Finally, Teamsters in Local 705 had enjoyed significant wage and benefits increases over the ten years Jerry Zero and his administration had run the union, including a $3,000-per-month pension payment for package delivery workers, a twenty-five-and-out plus $100 for every year of service over thirty for freight drivers, wage increases of 50 cents to $1 per hour per year, and some wages of $25 per hour or more.

While Paul was sitting in on bargaining with freight drivers and the management representatives left the room for a caucus, the Teamsters' conversation turned to wages, and it turned out that all the drivers in that room were more highly paid than Paul was in his professorial position. We may not be talking university administrators' salaries but better than those of most professors. No one there was looking for a different line of work, except maybe Paul.

These were the successes this administration could rest on. It was what it ticked off of its list every time it did it again, in preparation for the election in 2003. It is what the administrators used in their campaign materials and in talking to members during the six weeks leading up to the vote.

And now we waited nervously for the count.

Waiting for Returns

Paul asked me to observe the election in Chicago in December 2003. Jerry had already won two elections, and the staff, after many weeks of long hours campaigning in addition to its usual duties, was confident there was no question that Jerry would win, only by how much. The office pool gave it away. The numbers I saw, and talk I heard, showed Jerry winning by anywhere from a few hundred to more than 1,500 votes. Paul and I figured we'd be writing a paper about the ritual of elections and how in reality they mean very little except to ratify the current leadership's position and perhaps periodically build solidarity among the staff.

The staff helped get me into the back office to a building where the election officer had said no one but members was allowed. I wouldn't be near any ballots, and I wasn't a threat to anybody so long as I maintained a low profile, which I did. I listened to the election officer's announcements about the process. I watched each of the three slates assign each of the twenty-two tables for ballot counting to an observer from its slate.

One of the union's organizers had forgotten his photo identification, so he could not be an observer. After he calmed down, I took the opportunity to ask him about organizing targets.

"We've already started something at a trucking firm," he said. "It's about 300 guys. I think it'll be good. It's time we tackled something this big."

"Do you think maybe you'll get some more organizers?" I asked.

"Yeah, I'm counting on it. We've got two we could bring on right now."

I watched forty or so ballot counters file into the auditorium where Paul and I had attended so many membership and steward meetings. The ballots had gone out, now they had come back. The counters, hired from the outside, started sorting ballots in the center of the room. The day wore on as counters put the ballots in alphabetical order, then in the order of their company codes. Finally they checked each ballot against membership lists for eligibility. People had to be paid-up members of IBT Local 705 to vote in this election.

"I hope we win by a *thousand* votes," one BA said. "Then they'll finally leave us alone."

"It ain't gonna make a difference," another one said, shaking his head. "Somebody's always gonna be coming at us."

Paul picks up the story here.

The Election Campaign

These Teamsters are very physical, a physicality at first unfamiliar and uncomfortable to me. I wasn't accustomed to having burly guys—even wimpy academics—hug me or drape their arms over my shoulders and call me "Paulie." Frankly, I was a little nervous watching them get so familiar with Suzan, who, having lived in Chicago and seen these guys before, responded in kind. She told me to relax; it's just another way of communicating. I still had a hard time with it.

But the longer we worked with them, the more I came to appreciate the camaraderie of the physical contact. It was a sign of welcome, of familiarity, of belonging to get an arm shake or, among the Italians, a hug and a kiss on the cheek. I began to experiment with it myself, walking with a self-conscious Teamster swagger, chest jutting out, shoulders and arms swinging to the front and then to the rear, or putting my arm over the shoulder of someone I was talking with.

It was early morning in front of the largest of the package delivery's sorting facilities, a low horizontal form spreading over more than a square block of suburban territory. A large group of staff was there campaigning because the opposition had published a leaflet stating the most offensive and dangerous lies of the campaign yet: that Jerry Zero had said Emmett Till was a "n" who deserved to be hung. The incumbent slate had tolerated a lot of slander, but this it could never abide. Jerry's campaign staff had gone to court and won a temporary restraining order against the challengers to stop distributing the flier. But the damage had been done at this facility, the only one they had leafleted, where an estimated 90 percent of the 4,000 workers were African American.

We were standing in front of a revolving gate handing out palm cards. Other folks were guarding the other gates. With us was Becky, the popular BA from the facility. I began to understand why this facility has the reputation for being full of gang members.

Becky, a white woman, put an arm around the shoulder of a white man going into the gate and hoarsely whispered, "Remember that matter I handled for you?" as she handed him a card. He nodded.

I passed out cards and gave people the pitch as they came to or went from the facility. One older African American woman joined us with a nonstop line of comical commentary on Jerry's opposition, meant to taunt the burly feeder driver from the opposition who was also leafleting the facility for the opposition.

I knew the guy's name. Suzan had interviewed him in our telephone survey. I had seen him at meetings and had met him somewhere, probably at a stewards' meeting. He knew about our study. We never hesitated to explain what we were doing to anyone who asked. He approached me, got in my face in the way Reese had illustrated to the steward when we went to defend him against charges of lying to management, and hissed, "Doesn't this cross the line between advocacy and objectivity?" Mindful of the Teamsters watching, I held my ground, never lost eye contact, and drew myself to my full five foot eight, nose to nose with this guy, and hissed right back, "We discussed dat," trying to simulate the Chicago accent along with the Teamster body language. He backed down.

I got approving looks from my companions as I resumed leafleting.

Out of the other gate came a large young African American man. I strode to catch up with him, draped my arm over his shoulder, and passed him a card, feeling pretty proud of myself for mastering the walk and the physicality. As I returned to the gate, I saw Becky and Suzan looking at me in horror. They both told me, "Don't touch anybody. Not here."

"Oh, shit," I thought, "I broke some other rule . . . the race thing probably, maybe the gang-banger thing, maybe both."

By 8 a.m., everyone was in or out of the facility, and we joined the others in the crew to go to a diner for breakfast. The rep told the story of me approaching the African American guy and her apprehension that that was the last she'd ever see of me. (Suzan suggested later that draping my arm over a total stranger was the biggest infraction, with race, union affiliation, and the fact that I was trying to convince him to do something he obviously had no time for coming in second, third, and fourth, respectively, as reasons never to do that again.) I started a conversation about the status of the election. People seemed optimistic. I asked people to go around the table and assess their barns. Every one of them indicated that his or her barn was a shoe-in for Jerry. Solid.

In the car on the way to the union hall, I asked Suzan, "If all the barns are so solid, why are they campaigning so hard? Is this just a ritual to build solidarity among the staff? Is it to create a sense of us/them so the staff has some center of identity? Why so much work if they are so sure of winning?" That puzzled me.

Suzan pulled the car into the parking garage attached to the Teamster's building and went inside while I walked down the street toward the United Electrical Workers hall where Campbell had set up a phone bank. I worked the phones with a crew of three to five volunteers who came and went.

That night, just before 11 p.m., Suzan and I were waiting in the warmth of the parked car for Mark and Mike, both BAs, to arrive to leaflet a package sorting facility by the airport. I said, "Something's wrong."

"With what?" Suzan asked.

"All I've been hearing is these guys appealing to reciprocity. One way or another they're saying, 'We did something for you, now you owe us your vote.'"

"Well, yeah, I guess so," Suzan said. "That's what elections are about isn't it? This *is* Chicago."

"But it's not what our surveys told us. Something's wrong with those surveys. When the ethnography goes one way and survey data go another direction, I will always trust the ethnography over the surveys."

We had done the random sample survey of the union's stewards, but we hadn't completed writing the report. When I asked the leaders if they wanted the report on the results, they said no, hold on to it until after the election so nobody could claim it affected the results. I drew the sample from the list of all the stewards the union provided. Suzan called and interviewed the chosen ones. She typed in the numbers, and I crunched them. Suzan speaks for herself.

Reciprocity?

Paul said something about how the data showed that stewards didn't buy into the notion of reciprocity, but I hadn't spent much time thinking about that. I figured it didn't make any sense. Everybody knows that when you do people a good turn, they owe you for it. When we went out to help this crew campaign, it came as no surprise to me, especially after working several Chicago elections, that business agents told members, "Vote for Jerry. He's the one who got you a four-dollar-per-hour raise over the last four years."

Of course, that's what you would say in any campaign, I was thinking. You talk about results. You give people information about what you've accomplished, and they vote for you. Paul was shaking his head.

"Look," he said. "Some of the staff [we hadn't given them a chance to object on their surveys, and later efforts to ask the question again failed] is telling us it has nothing to do with reciprocity, and more than half of the stewards refused to answer the question because they objected to the notion of owing anyone in the union. But here this BA was saying, 'We won this for you so give us your vote.' And we've seen stewards out there doing the same thing. Our surveys must be wrong."

"They must be," I said, still not understanding what use that knowledge could be but figuring at the very least it would turn into some dig about sociologists and their surveys. So we were sitting the car discussing this in the middle of a cold, windy Chicago night. Paul tells what happened next.

A Cold Chicago Night

Mike and Mark drove up just then.

The November wind whipped at our faces as the clock marched toward midnight and we lay in wait for 705 members to spin through the revolving gate that protects the package delivery company's O'Hare Airport facility. In my fist in my jacket pocket was a stack of business card–size palm cards reminding people to vote for Jerry Zero's slate. I had staked out one quarter of the area to cover. Suzan, Mike, and Mark were guarding the other sectors so no one could escape to the parking lot without a card and a word from one of us.

Mike, the BA for the facility, told us that "his" chief steward had "flipped," gone over to the other side. He was worried what effect that would have on "his" members and warned us that we might see the man that night.

After a few minutes, Mike decided to go inside and see how things were going. We stayed and handed out palm cards.

"Hi, sister," said Mark to a statuesque African American woman exiting. "Remember the raise Jerry got for you?"

"You ain't *MY* brother," she said breaking her stride only half a step to say the words with an expression between a smirk and a sneer on her face.

"That race thing again," I thought.

"We're all union brothers and sisters," Mark said to her back without skipping a beat.

Mark handed each person who came his direction a card with the list of people on the Jerry Zero slate, pointed to Jerry's name, and said, "This is the guy who got you a four-dollar-an-hour raise. Can you hook us up?" In contemporary adult Chicago slang he meant, "Will you support us?" It was a classic appeal to reciprocity.

The workers' reactions were as chilly as the cold wind. People grabbed the cards and kept walking or answered curtly "I already voted" with a weird grin or a nod of dismissal. A short, burly man in a Carhart jacket and an opposition union button walked past saying "I already voted" and smirked.

"That's him. That's the chief steward," Mark said.

When Mike came out of the barn, he asked Mark what he thought of support for the slate out there. "It's not bad at all," Mark said. "I think you've got a good 80–85 percent here. Don't worry about it."

As we walked to our car, Suzan was muttering. I knew what the problem was. "I think they're lucky if they get 35 or 40 percent out of there, probably less. I don't know where that guy's getting his numbers from. If they had that kind of support, people would stop and talk to them, even in the cold, the stewards would help pass out cards, show their support. They wouldn't just leave and look at us that way."

"Uh-oh," I said, "What do you think about what we heard at breakfast?"

"Well, these are seasoned guys, but if they're reporting these kinds of numbers they're deluded."

Another evening I was with one of the higher-ups, a veteran of Chicago politics, going to leaflet another barn. I took the opportunity of the time in the car to ask him the same question I'd put to Suzan, "If the Zero slate is so far ahead, why work so hard?"

This seasoned politico had always been frank in his opinions and assessments. He said, "Better to run scared than confident" and left it at that.

I asked what the deal with the feeder drivers was.

"Fucking feeder drivers," he started as he explained how they expected the moon, they were never satisfied, they thought only of themselves and never of the rest of the union. The last contract had changed the procedure for them during layoffs. Their seniority would now be figured on the basis of their district instead of the entire Chicago area. That meant fewer feeder driver jobs if there was a layoff. The one massive facility in the southern suburbs was so big it was considered its own district. A layoff there meant a pretty quick, if temporary, fall to loader or package car driver, a horrible fate for these aristocrats of the package industry.

We got out of the car and leafleted the workers coming in and out of the facility.

Suzan and I had discussed a paper on the election as ritual—that is, actions disproportional to their stated objective of getting Jerry and his guys elected again. It must be doing something else, I thought, bringing the staff together through shared anxiety and distress, making everyone confident that they were in the same boat, something besides getting Jerry elected. Suzan picks up the story again.

The Count Comes In

As the afternoon of the vote count moved toward early evening, the tension in the office behind the auditorium began to increase. There were fewer funny stories and more hushed whispers. Supporters from all the slates began to stand at the back of the hall, outside the table barricade of the "counting floor," watching each slip of paper move from one place to the next. The leaders of the slates were watching the counters handling the envelopes, double-checking that envelopes were emptied out, carrying mail flats to the center of the room and back.

"We'll know in the first twenty minutes," one staffer told me. "Unless it's real close, it never changes after the first twenty minutes."

Finally, six hours after they'd begun, the counters began to separate ballots from their inner envelopes. Then, another hour later they began to sort ballots into piles—the Jerry Zero slate, the Steve Pocztowski slate, the New Leadership slate, and mixed votes.

Observers had pens and paper at the ready and tallied up the ballots as they landed in each mail flat. Floor captains walked behind them collecting the tallies. After the first twenty minutes I saw the Jerry Zero floor captain head into the back office. I followed him.

In the large leather chair was a small man with a pencil hovering over an accountant's book. Next to him was a woman taking down the numbers as the floor captain read them off to her. Jerry was sitting in a chair on the other side of the desk. Others were sitting or standing around, listening quietly.

"Jerry Zero slate: 58. Steve Pocztowski: 78. Jerry Zero slate: 52. Steve Pocstowski: 71. Steve Pocstowski: 68, Jerry Zero: 48." And so it went. The room fell absolutely silent. Then a cell phone rang. One of the staffers handed it to Jerry.

"We're getting killed," he said to his old friend on the other end of the line, one of the chief negotiators who had had to leave to attend a wedding. "We're getting killed, I'm telling you."

I watched that night as fifty of the most dedicated, bright, and articulate union staff members I'd ever seen lost their election and with it their jobs, their hopes, and, at least for the moment, their basic belief in justice—that balance between right and wrong where right always wins if you just hang in there long enough. I watched them cry. I talked to them about what they would do next. They stammered out answers, still kind enough to humor the researcher from Penn State even in their grief and shock. A few would go back to driving trucks. Others would retire. One proclaimed, "They're going to have to throw me out the window. I'm not leaving!" The staff has a union. They can only be fired for just cause. It could get interesting in the new year.

I was miserable when I called Paul to give him the news.

"It's a bad year for incumbents," Jerry said laconically in a staff meeting before they headed to a restaurant to commiserate with supporters. "I just hope the same goes for Bush."

On the way out of the auditorium, I stopped by the camper the opposition slate had used for its campaign and offered my card to the guys there drinking beer. I told them who I was, what we were doing, and asked them to have Steve give us a call. He never did.

What Happened?

When I returned, Paul peppered me with questions about the election and kept throwing out ideas about how we could find out what happened. A random sample of members was out of the question. We only had a couple of weeks before the new guys moved in, and a bunch of them had seen us join in the campaigning. There was little chance they'd take the time to understand what "participant observation" meant while they were trying to learn how to run a union. There was a good chance they'd see us as part of the Jerry Zero camp and not provide the access we'd enjoyed to this point. Paul suggested we get the current staff to distribute surveys to members as they visited their barns over the holidays.

"You've got to be kidding," I said. "You think these guys could care about our stupid study? They've just gotten thrown out on their butts, without any warning. They're feeling betrayed by everyone who said they supported them. They're bewildered as to why when they did such a great job they lost the election. It's *Christmas*! They're wondering what they're going to do for a living in January, and you want me to ask them to hand out a bunch of useless surveys to a bunch of truck drivers who didn't vote for them, get the surveys back, and get them to us?"

We argued about whether to approach the local about it, and finally Paul called and asked. Our contact person there said it sounded like a good idea and that he'd check with others. Paul got off the phone looking a little too triumphant for my taste. Then we got the return call, and the local had decided against it. It would be almost impossible since most of the staff was taking vacation for the holidays and not on the usual schedule. I felt vindicated, although disappointed that we wouldn't have a chance to talk to members.

A week later, Paul told me to go ahead and send the report he'd written to Jerry. He'd been following Jerry's advice to wait until after the election before turning it in. To make sure I sent the latest version of the file, I opened it and read the summary of conclusions. Right there in the second paragraph was the conclusion I hadn't really heard all that time.

Paul had written, on the summary page in front of the report, "there is little evidence of the traditional politics of obligation that BAs can use to build bases within the local. Almost half of stewards rejected the question and there is very little agreement among staff. This suggests that grievance handling and negotiating contracts do not translate into obligations that staff feel they can translate into votes."

"So it was a sampling problem," Paul said.

"What?" I responded, still a little stunned.

"Our conclusion that the surveys were wrong. The classical weakness of ethnography. We got too close to the people we were working with. We couldn't see beyond the handful of people we were in tight with. We didn't see beyond them to the rest of the union. We explain in elementary courses how you don't just talk to people in bars or just to people in churches. You have to have a random sample or else talk to everyone. And we were just in the churches. Or the bars. We didn't sample the whole union. The surveys were better for that and gave us the right answer after all. We just didn't see it."

"So that means ethnography isn't any good?"

"No, not at all. Without lots of ethnography, we wouldn't even know what questions to ask or how to begin to answer them. It's just as meaningless to count things you don't understand as it is to deny the importance of quantitative data across the board. There's a place for surveys and a place for ethnography. The trick is to figure out the proper place of each."

Democracy?

So we learned once again a classical lesson about sampling and about the relationships between ethnography and survey data. But we learned so much more. The conversations in the next days and weeks were like conversations friends and relatives have when someone dies unexpectedly. "It was fate," "it was an accident," "it was . . ." searching for pattern, searching for meaning.

One lesson: one-person, one-vote elections are not the acid test of democracy. But we knew that from our experience as Americans. As is the case with the rest of us, only a small portion of the members voted. As one staffer said, he figured the real winner would be "I left my ballot on top of the refrigerator." Only a dozen more voted in this election than had done so three years previous. The last time there were five opposition slates. This time there were three—three of the previous slates had united as one stronger slate. With the same number of voters, they won. That was enough to explain it, just the dynamics of voting.

But still, the questions remained. People were not satisfied with the answers. Maybe that's the thing about democracy, as with anthropology; we have to keep asking the questions.

References Cited

Doukas, Dimitra
2003 *Worked Over: The Corporate Sabotage of an American Community*. Ithaca: Cornell University Press.

Durrenberger, E. Paul, and Suzan Erem
2005 *Class Acts: An Anthropology of Urban Service Workers and Their Union.* Boulder: Paradigm.
2007 *Anthropology Unbound: A Field Guide to the 21st Century*. Boulder: Paradigm.

Durrenberger, E. Paul, and Tom King
2000 Introduction. In *State and Community in Fisheries Management: Power, Policy, and Practice,* ed. E. Paul Durrenberger and Thomas D. King, 1–15. Westport, CT: Bergin and Garvey.

Erem, Suzan

2001 *Labor Pains: Inside America's New Union Movement*. New York: Monthly Review Press.

Fones-Wolf, Elizabeth

1995 *Selling Free Enterprise: The Business Assault on Labor and Liberalism*. Champaign: University of Illinois Press.

Frank, Thomas

2005 *What's the Matter with Kansas: How Conservatives Won the Heart of America*. New York: Holt.

Leaf, Murray

1998 *Pragmatism and Development: The Prospect for Pluralist Transformation in the Third World*. Westport, CT: Burgin and Garvey.

Soros, George

2008 *The New Paradigm for Financial Markets: The Credit Crisis of 2008 and What It Means*. New York: Public Affairs.

Trawick, Paul

2002 *The Struggle for Water in Peru: Comedy and Tragedy in the Andean Commons*. Palo Alto: Stanford University Press.

FOUR

With God on Everyone's Side: Truth Telling and Toxic Words among Methodists and Organized Farmworkers in North Carolina

Sandy Smith-Nonini

Moral authority and religious faith have been important components of social struggle during both the civil rights movement and farm labor organizing struggles. From his earliest efforts organizing in the fields, former United Farm Workers (UFW) president Cesar Chavez worked closely with the fledgling California Migrant Ministry (CMM), which assigned staff members to assist with his labor campaign (Hoffman 1987). The new partnership of the UFW and progressive religious supporters involved a gradual shift from charity and service work to social justice advocacy as a central focus for mobilization. This shift was facilitated by several factors, including the late 1960s culture of youth mobilizing for social change, Chavez's adoption of Gandhian nonviolent organizing techniques, and the Catholic Church's authorization after Vatican II of liberation theology, with its focus on building solidarity at the grassroots through practices that involved social action to alleviate poverty and other forms of oppression. Even today, after a period of growing influence by Protestant evangelicals and charismatic churches in Latin America, about three-quarters of Mexican American farmworkers grew up Catholic, and the traditions of liberation theology and rhetoric about class solidarity among rural workers dating to the Mexican revolution resonate with many from their pre-immigrant lives in Mexico (Hoffman 1987; Holt and Mattern 2002).

In 1972, as the UFW expanded into other states, the CMM folded itself into the newly formed National Farm Worker Ministry (NFWM) to build a national leadership within the churches in support of consumer boycotts supporting farm labor (Hoffman 1987). Such boycotts have proven to be a crucial strategy for agricultural workers who lack the protections for strikes and collective bargaining the National Labor Relations Act provides to other categories of workers. Although farm labor continues to be one of the most dangerous and poorly paid occupations in the United States, the nation's increasingly Mexican American workforce faces many obstacles in seeking reforms, including lack of understanding English, fear of deportation, and chronic poverty that causes many workers to accept deplorable conditions in exchange for employment. Growers, when facing a labor dispute, have often taken advantage of these vulnerabilities by seeking replacement workers to undercut strikes (Edid 1994).

Emulating the UFW, the Farm Labor Organizing Committee (FLOC), based in Toledo, Ohio, pursued a similar boycott strategy targeting the Campbell's Soup Company during the 1980s on behalf of Midwest tomato and cucumber pickers. FLOC's eight-year boycott, combined with moral pressure on Campbell's, ended in a three-way contract among farmworkers, growers, and Campbell's Soup—which set a precedent by involving the corporate processor in the grower–farm labor relationship. In 1999 FLOC began a new campaign in North Carolina that again targeted a corporate processor—this time, the Mt. Olive Pickle Company, which had attained second place in the nation in sales of supermarket shelf pickles.

The NFWM was a key ally in building the "communities" on which the UFW and FLOC relied to support and promote their consumer boycotts. Their community building involved outreach and networking with people of faith, students, other unions, nongovernmental organizations, and community groups in urban centers (Barger and Reza 1994). Like Chavez, FLOC president Baldemar Velasquez, ordained as a charismatic minister, drew on biblical prophecy and Christian inspiration in defending farmworkers' rights. As with the UFW, priests, nuns, and Protestant clergy often provided accompaniment during FLOC's public marches, which offered a level of security for workers. Religious grounding also helped to validate union claims and build a bridge between poor, often undocumented immigrants and middle-class consumers with little knowledge of agribusiness.

My involvement in FLOC's North Carolina campaign as an anthropologist and farmworker advocate came about after a chance encounter with an organizer the NFWM had sent in 1998 to help lay groundwork for the campaign among people of faith. In 1999–2000 I helped organize a Unitarian Universalists (UU) project to provide statewide education about farm labor in support of the FLOC campaign. Many of the denominations and individual churches that supported the campaign had social justice traditions that included support of labor and immigrant rights. In addition to the UU, early supporters included the United Church of Christ, the Catholic Church, and Quakers.

The campaign for a contract with Mt. Olive lasted five years and ended in a contract signed in September 2004 among the company, FLOC, and the North Carolina Growers Association (NCGA), an H2A "guest-worker" brokerage that provided labor for most Mt. Olive growers. According to observers close to the negotiations, a key factor that prompted Mt. Olive's CEO Bill Bryan to negotiate with FLOC was the decision by the United Methodist Church earlier that year to support FLOC's ongoing boycott of Mt. Olive pickles. The National Council of Churches, representing thirty-six Protestant, Anglican, and Orthodox denominations, had endorsed the boycott the previous November, as had many individual denominations.

Bryan, a Methodist, had lobbied personally against the decision at the church's General Conference in May, and he had previously rallied conservative Methodist supporters in North Carolina's eastern counties to oppose FLOC's efforts. Early in the campaign NFWM organizers found the state's churches deeply divided on the issues of the rights of immigrant workers and organized labor. Both clergy and lay leaders of white Protestant churches, especially in rural counties, tended to side with local farmers over undocumented immigrants, who many saw as interlopers. Black churches, weakened by a shortage of clergy in rural areas, tended to be more sympathetic toward labor, but their congregations found little common ground with immigrants, who many saw as competing with African Americans for jobs.

We found that the national leadership of denominations often took more pro-labor stands than did regional leaders and that urban congregations were more receptive to FLOC's message than were those in rural areas, which had been hit by twin economic blows from the loss of manufacturing jobs and the scaling back of federal support for tobacco. For example, as early as 2000, members of the staff of the Washington-based Methodist General Board of Church and Society were sympathetic to the FLOC effort, but a lobbying effort by farmworker supporters at the 2003 national Methodist General Conference failed to gain endorsement of the boycott. As noted earlier, the vote went in FLOC's favor at the Methodist General Conference the following year.

Thus, clearly, "communities" in solidarity with immigrant labor cannot be assumed but must be built. Certainly, ethnic differences, reinforced by the language barrier and a class divide, have made it easier for farmers (and consumers) to rationalize poor living and working conditions for farm labor. This sentiment was rarely expressed in public but came out at times in private conversations. One wealthy grower in his sixties gave me a tour of his labor camps, shrugging off concerns about the stark barracks and tiny tin roof–covered rooms. "I don't have no fancy labor camps, but they're better than the house I was raised in," he said, lamenting about the money he spent on repairs each year: "Some people don't know how to take care of things. . . . I'll provide the mattresses and soap and hot water, but I'm not going to wipe their behinds."*

Most of the time, the FLOC campaign's public debates were civil exchanges. Bryan in particular projected a pleasant demeanor and quiet diplomacy in representing Mt. Olive to the public. The hostile encounters that occurred tended to take place in the countryside. During 1998 one grower famously confronted a FLOC organizer, asserting: "The North may have won the [Civil] War, but that was just on paper. We still haven't given up our slaves." Other times, ethnicity was indexed by paternalism. On one of her first outings, an NFWM volunteer knocked on the door of a grower's house and was asked pointedly, "Why do you want to visit '*my* Mexicans?' " Confrontations took place most often on large tobacco farms in eastern counties. In contrast, on some smaller farms I visited, workers told me of farmers who kept a relationship with the same group of workers year after year, even learning basic Spanish to improve communication. As anyone familiar with farmwork knows, having a boss of common ethnicity is no guarantee against exploitation—many unscrupulous non-H2A crew leaders are Mexican Americans.

I was a participant-observer in an early skirmish among Methodists over the FLOC campaign when Bryan supporters in eastern North Carolina or-

* This and similar quotations are from personal interviews with FLOC organizers and volunteers conducted during my work in North Carolina.

ganized a Methodist-sponsored conference in late April 2000 with an anti-labor theme. In this chapter, I use the experience and aftermath of this event to reflect on the historical relationship among religion, race, and labor relations in the South. This history is especially relevant, given the recent wave of Latino immigrants to the Southeast and the rise of anti-immigrant sentiment that followed the spring 2006 marches for immigration reform.

The conference, entitled Mediating toward Justice for All: The Pickle Industry, grew out of a pledge Bryan had made at a North Carolina Council of Churches meeting six months earlier. Frustrated at Bryan's refusal to meet with FLOC leaders, a Methodist lay leader put Bryan on the spot by challenging him to agree to attend a church forum to discuss farmworker concerns with FLOC. He agreed and in the months to come received gentle pressure from farmworker advocates to follow through on his pledge. Methodists living near Mt. Olive who supported Bryan's anti-union position, in league with a conservative Methodist lay leader in Raleigh, hijacked the idea and obtained backing from the regional Methodist conference, which represents parishes in eastern North Carolina.

As a former member of a more liberal Methodist church in Durham, North Carolina, where I grew up, I was intrigued to learn from the FLOC staff that the conference, initially conceived as an event for reconciliation, had morphed into an anti-labor event. Although FLOC had been invited to the conference with a month's notice, it was not invited to participate in planning the dates or the agenda. It was not until the last week that the union staff saw the conference's preliminary agenda, which stated that a key goal was to seek an "alternative to labor organizing farmworkers."

In addition to Bryan, representatives from the NCGA (the H2A "guest-worker" brokerage that supplies seasonal workers to three out of four Mt. Olive growers), the owner of one of the state's largest farms, and staff from the state Departments of Agriculture and Labor were invited. It appeared that FLOC was invited almost as an afterthought—the preliminary agenda listed the last speaker on the panel as "a representative of a farmworker union (such as FLOC)." No other Latino or farmworker advocacy organizations were invited, although many exist in North Carolina.

The FLOC staff was cautioned by the Methodist organizers that the conference would not be open to the public and that each of the represented interests would be limited to bringing three to five observers, in addition to the main spokesperson. The meeting was held in Goldsboro, a few miles from the town of Mt. Olive in eastern North Carolina's tobacco belt.

Interestingly, very few Methodists other than staff of the church's state and national offices attended, although clergy from Catholic and Presbyterian parishes and the North Carolina Council of Churches were present. During the meeting, organizers noted that they had invited administrators of other pickle processors and other farmers to attend but all had declined, which was not surprising. Both groups had previously kept a low profile during the Mt. Olive–FLOC controversy.

FLOC president Baldemar Velasquez also declined to attend in person, citing the "anti-labor" bias of the agenda, but he did send a letter to be read aloud. The union's vice president, Fernando Cuevas, did attend, as did a handful of FLOC supporters from the religious community. Several vanloads of farmworkers invited by FLOC also showed up—much to the chagrin of the Methodists, who seemed to have worked hard to avoid publicizing the event or putting leaders of "the pickle industry" in a confrontational situation.

The classic Georgian red brick chapel of Pine Valley Methodist Church (a pseudonym) fronted a busy four-lane highway that sliced through Goldsboro's commercial district. As a former member of a liberal congregation, I felt somewhat miffed by these conservative Methodists, so I decided to cast aside my secular humanist materialism and go slightly undercover in the interest of social science. I hurried up the steps between the white columns, distancing myself from the farmworker contingent that had just arrived.

Not having been officially invited, I was concerned about being turned away. I shook the hands of the gentlemen in suits hosting the conference with as much southern charm as I could muster. Delighted to be there, I slipped the name of my childhood Methodist church into the chitchat when they asked what group I was with. They handed me a name tag and introduced me to the effusive elderly minister who would moderate the meeting. In this account I call him Rev. Samuel Jones, and in what follows I use pseudonyms for all participants who were not acting in their official capacity as organizational spokespersons. The Mt. Olive contingent and a handful of invited religious observers had already arrived. I watched as the first contingent of scruffily dressed farmworkers with women and children in tow came through the doors and the good Methodists' plans began to go awry.

With no one to translate, the next few minutes were a cacophony. The entry hall filled with brown-skinned, Spanish-speaking men and women, many of them hesitant and waiting for directions. The first few were welcomed with good cheer, but as more and more arrived, the gentlemen in suits frowned and whispered among themselves. Someone was sent in search of the FLOC leaders. Fernando Cuevas and his staff were cornered by the men, who reminded them in stern tones of the limits set on participation for each interest group. The FLOC staff pointed out politely that the agenda of interested groups was heavily biased toward "pickle industry" representatives who opposed reforms to farmworkers' living and working conditions and that farmworkers' voices needed to be heard. This rationale gained no traction. The Methodist men and the union finally reached a compromise, allowing eight farmworkers into the meeting room as observers. They shunted the others, including most of the women and children, into the empty sanctuary and asked a church lady from the kitchen crew to help with child care. My shaky cover as a neutral Methodist began to slip as I joined other farmworker advocates present in protesting this exclusion, which neatly divided the mostly white, educated English speakers from the apparent threat of Mexican workers—was it their language, skin color, the sweat stains on their clothes? I had not seen such overt ethnic segregation in years.

The Methodist delegate from the denomination's national office was visibly disappointed that things had gotten off to such a poor start. Although farmworker advocates regarded him as an ally, at this moment he was taking out his ire on a FLOC staffer. "Why did you bring so many people?" he whispered in an annoyed tone. The national office very much wanted to resolve the conflicts among Methodists over this issue.

An elderly lay leader, who I later learned was a Raleigh-based conservative advocate within the Methodist state leadership, took umbrage at my suggestion that the policy of excluding the Mexicans was discriminatory. "They were not invited," he told me bluntly.

"I was not invited," I pointed out. "Why did you let me in?" The man glared at me but offered no reply. Finally, a group of about ten farmworkers decided to leave and went to their vehicle.

In the meeting room, eighteen spokespeople for the invited parties were grouped around a long rectangular table. They included eleven representatives of different players in the pickle industry such as farmers, the processing plant, and the NCGA "guest-worker" program; two representatives of regulatory divisions of the state government; and five spokespeople for FLOC, including two former farmworkers. Reverend Jones, the moderator, took charge with a no-nonsense Cotton Mather management style and designated the remaining thirty to forty attendees (including myself) as observers. We were asked to sit around the periphery of the room and informed that only those at the table would be allowed to speak.

The large room could have easily accommodated the farmworkers who had been sent to wait in the sanctuary, but Reverend Jones's show of authority had us all acting like sheep in the hope that some meaningful dialogue could still take place. The migrant families would not have understood the bulk of the meeting in any case, as it was conducted in English with no translation. I felt bad for the eight farmworker observers lining the wall nearest the speakers' table. A bilingual observer sitting nearby leaned over to whisper the gist of the proceedings to them from time to time, but she was hampered by Reverend Jones's edict that observers stay silent. Luckily, he ignored my tape recorder on the table, so I was able to record the proceedings. (Quotations from the meeting were transcribed from that recording.)

Reverend Jones set the tone of the meeting in his opening statement, which included this comment: "The principal players [in the pickle industry] must be fairly rewarded. . . . This can be done through a competitive, fair, and just commercial enterprise. However, this industry . . . cannot achieve the goals just stated with tactics used of threat, intimidation, raw power, and bad faith." He went on to call for a "zone of truth, fairness, and goodwill" and asked the speakers to "offer solutions that speak to the needs of all the parties involved."

At this point he permitted a farmworker advocate to read the letter from FLOC president Baldemar Velasquez, who explained his nonparticipation because of the conference's anti-union nature and called on North Carolina Methodists to answer a central question: whether farmworkers have a right to form a union. "If the answer is yes," he wrote, "then you would listen to that voice and allow self-determination to prevail." The alternative, he said, would be to "join the ranks of prevailing paternalism in North Carolina, where everybody knows what is good for the farmworkers."

After the letter was read Jones qualified his tolerance, saying, "Without knowing the contents of that letter, I permitted it to be read." He then introduced Bob Harris, whose 3,500-acre farm in Nash County supplies 15 percent of Mt. Olive's North Carolina–grown cucumbers, with rhetoric that gave new meaning to the notion of paternalism: "We are seeking understanding, not decision making. . . . Words like boycott, unionizing, threats, these are toxic words, toxic expressions, and when they are used in certain ways, they divide rather than bring together."

In an interview I conducted with Harris a few months prior to the conference, he had boasted that he had inherited much of his land from his grandfather, who in his day was Nash County's largest farmer. Harris's large farm depended on a non-H2A labor broker that supplied 600 migrant workers during the growing season each year, and his farm had revenues of $30–$35 million annually. Harris's comments at the conference emphasized heightened competition from globalization, a theme that became a frequent discourse for pickle industry participants:

> We are in a global market. We have to compete, not with our neighbors, not with other farmers in the United States so much but on a worldwide basis. We have to compete with really cheap wages in India, Central America, Mexico. Their production is going up, up, up, and we cannot compete. The consumer in this country wants cheap food. The percentage of income spent on food in this country is the least in the world, and food imports are rising. . . . The U.S. consumer is wanting [his or her] food to be grown overseas. . . . And the wages in the United States vs. foreign wages . . . there's just a lot of difference in them. And that's the reason we're losing market share.

Later the same day, Harris added a new twist to the issue of competition from Mexico and Central America, claiming "we're competing against a tremendous amount of drug money that finances these operations." Both in our interview and at the meeting, Harris frequently mentioned the large sums of money he spends on his labor force: $30,000 a month for utilities, $130,000 to purchase port-a-johns. He attributed these costs to government regulations:

> A lot of [these regulations] are made up there in Washington, and they just have no idea in the world what they have to do with reality. . . . What hurts our farm operation is we have to put up with certain regulations that other people don't. I think something constructive that this group could push for is workmen's compensation for everybody. The small farmer doesn't pay workmen's comp, doesn't have to. But workmen's comp is a very, very big expense of our operation. And every time I've tried to get the legislature to consider this, the Farm Bureau fights this tooth and nail. They say they're looking after the small farmer. The other thing we have to do is pay minimum wages. The small farmers—they have certain exemptions from minimum wage that we don't have.

Later in the day he reiterated his opposition to small-farmer exemptions, claiming they make "people like us be on a very un-level playing field." Interestingly, in our private interview a few months earlier, Harris had described a playing field tilted a different way. In that setting he proudly recounted how he had built his business through buying up land lost by smaller farmers who could not handle the high interest rates in the 1970s.

Globalization again came up later in the day when Bill Bryan spoke. In this conference setting he emphasized how he was resisting attractive offers to do more business abroad so he could buy more pickles from North Carolina growers. However, in an interview with me two months earlier, Bryan had dismissed FLOC as a threat in North Carolina, emphasizing that his company now bought a larger percentage of its pickles from other states and was responding to consumer demand by marketing more "fresh-packed" pickles from India, Mexico, and Honduras.

In his testimony, the NCGA spokesman touted the brokerages' adherence to federal H2A requirements for workers' compensation above minimum wages, housing inspections, and a new program of bilingual pesticide training—his point being that union representation was not needed for workers to get fair treatment. H2A workers harvested about three-quarters of Mt. Olive's North Carolina–grown pickles. Because of the tight labor market at that time, he argued that the association had nothing to gain by abusing workers. Naturally, he did not refer to the many complaints and lawsuits filed against his organization or to the fact that union leaders and legal aid lawyers were barred from attending worker orientations at which workers were instructed that farmworker legal services were "the enemy of the H2A program."

A retired staffer from the North Carolina Department of Labor and the state's only bilingual pesticide inspector spoke next. Both speakers told a tale of gradual improvement in protections for farmworkers since the 1960s and 1970s. Farmworker advocates and attorneys present attempted to correct what they saw as whitewashed accounts, but Reverend Jones denied them time to respond, pointing out that they were not among the invited speakers. When I later transcribed the day's proceedings, I found that the forces resisting any change in the status quo—for example, spokesmen for the pickle company, the farmers, the NCGA, and conservative voices from state agencies—accounted for four times the number of pages of transcribed testimony as did FLOC and farmworker testimony. The information from farmworkers conveyed in the meeting required constant jousting with Reverend Jones, who resisted attempts to allow this testimony at three different points during the day.

After the state speakers had finished, Fernando Cuevas of FLOC requested that a farmworker be allowed to speak. Reverend Jones resisted, saying he wanted to follow his agenda, which had the "pickers," as he called them, last. But several observers in the room supported Cuevas. Finally, Jones conceded. He turned to the row of farmworker observers along the wall and said loudly in English: "Do we have a picker?" The workers appeared confused since no one was translating the proceedings.

I called out to Jones: "None of the Hispanic people here understand. They are not part of this conversation."

Jones frowned and said "They're going to get translation." He asked Cuevas to interpret.

"One thing I want to say up front," said Cuevas, "is for these workers it takes a lot of guts to stand up here and say anything. So I want to make sure the workers don't get any harassment or don't get blacklisted and fired when they go back to work tomorrow. I'm going to take their names down, and if anything happens like that to a worker, I'm going to take somebody to court." He looked at a well-known Goldsboro-based produce grower sitting among the conference observers as he said this. "We should feel free to talk about our futures, our lives and concerns without somebody firing us."

He introduced a woman named Mary Lu who had previously worked as a farmworker. Her testimony touched on health issues: "I've [seen] people working where they could not even bring them water. If they get sick, they don't have no medical insurance. I've seen in one house twelve to fourteen people living together. I've seen a lot . . ."

Reverend Jones interrupted, "Is that a law? Is that a regulation? There's not a regulation that you get healthcare?" This was followed by a cacophony of comments on the rules and regulations from observers, but, as before, they were cut off by Jones in a pattern that began to be apparent. While Jones allowed Harris, the speaker for the growers' association, and Bryan to talk at length without interruption, he frequently intervened when farmworkers or their advocates brought up regulations—in some cases revealing his basic ignorance of issues (as seen earlier), at other times summing up a complex issue with a cliché or dismissing it as irrelevant.

I was sitting next to Sr. Evelyn Mattern, a highly respected elderly nun (now deceased) who headed the farmworker task force for the North Carolina Council of Churches. I had noticed her frustration in several attempts to get Reverend Jones's attention. Finally he turned to her. "I saw you jumping up over there, Sister Evelyn," he said, as if chastising a five-year-old.

Sister Evelyn winced and said, "I thought it would be important that everybody know that when the basic labor laws were formulated about sixty years ago in the United States, farmworkers were excluded. There have been attempts in North Carolina, bit by bit, to get workers' comp, to get some kind of healthcare coverage, to get some wage benefits like other workers have, but they've all been defeated in the North Carolina legislature. So we're really dealing with a situation where farmworkers are excluded from all the kinds of protections that even small business owners have to provide for their workers."

"So what you're saying is that this issue belongs to the state of North Carolina?" asked Reverend Jones.

Sister Evelyn replied, "No, I'm not saying that. I'm simply commenting on . . ."

Jones interrupted her: "If they haven't made the regulation, it belongs to them."

I remember thinking, what an odd, yet convenient, way to put it. The moral neatly spliced and separated from the legal—a common stance in a rural area where disdain for government intervention holds sway but an odd one to see a minister proclaim.

Jones again turned to Cuevas, who introduced a Spanish-speaking worker named Pablo. Jones again aggressively tried to control the testimony, interrogating the farmworker speaker over his reference to "most" farmers, sometimes dismissing the content with jokes, and contesting with Cuevas over whether workers should be allowed to speak.

> JONES (*to Pablo*): I know you belong to FLOC, but can you speak [about] the workers, not siding with organizing labor? (*Cuevas translates.*)
>
> PABLO: Sure. My English is not so well.
>
> JONES: Mine's not either, but go ahead. (*laughter*)
>
> PABLO (*speaking in Spanish, interpreted by Cuevas*): The only time [he] sees the posters put up with pesticide prevention information is right after an accident. In other words, an accident has to happen where somebody gets hurt before they put up the poster saying be careful.
>
> JONES: You lock the door after the horse is out. Are there other issues you'd like to speak to where the workers are concerned, besides the posting of regulations?
>
> PABLO (*Cuevas translating*): You know when the work is over at the end of the season, as soon as they don't need you anymore, most of the farmers throw you out of the housing right away. That's very upsetting.

JONES: Talking about truth telling just a little bit . . . how does he know it's most of them? See, these words are very toxic . . . most, always, shoulds, and all these kinds of statements. Can you give us some information that would help us?

PABLO: The majority of farmers . . . (*Cuevas begins to translate, Jones interrupts him.*)

JONES: So you have found that to be true in other situations?

PABLO (loudly): I've worked here for a long time. And I know. I've been working here since 1974—in North Carolina. Now I live here.

JONES (boisterously): Welcome to the state. (*Jones abruptly turns away from the worker and looks at Cuevas.*) And now you said you would speak. (*Cuevas speaks in Spanish to a farmworker. Jones looks annoyed.*)

CUEVAS (*responding to Jones*): When you asked before if anyone wanted to say anything, he stood up.

JONES: I know he did. But he didn't speak.

CUEVAS: I was just making sure whether he still wanted to say anything.

JONES *(to Cuevas)*: Would you speak to the issue we're talking about? I'm asking you to speak, and you keep on asking someone else to do it. Will you speak to the issue?

VOICE FROM OBSERVER SECTION (*to Jones*): Don't you want to hear from the workers?

CUEVAS: I will speak at any time, but . . .

JONES: I'm asking you to right now.

CUEVAS: It's very rare that a migrant worker gets the opportunity to speak for himself. Very rare. I'm willing to speak, but I want Bryan to see that it's not Fernando Cuevas saying this thing and that thing . . .

JONES: Hey, I asked him to speak and no one is speaking, so either he speaks or he doesn't speak. (*Jones is gesturing to the row of workers while talking in English, not waiting for translation. Finally, the worker Cuevas spoke with signals that he wants to speak.*)

JONES: Okay, good show.

CUEVAS (*translating*): His name is Fidel Martinez (*pseudonym*). He says when we go to eat, they don't give us soap or water so we can wash, and the toilets in the fields get so full they're disgusting. . . . He says the workers need protection from pesticides—he calls them poisons—on the plants. He is talking about an experience that happened last year with some of his coworkers. As they were harvesting, they got some kind of blisters on their hands, and the grower didn't do anything about it, no one did anything or recommended to them what to do. And they got so severe they paid out of their own pocket to go to the doctor. And they paid for their own medical expenses and prescription expenses.

At this point the state pesticide specialist, Peyam Barghassa, broke in to instruct the worker in Spanish on how to file a complaint with the state and offered Martinez his card. Martinez told the man to give the card to Cuevas. This prompted Reverend Jones to intervene.

JONES *(to Barghassa)*: If I understood, he said to give your card to FLOC? What about going to you?

BARGHASSA: Well . . . [it's an issue of] how I can get the cards out to workers and tell them to call us and tell us what the problems are. If we don't know about the problems we can't do anything. We have inspectors . . . but there's a difference between an inspection and someone calling and saying this is occurring.

JONES: Do you consider yourself an advocate for the workers?

BARGHASSA: We're a pesticide agency, which is a government . . .

JONES: Are you an advocate for them?

BARGHASSA: I care about the workers . . . we care about workers.

Repeatedly, the issue of farmwork regulations—always described as the realm of the state—became the neutral ground sought by both pickle industry spokespeople and Reverend Jones as proof that there was no need for a union. While Harris, the large farmer, had decried what he saw as an excess of regulations, Bryan of Mt. Olive took a different tack. Bryan had often pointed out in public forums on the union campaign that his company did not hire workers directly, and he usually distanced Mt. Olive from farmers' relationship with labor. But in the setting of the Methodist conference, he sought to shift the responsibility for taking action to the state.

Bryan said, "Our understanding was this was to be a conference about farmworker concerns. Legal solutions seem one way of dealing with those problems. It has been a long time since legislation of that type was debated in the [state] general assembly." A well-known farmworker advocate in the observer section interrupted Bryan to observe that state legislative proposals to provide workers' compensation for farmworkers in the past had never been voted out of committee.

"There were fourteen to fifteen years of public hearings before the field sanitation rules were passed, and it took two court orders before that law was put into effect," she added.

This promoted Sister Evelyn to stand up and pose a question to Bryan, eliciting another effort by Reverend Jones to trivialize her comments:

SISTER EVELYN: The proposal to cover farmworkers under workers' compensation laws will go back before the legislature in this next season. It would be wonderful if a good-faith effort could come out of this meeting. So I'd like to pose the question whether Bryan will endorse that legislative effort?

JONES (*in a sympathetic tone, to Bryan*): Do you feel like a bad man?

BRYAN: Yes. It is a terrible tactic this organization has taken.

SISTER EVELYN (*annoyed, stands up, speaking to Jones*): You just diminished the issue I raised by personalizing it. It is an important issue.

BRYAN: You could have posed that question to all the people here.

SISTER EVELYN: I would like to see the pickle industry supporting it.

JONES (*in a dismissive tone, to Sister Evelyn*): Thank you.

After lunch, Bryan made a lengthy statement (four single-spaced typed pages in my transcript) in which he emphasized that Mt. Olive did not employ farmers directly or hire farmworkers. He accused FLOC of unfairly targeting Mt. Olive, which he described as having "responsible" practices: "I think perhaps the greatest moral obligation that our company has is to provide our customers with quality, wholesome products that represent a clear value to the consumer. . . . We try to be a good corporate citizen. We look for good suppliers. We want to do business with good operators."

Like Harris, Bryan justified his company's practices by citing globalization: "We purchase cucumbers in about a dozen states, and we purchase in Mexico, in Honduras, in India," but he explained that this strategy was necessary to meet market demand for "fresh-packed" products and to enable the packinghouse operation to operate year-round. He said he had turned down offers to contract out pickle packing to Mexico because of a desire to keep jobs in North Carolina. On the other hand, one might read in this discourse a veiled threat that if workers coming to North Carolina were to unionize, Mt. Olive would do more purchasing and packing abroad.

But Bryan closed by emphasizing his company's homegrown "Americanness," in tropes that could only be read as a counterpoint to the foreign workers the union sought to defend: "What we're being criticized for is doing business with American citizens who are operating within the rules and regulations we have established, the standards of this country, and that are subject to oversight from our federal and state agencies."

At this point, Reverend Jones attempted to end the part of the meeting devoted to testimony from interested parties and proposed breaking the group into small discussion groups. This surprised many of us as FLOC had not yet been given the floor, except when Cuevas was asked to translate for individual farmworkers in brief exchanges.

JONES: Now what I'd like us to do is to go to the section groups we want to have.

SISTER EVELYN (*raising her hand*): When are you going to let FLOC speak?

UNKNOWN OBSERVER (*to Jones*): It is on your own agenda.

JONES (*to Sister Evelyn*): (*Inaudible*) . . . speak to the issue?

SISTER EVELYN: It's not for me. I'm following what I heard you say this morning. (*This was followed by a long pause by Jones; many voices heard speaking at once in background.*)

JONES: Who, uh, wants to represent FLOC?

Another set of tense exchanges then took place when Cuevas said he wanted to speak first about his personal experiences in farmwork. Jones objected and asked him to just address union issues. But Cuevas insisted, and Jones backed down. Cuevas stated:

> I was born and raised in Brownsville, Texas. I come from three generations of U.S. citizens, even though I've always been treated as Mexican. Yet people say, "Why don't you go back to Mexico, where you come from?" . . . Ever since I can remember it's been a struggle for my family, as well as all the farmworkers I know, to make ends meet. . . . I have a ninth-grade education [because] I had to drop out at sixteen to work full-time. One thing I will always remember is when my grandfather got kicked in the rear by a grower because the grower wanted him to pick more red tomatoes. He kept repeating it to my grandfather, but he didn't understand. My parents and my grandparents had a lot of trouble learning English. It's not an easy situation to be picking alongside your grandfather and seeing a grower swearing at him and then kicking him in the rear, and my grandfather just went swooping down into the vines and got tomatoes squashed all over his face. I remember I got very angry and I actually jumped at that grower. You know what happened next? My parents and my grandfather dragged me off and beat the heck out of me. They said, "You will not bite the hand that feeds you. You cannot lift a hand against your employer. You have to be very dedicated to your employer." And that's rammed into us, if you're born and raised as a Hispanic. It's almost like they're gods, our employers. I argued [with my parents], "That's not right. That's not what we're learning in school. [We] learned that we're all people. And I learned that we have the same rights in this country, no matter if we're richer or poorer."

The tactic of stressing the personal worked well in this setting. Cuevas's testimony ended in probably the most productive set of exchanges that day as he and Bryan went back and forth in a civil tone, clarifying details of how FLOC's union contracts work and how Mt. Olive sets the prices paid to farmers for cucumbers.

The meeting's main accomplishment came shortly thereafter when Bryan and a large cucumber grower from the Goldsboro area (Harris had left early) agreed that they would be willing to attend a future meeting with other growers and FLOC to work toward mutual understandings. While the projected meeting did not come to fruition until years later, it was clear by the end of the day that, in spite of Jones's antagonism toward the union and farmworker advocates, the major parties had gained a greater respect for each other. In conversation afterward, both the grower and Bryan separately said they found Cuevas to be "someone [they] could deal with." (They seemed to be contrasting Cuevas with FLOC president Baldemar Velasquez, who they regarded as more hardnosed).

A few days later the local newspaper, the *Goldsboro News-Argus*, and the Associated Press ran stories quoting Mt. Olive officials who painted the meeting as a conciliatory gesture on the part of the pickle company, whose sales they claimed had not been hurt by the boycott. The articles referred to the event as a "mediation session." This led to a public disclaimer from FLOC, asserting that no negotiations had in fact occurred.

Clearly, despite Reverend Jones's bluster, the conference had humanized farmworkers and the union in the eyes of the other parties. But it was Jones's behavior that stuck in my gut. In retrospect, I think I was annoyed by his uncanny resemblance to my patriarchal southern grandfather.

Hard work might have been my grandfather's middle name. He earned his living as a postman but as a younger man had once aspired to the Baptist pulpit. Farming, however, was his obsession, and he labored long hours over his half acre of vegetables each summer. While I grew up next door to him and loved him dearly, my parents had distanced themselves from his authoritarian tendencies and his occasional lapses into Jesse Helms–style rants that seemed guaranteed to offend someone—usually blacks, women, or the long-haired teenage males his granddaughter brought home. My parents' choice to join a new Methodist congregation in Durham after they married had been, in part, a move to escape the conservatism espoused by my grandfather and his beloved Southern Baptist Church. And like Reverend Jones, my grandfather talked a blue streak, seldom restrained by social graces in sharing his opinion with all who would listen. If I replaced the Mexican workers of today in my mind with 1960s' "colored people," I could well imagine my grandfather mouthing the same platitudes and dominating the discussion just as Jones had done. He would have been terribly hurt if anyone pointed out how rude he had been. He would have insisted that he only meant well.

In an interesting twist on ethnography close to home, I had by this point so distanced myself from my grandfather's South that my reaction to Jones was more a knee-jerk rejection than any measure of understanding. For the past twenty years, much of it spent living in or writing about Central America, my own identity had been shaped by the materialist humanism and universalism of liberation theology Catholicism. What was the religious tradition from which my grandfather and Reverend Jones had sprung? How did Protestant beliefs become so strongly linked with ethnic pride and antilabor politics in the Old South? The "familiarity" of my own southern past had dulled my intellectual curiosity. I simply had not thought to ask the question before.

On looking into the literature, I learned that the matter is complicated by a great deal of misleading southern cultural history that conflates the ideology of the Old South's aristocracy of cotton planters with the far more numerous white yeoman farmers, some of whom owned small numbers of slaves and some of whom did not. Yeoman farmers predominated to a far greater extent in North Carolina than in the Deep South. In a recent historical study of labor and religious views among "plain folk" in the South, Carl Osthaus (2004) distinguished this "Big House" school of writings, which emphasized the southern gentleman's laziness and contempt for menial labor, from more recent community-based studies of small farmers, who held a far greater respect for hard work. In an exhaustive study of diaries and other accounts of yeoman farmers in the mid-South, Osthaus draws a portrait of "a sturdy, industrious, self-sufficient folk, tough, proud, and fiercely independent . . . [with] a desire to control their own destiny and scorn of being controlled" (2004:751–752). Accumulating some wealth through hard work was one of the keys to independence for such folk, but respectability among these farmers, Osthaus wrote, depended more upon a man and his family being perceived as self-sufficient, and status was often reflected through standing in a religious community. Yes indeed, I thought, these accounts perfectly described my Appalachian-born grandparents.

By the early 1800s the Baptist, Methodist, and Presbyterian evangelical movements had successfully challenged the elite and hedonistic values of planter culture in many areas, and over the next century ascetic values associated with common folk such as frugality, hard work, honesty, and sobriety came to dominate in the mid-South. These characteristics took on religious overtones and became measures of faith and moral fiber (Wills 1997). Again, bull's eye on the grandparent front.

Among yeoman farmers, Osthaus wrote that class lines were often blurred through the central role hard work played in notions of honor and a sense of Christian "right living." A respectable farmer took pride in the fact that he worked alongside slaves or hired help. Work was often the measure of respect used for others, in that a hardworking slave was often spoken of with respect, just as a wealthy man might be, provided he was seen to work hard and to be a good neighbor. Upward mobility was, in fact, a goal motivating the hard work of the yeoman farmer, so achieving wealth was not frowned upon; the idle rich were denigrated, however, as were poor people, or "white trash," who gained a reputation as thieves, vagabonds, or layabouts.

Importantly, however, menial or servile work done under the direction of another was not highly regarded. This was considered the work of slaves. It was manual labor undertaken by free citizens that held the promise of self-sufficiency that drew respect. Owning land was a key part of achieving this independence and avoiding the stigma of extreme poverty (Osthaus 2004:780). Since access to land tended to be a while privilege, even decades after emancipation, few blacks could aspire to this measure of status. The Civil War actually strengthened what was already a strong nativist element among southern farmers.

In the aftermath of the war and reconstruction, many poor white farmers found themselves in debt to urban-based farm suppliers while struggling to hold onto their land and social standing in a new situation without slaves, relying instead on hired labor or tenant farming. Influential farmers, backed by local sheriffs and white politicians, scrambled to regain the upper hand over "uppity" blacks in local politics. Eastern North Carolina was an area where the Ku Klux Klan thrived well into the 1960s. Just a few miles from Goldsboro, outside the town of Smithfield, a Klan billboard welcoming tourists was still visible from a major highway during the 1970s. The large tobacco farms that dominate in these counties are the same farms on which pickling cucumbers are grown, and they are the areas where large landholders continued to dominate county politics long after other trappings of the antebellum South had fallen out of favor (Hall 1986).

In the postwar chaos and economic turmoil, white farmers of all ranks felt victimized by a hostile industrial economy to the north and often found common cause in public events such as evangelical revivals, the Klan movement, and anti-Catholic crusades. Christian ministers in many cases sanctioned these gatherings, which provided a vicarious sense of communal victory. In these charged public spaces it became common practice and a source of native pride to vent against more vulnerable antagonists or anything viewed as strange or foreign and therefore potentially evil (McDonogh 1995; Woodward 1938).

After World War II, corporate leaders seeking to expand into the South found common cause with North Carolina's state leadership in developing economic policies designed to attract labor-intensive industries such as textile and apparel mills from the Northeast. The state's large population of poor farm families, combined with the Piedmont's geography of small rivers and a taxpayer-supported community college system aimed at training industrial workers, were attractive to northern textile companies, which sought to cut labor costs and avoid unionization efforts. The rural industrialization brought stability to family farmers. Having one family member bring home a regular salary from a mill eased the financial instability of relying on income from farming. But private industrial recruitment boards and legislators took pains to spread industrial development thinly across the state's rural towns, in part as an effort to thwart unionization efforts, which were known to be more likely to succeed in urban settings and company towns with large concentrations of workers (Myerson 1978; Wood 1986).

In line with these goals, North Carolina legislators quickly took advantage of new anti-labor legislation like the Taft-Hartley Act in the late 1940s by passing "right-to-work" laws (still in effect today) that required unions to extend benefits from contracts with employers to nonunion members and forbade a "closed shop." Organizing efforts such as the 1958 textile strike in Henderson, North Carolina, were met with violence when political authorities allowed the use of state police and the National Guard to repress strikers. Segregation served the goals of bosses who used racial divisions and whites' fears of losing good jobs to blacks to undermine the efforts of union organizers (Wood 1986).

Mills were dispersed in distant, far-flung rural communities that formed a close-knit paternalistic world of company housing, company stores, and mill-owned churches where the pastors equated unions with the fires of Hades. The South's pervasive poverty made the lure of a job, however modest, far more potent than a union's vague promise to fight for better pay and conditions. General poverty also ensured an eager supply of hungry workers off the farms who would be ready to take one's job if that person did not seem to want it. Just as it did with politics, culture trumped economics. There was something foreign, menacing, un-southern about unions, so it was easy to tar the union movement with what historian James C. Cobb called "the triple bugaboo of Yankeeism, race-mixing and communism" (quoted in Applebome 1996:188).

In his study of southern politics, Peter Applebome cited Cobb again in reference to the way Senator Strom Thurmond of South Carolina, over the decades, had come to accept blacks but still held animosity for union organizers. Cobb called anti-union sentiment "the South's most respectable prejudice" (Cobb 1993, cited in Applebome 1996:192).

These sentiments were reinforced during the Cold War, when unions were routinely equated with communism. The strong economic growth during the 1960s, combined with welfare state policies such as the G.I. Bill, Social Security, and Medicare, allowed a wide measure of prosperity that many workers came to associate with capitalist ideals. In eastern North Carolina politics, former senator Jesse Helms, whose racism and antipathy for unions were legendary, became an outspoken beacon of conservative values for more than thirty years. One of the practices that kept Helms in office term after term was his diligence in responding to his constituents' concerns, often with personal attention. Helms's legacy illustrates the degree to which the most effective politics in the rural South is a personal politics. Paternalism is not understood (in the white working class) to be an offense; rather, it is a show of neighborly concern.

Helms's conservatism was refurbished during the Reagan era as a form of "authoritarian populism" that appealed to white working people because it provided a framework for explaining a variety of social ills affecting their lives by linking radical political movements and other turmoil of the 1960s (including the civil rights struggle) with developments such as the decline of small farms and the loss of blue-collar jobs (Omi and Winant 1994). Conservative politics, often packaged together with God-fearing Christianity, encouraged working-class whites to lump blacks, "communist" union organizers, and feminists together as causes of economic dislocation.

Neo-liberal rhetoric about emerging markets, the inevitability of global competition, and the "backward" aspects of rural economies has further conflated the issues of what's good for business and what's good for rural America. By 2000 when the Methodist conference took place, rural North Carolinians had endured two decades of declining manufacturing jobs, accompanied by an unprecedented influx of Mexican immigrants who have visibly shifted the landscape of rural culture. Considering these changes together with the infusion of conservative sentiment in national politics and on talk radio, it is not hard to understand why a circling of wagons in communities of faith could seem like "right action" indeed.

In the days that followed the pickle industry conference, I remained in a state of high dudgeon. In recent years the closest I had come to organized religion was my participation in a Unitarian Universalist farmworker advocacy group, so my advocacy self was outraged by the anti-union sentiment at the event. But I had been active in a liberal Methodist youth fellowship during most of my teenage years, so in deference to my Methodist past, I felt embarrassed by these conservative Methodists. I spent the two days after the event transcribing my tapes of the proceedings. Then I wrote a short, anonymous critique of the conference. By then, my goal was no longer cultural research; it was activism, plain and simple. I printed out the proceedings and my critique and mailed them to North Carolina offices of the Methodist Church. Encouraged to learn about a forthcoming regional Methodist convention, I sent them to every Methodist lay leader for whom I could find an e-mail address. I cajoled my parents into writing a letter to the state office. I arranged a meeting, accompanied by another UU farmworker advocate, with Jimmy Creech, a well-known dissident Methodist minister who had spoken out for gay rights. Reverend Creech wrote a letter to the state office. In short, I caused quite a bit of turmoil among Methodists. Efforts toward reconciliation ensued. Calls and letters were returned. A set of short, inoffensive minutes of the conference were produced. Roiling waters were soothed. I hoped the right feathers got ruffled. But I am sure that from the point of view of Reverend Jones, my truth telling was his equivalent of "toxic words."

I think Thomas Wolfe was right about not being able to go home again. My effort to delve into the history of religion, race, and labor in the state I grew up in set in stark relief the many ways faith and community can be built on both love and hate at the same time. On the other hand, the Methodists finally came down on the side of the farmworkers when it counted by supporting the boycott in 2004, which helped get Bryan to the negotiating table. Perhaps the Goldsboro conference and its aftermath played a role in that process. I want to have faith in community. And I am nourishing an ecumenical faith that the new FLOC contract with Mt. Olive and the North Carolina Growers Association will help build bridges across the crevasses of race and class that divide our social landscape.

References Cited

Applebome, Peter

1996 *Dixie Rising: How the South Is Shaping American Values, Politics and Culture.* New York: Times Books, Random House.

Barger, Ken, and Ernesto Reza

1994 *The Farm Labor Movement in the Midwest: Social Change and Adaptation among Migrant Farmworkers.* Austin: University of Texas Press.

Cobb, James C.

1993 *The Selling of the South: The Southern Crusade for Industrial Development, 1936–1990.* Urbana: University of Illinois Press.

Edid, Maralyn

1994 *Farm Labor Organizing: Trends and Prospects.* Ithaca: ILR Press.

Hall, Bob

1986 *Who Owns North Carolina: Report of the Landownership Project (Part II).* Durham, NC: Institute for Southern Studies.

Hoffman, Pat

1987 *Ministry of the Dispossessed: Learning from the Farm Worker Movement.* Los Angeles: Wallace.

Holt, Alexandra Okie, and Sister Evelyn Mattern

2002 Making Home: Culture, Ethnicity, and Religion among Farmworkers in the Southeastern United States. In *The Human Cost of Food: Farmworkers' Lives, Labor and Advocacy*, ed. Charles D. Thompson Jr. and Melinda F. Wiggins, 22–52. Austin: University of Texas Press.

McDonogh, Gary W.

1995 Constructing Christian Hatred: Anti-Catholicism, Diversity and Identity in Southern Religious Life. In *Religion in the Contemporary South,* O. Hendall White Jr. and Daryl White, 67–78. Athens: University of Georgia Press.

Myerson, Michael

1978 *Nothing Could Be Finer.* New York: International Publishers.

Omi, Michael, and Howard Winant

1994 *Racial Formation in the United States: From the 1960s to the 1990s.* New York: Routledge.

Osthaus, Carl R.

2004 The Work Ethic of the Plain Folk: Labor and Religion in the Old South. *Journal of Southern History* 70(4): 745–782.

Wills, Gregory

1997 *Democratic Religion, Freedom, Authority and Church Discipline in the Baptist South, 1785–1900.* New York: Oxford University Press.

Wood, Phillip J.
1986 *Southern Capitalism: The Political Economy of North Carolina, 1880–1980.* Durham, NC: Duke University Press.

Woodward, C. Vann
1938 *Tom Watson: Agrarian Rebel.* Savannah: Beehive.

FIVE

Buying Out the Union: Jobs as Property and the UAW

Peter Richardson

American companies and government institutions have shunted unions out of a role in regulating the labor process since at least the early 1980s. In a process David Harvey has referred to as accumulation by dispossession (Harvey 2003),[1] they have deprived union memberships of rights. Dispossessing unions of wages, benefits, and work rules (i.e., rights in the workplace) has been part of a process economists insist is necessary for the American auto industry to return to profitability.[2]

To provide an extended case study of how workers' perspectives have changed over time in the face of different waves of buyouts, this chapter takes an ethnographic look at buyouts offered to autoworkers at the Sylvania parts plant outside Detroit between 2003 and late 2006. A focus on change and temporality (including imaginings of the future) brings insight into how persons and social institutions interact and into what is contingent, local, and path-dependent.

The buyouts Detroit auto manufacturers have offered to United Auto Workers (UAW) members have given them varying sums of money for relinquishing the contractual rights their union—the UAW—has negotiated for their jobs, healthcare, and pensions. These are promises the auto companies (here Ford and its spun-off parts supplier, Visteon) have made over the past decades. A pension promise made to a current worker may stretch back forty years, to when that worker first took a job. The buyouts transform what were collective rights the union had negotiated into private, transferrable property people can sell.

This process of dispossession has occurred through the interplay of economic and governmental institutions on the one hand and the union on the other. Following the recent work of Don Kalb (and others) calling for a return to the social, I argue that this interplay has produced the particular global "path-dependent" situation I document here (Kalb and Tak 2005). Rights such as healthcare, pensions, and work rules on the shop floor are being taken from UAW auto workers, thus "(re)commodify[ing] aspects of social relationships and social reproduction that were the object of state or community regulation, social entitlements and protection, and expanding and deepening the circuits of capital" (Kalb and Tak 2005:194; also Harvey 2003).

I will look at three periods of the transformation of rights into property: (1) prior to approximately 1980—before unions came under heavy fire; (2) from 1980 through the early 2000s—the period when union jobs started to become property but a kind of collective, family property (given by parents with power in the union to their children); and (3) the present, where buyouts represent the conversion of union jobs into individual, transactable, alienable property.

The shocks the auto industry and auto workers have taken since 1980 have been coordinated with shifts in regulation and other crises of capitalism, in particular the ascent of neo-liberalism and threats to and shifts in oil supply.[3] Michael Watts has argued that the neo-liberal age, rather than pursuing free markets, has been marked by state intervention against the working class: "[T]he U.S. working class is one of the first victims of U.S. imperialism" (2006:36). Changing definitions of property are part of this process.

The interplay of past promises and future expectations and relationships both within the plant and outside it (e.g., with family) determines what union members have considered property. The first section of this chapter will discuss the relationships between union jobs and property. The second section will discuss "familism" in the UAW and at the local I studied. The third section details the buyouts and workers' responses. The conclusion suggests how unions might reproduce union rights without turning them into forms of property people fight over.

Union Property?

Ford spun off its parts-making capacity into a new company, Visteon, in 2000. Since then, workers in the Sylvania union local (attached to a parts plant that went from Ford to Visteon) have had to deal with three strategies initiated by corporate governance in concert with financial capital to reduce labor (and other) costs: (1) two-tier plans, (2) bankruptcy threats, and (3) buyouts.[4]

Two-tier plans bring new hires into the plant and union on a greatly reduced pay scale (on two tiers, see Richardson 2007). Bankruptcy has been used to strip workers of their vested pensions and promised retirement healthcare because current bankruptcy law puts such contractually negotiated claims at the bottom of any list of creditors.[5]

The third strategy is more ambiguous. On the surface, buyouts seem like largesse from the company, thanking workers for their service. Examined more closely, buyouts are not parting gifts from the automaker but instead the conversion of collectively held union rights into property and the corporate purchase of that disaggregated property from workers. It is not going too far to say that with buyouts the automakers are buying the union itself, job by job.

Unlike most of recent social theory and criticism's objects, unions represent a history of integration, the joining together of persons into new groups rather than the fragmentation of old identities. Companies and the UAW's International (the union's "upper management") tell workers that buyouts represent the companies' goodwill. But because union members have come to see their jobs and benefits as forms of property, buyouts parcel out and sell the collective power of the union back to the company as property, worker by worker, as a series of fragments of a once-powerful social formation that could bend government and corporate power to workers' collective will.

All three corporate strategies eliminate the union in its present form: the two-tier plan by breaking the union into higher and lower positions, bankruptcy by drowning the union's claims on the company in (often fictive) debt, and buyouts by individuating interests. If any union survives, it will be vastly downsized and subject to what are called COA (competitive operating agreements) that, as one example, limit workers' rights in the name of granting managers greater flexibility (i.e., arbitrary power) in the workplace.[6]

The anthropology of industry (e.g., Burawoy 1979; Fernandez-Kelly 1983; Mayo 1933; Ong 1987) and of the auto industry (Beynon 1973;

Briody and Baba 1991; Brondo et al. 2005) has stressed themes too various to summarize. The anthropology of unions is a relatively new subfield arising out of the anthropology of work, spearheaded primarily by the work of Paul Durrenberger and Suzan Erem (1999b, 2002, 2005a). While some work has been done outside the United States, including some of a historical anthropological nature (Kalb 1997), recently the anthropology of unions has been mostly an Americanist genre.

Anthropology has a long history of acknowledging the heterogeneity of property institutions, undermining the self-evident and unitary notion of property proposed by the liberal tradition. On the one hand, the classic definition of property rests upon a right to exclude; on the other, property is social (the right to exclude exists only in relation to others). Property is triadic; "'A owns B against C' where C represents all other individuals" (Cairns in Hallowell 1967:239). It is not property unless *someone* is excluded from use; if the person excluded enjoyed use rights in the past, then we can clearly call what has occurred "dispossession," as used by Harvey.

Property is once again a central topic of anthropology, as recent work by Katherine Verdery, Marilyn Strathern, and many others attests. Verdery's studies of the creation of private property in post-socialist Eastern Europe show how the "decollectivization" of socialist state property and the de facto creation of individual property rights did not create "effective ownership" (Verdery 1996:348). Verdery defines property as a "political symbol and active force in the contemporary world, as a basis for appropriation, as social relations conjoining people and things, and as a process of determining the values those things hold" (1996:355).

The post-socialist process is resonant with that described here if we think of the union as the collective entity being dismantled. Dispossession through buyouts relies on transforming collective rights held in common (incapable of being individually transacted) into alienable private property the company can buy lock, stock, and barrel. As in Verdery's example, effective ownership never arises because only in the selling of them do rights become acknowledged as property. In the history of the United States, the forced privatization and individuation of land ownership on many Native American reservations (and the consequent acquisition of much of those lands by land speculators) followed a similar pattern.

Marilyn Strathern has argued that property arose in the process of forging relationships and that it generated relationships. Moreover, she argued that in the emerging global legal system, property has become loaded with more meaning as groups try to establish rights to seemingly intangible forms of property such as culture, tradition, and knowledge. Property can "mobilize relationships" through transactions, and many kinds of property exist only as relationships. She has observed that "in certain respects 'traditional' Melanesian societies belong much more comfortably to some of the visions made possible by socio-economic developments in Europe since the 1980s . . . turn[ing] some of the ways in which relationships are contested in late capitalist society into a new resource for apprehending Melanesian social process" (1998:222).[7]

The next section details the interdependence of mutations in property's form with changes in relations of production during the 1980s and 1990s in the unionized auto industry. As James Carrier and Daniel Miller (1998) have also argued, idealized discourses about property should never be mistaken for the actual practices surrounding property, practices generating possession and dispossession.[8]

Familism and Jobs as Property

After one meeting at the union hall I noticed Beth, a union officer, doing a funny duck-walk while cooing to a baby that wasn't hers. It was a Saturday morning, so many had brought their children to the meeting, a common practice. Beth couldn't get enough of the baby, and behind her a few other women were taking turns with two more babies— holding them up, cherishing them as the rest of the children darted around in unorganized chases. Women, African American and white, were sharing a motherly moment with their children in common.

Our institutions do everything to spatially insulate family and work such that they intersect, at most, at a yearly picnic. Arguably, the union has become a limen between the purified spaces of work and family: uniting them while also keeping them safely at a distance. Many union meetings resemble family reunions, with people lavishing attention on each other's babies and disciplining each other's children. The presence of the children makes the blurring of family and union obvious.

In the UAW auto parts plant where I conduct research, relations both of and within production include workers' families. This fits Don Kalb's concept of *familism* (1997). Kalb's historical anthropological study of the Philips Corporation in the Netherlands (centered on the early twentieth century) describes a situation in which the father of a family was given full-time work on the condition that his daughters were available to be brought on and laid off at the company's will; the daughters became a kind of flexible labor used as demand waxed and waned. Since 1980 within the U.S. auto industry and the UAW, conflict over remuneration and jobs has become a family issue and an issue between families: in other words, the family (the sphere of social relations supposedly excluded from the market) has internalized conflict between workers and between workers and the company.

This section discusses how, after major shocks to the U.S. auto industry beginning around 1979, jobs in UAW-represented auto plants became the property of families. Access to scarce jobs became something traded between the company and the union, and when one of the rare jobs became available, those with the power to do so directed the job to a family member—usually a son or daughter. For a generation, access to jobs became heritable (like membership in a guild), but such a structure could not last and could not reproduce the union. While solidarity between workers is one defining facet of unions, so too is limiting access to jobs in specific workplaces, trades, or professions. At Sylvania and other UAW locals and plants, for the past quarter century the limiting of access has taken on a specific contour: to kin and kindred, to family and close friends.

When auto manufacturers began hiring in any significant numbers again during the mid-1990s, the number of UAW members who wanted well-compensated jobs for their sons or daughters far exceeded the available jobs, and nepotism quickly became a practice. Using their power in the union to take control of jobs and make them a form of heritable property, families with such influence used it to get their offspring UAW jobs.

Unions like the UAW were shaped by legal strictures such as the Taft-Hartley Act (1946) that were supposed to make unions and companies partners but have instead served to clip unions' most effective talons, such as the right to strike and organize. As the industrial sociologist Clark Kerr (1948) observed, Taft-Hartley (and the "industrial peace" it was supposed to usher in) institutionalized unions as representatives of their members' individual interests against management rather than as social movements seeking justice in and out of the workplace through collective action.

Taft-Hartley also enshrined the right of managers to make all decisions as long as bargaining unit employees were paid what their contract stipulated. This foreclosed unions' concern with anything but remuneration and grievance handling. This singular focus on individual interests became the basis on which union jobs were transformed into disposable property.

But in the intervening decades, illegal wildcat strikes against "speed up" occurred beginning in the late 1950s, and the early 1970s witnessed a shop-floor revolt against the institutionally mandated focus on interests. Autoworkers made it clear that while they deserved and desired a living wage and decent benefits, the division of labor within the managed labor process needed to be changed. Alienation and domination, not just exploitation, were issues. This is a populist as much as a class vision that Dimitra Doukas has argued is an enduring theme in America's culture of work: "American culture envisions universal autonomy, universal social and political adulthood, without slaves or masters" (2003:155).

The Taft-Hartley rules for the relations among capital, labor, and company management "provid[ed] a rigid institutional framework for the conduct of class struggle" at the point of production aimed at the "control [of] labor costs as a stable factor of production" (Aronowitz 1973:66). Even if fatally flawed, the Fordist compact among labor, capital, and government that made unions part of industrial organization also created union jobs that came with rights previously held only by the propertied. The UAW and other unions gained access to healthcare, pensions, and, through work rules and grievance procedures, rights in the workplace. The union negotiated these rights as a function of the collective power of its members.

When the auto industry was expanding, strategies for job recruiting cast a wide net. During the 1970s cars with loudspeakers still drove around Detroit's ghettos blaring "Ford's hiring." Prior to the late 1970s, union jobs were not considered property; there was no need to exclude others because there were enough jobs for all. When there are plentiful jobs and a cooperative government, unions face fewer barriers; when the union's membership was expanding, the UAW faced no conflicts impeding its reproduction. Moreover, there was no pressure to turn jobs into exclusive property when union jobs in the Detroit area were widely available. The jobs generated new relations, as Strathern argued about property, but were yet in no way property; the transfiguration into property came only as jobs became scarce and contested.

In 1979, after a few years' downturn in hiring, the American auto industry effectively collapsed. Massive layoffs shook the Detroit area. No one imagined that the layoffs represented a permanent downsizing of American auto production or that no significant numbers of new jobs would appear in Detroit-area factories for a generation. Ironically, it was around this time that the first serious efforts to introduce "Employee Involvement" (EI) programs began, meant to both ameliorate the alienation crisis and reap the latent gains of "teamwork" thought at the time to be behind Japanese automakers' greater quality and efficiency in production.

After the early 1980s when jobs again became available, UAW jobs were the only ones in the Detroit area that paid well. Management created individual interests for UAW leaders by giving them a resource—jobs they could dispense. In accepting the bribe in return for concessions, the union's leadership became complicit in the transformation of the union from an agency of workers' collective action to a bureaucratic dispenser of property rights to the privileged.

Greg Shotwell, a leader in the dissident auto workers' group Soldiers of Solidarity, recently said that the union became an adjunct of companies' HR departments. Another way to look at it is that people who were excluded from the process have no future interest in the union, as they are excluded from the realm of its collective action. In the process, the UAW has lost the appeal to the rights of labor and to autonomy that stirred so many to the union's side as it was born.

Since the late 1990s, a lottery has distributed applications for scarce jobs. Most claim the lottery must have been rigged because, miraculously, union officials' children almost always won. Parents gamed the system for their children, but in the process they undermined union solidarity, the basis of collective action that gave union jobs their relative advantages. Those of the senior generation who failed to get applications for their children grew cynical about the union; when the lottery process loosened it up a few years ago to distribute applications for the much lower-paid second-tier jobs and their children did begin to enter the plants, the children's ethos seemed shaped by a sense of thwarted union brotherhood and undermined collective action.

During this period, it is significant that a union job could be bought. People could bribe union and company officials to usher their children into jobs, or a union official could make a side deal with the company to get his or her child a position. Spots in the lottery were bought and sold on the shop floor: a worker named Hugo said his brother bought him four spots in the lottery before he finally made it into the plant as a second-tier Visteon worker in 2004.

Roy Hill, a retired chair and past president of the local, said that when the UAW agreed to concessions in the early 1980s (while he was president of the local), he never imagined he was putting a burden on his grandkids.

The neo-liberal onslaught was just emerging and no one imagined the hiring freeze would last almost two decades, skipping generations and leaving teenage children of then-current auto workers with no access to union jobs. Making concessions to the company was the rational thing to do at the time.

The fact that members of a workplace-centered structure like an auto workers' union would expect the union to consider the futures of their children and grandchildren contradicts an image of the union as a means to achieve individual interests for the privileged. During the 1980s UAW members with children who had been unable to find decent work started to legally adopt their grandchildren as dependents to give them access to healthcare closed off to their parents: the UAW's and the Detroit area's lost generation who had not held union jobs and benefits. These grandchildren, in a way, were being adopted by the union, but only to provide privileged access to resources, not as a matter of collective action for common interests.

Buyouts

Prior to the collapse of the American auto industry around 1979, auto workers were focused on the labor process as alienating and dominated by managers. The collapse made possible the shift in property relations through access to jobs discussed in the previous section. The three waves of buyouts discussed in this section took the nebulous relations of property in jobs inhering within the structure of the union and families and reified them a further step toward property in the full liberal sense—as alienable, individually transactable property.

The relation between jobs and family still mattered during the buyouts, but the family that mattered now was not the senior generation in the plant who could get someone a job but rather the domestic household of spouse and dependents only loosely connected to the union and autowork. In fact, the contours of who took a buyout and who did not are best explained by the fact that the incentives were for economic individualists pursuing their own interests, not those reasoning about dependents, spouses, and other relations—including social relations on the shop floor. What linked the person holding the job, the domestic family, and the union together was not so much the wage but the benefits that came with a union job—healthcare in particular.

Having seen the paucity of benefits that came with second-tier jobs, parents were fully aware that their families' futures hung by the thread of those benefits. The social insurance of benefit programs is now reinforcing cross-cutting ties emanating from the workplace: the labor of present workers today supports everyone in the union's children and spouses on the one hand and their parents (the retirees) on the other.

While the two-tier approach's apparent ageism may make it seem so, conflict over jobs does not occur only between generations. It began within senior generations over the fate of their children and the children of their close friends and continued with their children's understanding of union sibling-ship as a two-tier system (you could say the two tiers of union families' access to jobs preceded the two tiers of pay and benefits the company imposed). Not a conflict between generations, then, but instead one among economic individualism, familism, and collective interests. For decades the UAW (like capitalism) "expanded" its way out of this contradiction: if the pie is growing, if ever-increasing union jobs are appearing, there is no need to make a choice.

An aspect of the Fordist era in America is that corporations provide social insurance, such as pensions and health insurance, that governments provide in other countries. Unions negotiate specific benefits for their members through collective bargaining. Auto companies would most like to limit or shed altogether this responsibility for providing social insurance, particularly pensions and healthcare for retirees. They regularly represent the coming due of promises made over thirty years ago. Responsibilities to retirees, in essence, are nearly breaking the backs of unionized auto companies because as a result of shrinking employment, UAW retirees now outnumber active workers.

Other than a buyout offered in 1980, which was opposed by the union and only garnered one volunteer at Sylvania (back when the plant still employed about 2,000 workers), the first wave of buyouts took place in 2003 when automakers and their spun-off parts divisions were trying to implement the two-tier wage system.[9] The parts makers were losing money, and there was talk of bankruptcy (which happened to Delphi in 2006). Workers who had worked for Ford when Visteon spun off in 2000 had remained Ford employees: if Visteon were to close plants or go belly up completely, the contract guaranteed these "Ford" workers the right to "flow back" to another Ford facility while retaining their first-tier pay and benefits.

At the time the buyouts, aimed solely at getting older workers to retire to make room for more second-tier workers, had few takers. In 2003 Ford and Visteon had a workforce heavily skewed toward those on the verge of, or already eligible for, retirement. Alongside these older workers were a smaller number of younger workers hired beginning in the late 1990s, after the two-decade freeze (about one-fifth of the total in the plant considered here). The younger workers were divided between those on the same tier as older workers and those on the second tier, with vastly reduced wages and benefits. To encourage older workers to retire to make way for younger workers on the second tier, the companies offered "buyout" incentives to those willing to retire.[10]

Many younger workers, particularly young males, grumbled that older workers should retire to allow them access to the better jobs in the plant that the older workers held, such as positions within the skilled trades that had long waiting lists of people who had passed the tests for those jobs, which offered better pay and greater workplace autonomy.[11] Many accepted the basic logic that it would be nice if somebody would retire to make room for the new generation, but the idea of "taking one for the team" garnered few volunteers. And some said it was unfair to expect older workers to retire from jobs that provided them with satisfaction, not so much from the work but in the sense that the workplace was a second home for many and offered a vibrant social life that would end if they retired.

In early 2006, after Ford and Visteon had already established and rescinded the second tier and auto parts plants in the United States previously owned by Visteon were transferred to a limited liability company called Automotive Components Holdings (ACH), buyouts were offered again. But this time the offer was made to anyone willing to take the incentives to leave through an auction of sorts, with seniority as the bid: (1) either retire with benefits (for about $35,000) or, if too young to retire, (2) take a onetime payout of $100,000 to leave with no further right to insurance and other benefits, or, lastly, (3) take an educational buyout that promised four years of tuition (up to $15,000 a year) and half of the worker's average annual wages and benefits during that time as long as the worker made progress toward graduation.[12]

At the time the buyouts were offered, the Sylvania plant had already been scheduled for closure, with the workforce slated to move in toto to a nearby plant (with acres of empty floor space) along with the machines they worked. Rumors circulated, including one that purported that only a portion of those at Sylvania would be going to the new plant and one that held that there would be a wider round of buyouts in which the company would sweeten the pot. An international union representative came to the plant and addressed all the workers on each shift, assuring them that everyone who wanted them, including the lowest-seniority workers, would have jobs in the future. I went into the plant regularly around this time to get a real-time portrait of how people's perceptions of the impending changes were coalescing into action.

Idioms of discussing and justifying one's decision converged throughout the factory as people discussed and compared their plans, coalescing into two broad visions of the future (leaving aside retirement for now). The plant's rumor mills were largely responsible for aligning people's views and generating consistent idioms as they debated common goals and traded information (even if what passed as information was often lightly disguised hopes and fears).

The aspirations of those taking the buyout usually centered on economic individualism and success gained through moving to a better occupation (for most, through education to allow them to qualify for a white- or a pink-collar occupation). Without the complicating responsibilities that come with spouse and children, those taking the buyout viewed it as facilitating freedom to make themselves anew; their vision was of a personal future and self-interest. The increase in wages that would come with an education and its "skills premium" was matched for many by a possible escape from the status humiliation of being an autoworker to the increased status of higher education and white-collar work. Two young men I talked with made no mention of increased wages. They had no familial responsibilities and hence were the most strongly wedded to individual interests.[13]

There was a striking regularity to the way some in the plant referred to the amount offered in the second buyout as $65,000 rather than $100,000. If you wanted the buyout, the figure was $100,000; if you didn't, it was $65,000 (the approximate after-tax amount). Among the younger workers in the plant, the childless, single males (and some females) imagining life after the buyout saw it as an escape but also as opportunity. The $100,000 would be a catalyst toward a better future. But those for whom the most secure future was sticking with their job and its benefits said the amount was really $65,000 and noted that this was just a little more than a year's wages (interestingly, only if considered before taxes).

Younger workers expressing a preference for either taking or not taking a buyout were constrained by the fact that they were at the bottom of the seniority ladder. Most thought at the time that it was entirely likely that they would end up with no job and no buyout but would simply be laid off. Sam (a younger worker who had entered the UAW on the second tier and attended the University of Michigan on an engineering scholarship) said there was no use in him even thinking about the buyouts: he had no control over what was going to come about, although he would prefer to keep the job he had.

Leaving aside the motivations of older workers, many of those who stayed with their jobs mentioned children as central to their reasoning. I asked Sam's aunt (who had gotten him the application) if she was taking a buyout. "No way," she answered. She cited the fact that she was a mother who needed insurance and benefits for her child. She said "Kids come first, and I'm a worrier, 'what if?' . . . I just want to give my little boy everything he needs. If it was just me, I'd take it." Parents, no longer affording themselves the luxury of unbridled individualism, must account for others and their futures—their domestic family, the group of people receiving rights to healthcare and the support provided by a living wage. For most in this position, the benefits were the reason for staying (although some divorced fathers mentioned that their child support payments would not go down while their income was reduced as they sought an education).

A substantial number of single males said they were staying. All of them made reference to the economic rationality of doing so (e.g., the $65,000 after-tax number kept popping up). A few single males noted that even if they were laid off in a year, they'd get a year's unemployment compensation afterward, so for them the $65,000 had to match a year's wages plus a year's unemployment (no mention was made of wages they might otherwise earn in that time). These young men were drawing extra future income into their argument for staying—diluting the appeal of $100,000 in an alternate calculation. A few of these males were using their very high incomes for men in their early twenties to (what else?) party. Individual interests here did not mean moving on to another occupation. Their interest seemed to be in staying with a wage they were fairly sure would not otherwise be available to them, even with a college education.

Yet I heard no one express unbridled optimism about the future of union jobs in the auto industry; part of the reason for speaking about the equivalence of the buyout to one year's pay may well have been that this was about the horizon within which they felt their jobs were completely secure. Some seemed to be admitting that they had no choice but to stay; they did not think they could replicate the lifestyle they were living with any other job, so when they imagined a future, it was the only one available that they could accept.

The younger workers not taking the buyout insisted they were making the best choice with as much conviction as was shown by those taking the buyout: were persons not taking the buyout pessimistic about their personal futures outside a union job? This would not explain the correlation with being a parent; in some ways, the future imagined by each group emerged out of the degree of responsibility to others.

The young singles not taking the buyout were not so much pessimistic as they were convinced that they had no agency. There was no way for them to create a personal future—the future was just going to happen to them. Imagination of the future is constrained and enabled by what is possible even as what is possible is filtered through fantasy (e.g., an economically rational calculation, seeing the very same buyout offer as a higher or lower amount—as either $100,000 or $65,000, depending on one's view). Choosing to stay with the company did not translate into optimism about the company and the long-term stability of the current wage and benefits package; it seemed to have been more a short-term hedging strategy.

Other subgroups had distinct attitudes about the buyout. One young woman noted she already had a college degree, so the buyout would do her little good. She seemed cynical about the supposed "skills premium" a college education was supposed to bring (another young man noted that he had friends with masters degrees and he was making a lot more money than they were). Another young mother had a spouse who covered her family's benefits, so she was taking the buyout while still reasoning through the collective interests of her family.

One of the first people I always talked to when I came into the plant was Curtis, a sixty-year-old worker. He complained that young people who griped about the union had grown up in a fancy house on the union wage. Curtis is a union man; he would spread the advantages he has as a member of the union as widely as possible: "I don't mind paying more so another American can have a living wage," Curtis said of buying American. On the topic of the buyouts and pensions, Curtis held a consistent position: "I'm not ready to retire, to cut my salary in half" and "I don't want to go home and sit down. . . . I've seen too many people in perfect health retire and die within six months." Commenting on the airlines and steel manufacturers breaking health and pension promises, Curtis proclaimed: "The hundred thousand ain't gonna last. I've seen too many of these gigantic companies renege on their promises." As for what he saw the Republicans doing with Social Security, "I don't want to get out of here and not have shit."

In contrast to his pension and Social Security, of which he argued he was in danger of being dispossessed, Curtis saw the wage as the only source of security with full jural backing. He quipped, "If I come in here and do work they have to pay me or I'll go postal on their ass." If he kept the job, he had a secure source of income, whereas pensions and the buyout were insecure sources of income accompanying an insecure future. The most secure future available was staying at work; it was the only thing that obligated the company and the government to provide him with a living wage.

The only people who said this was the best job around for them and they were sticking with it were older workers with largely closed paths to new personal futures compared with the open future imagined by young takers of the buyout. There were those who, as one older male put it, think of work in the plant as like being at a "country club": that is, the work is relatively easy and unchallenging. This attitude is something of a holdover from a time when the standard of comparison was the heavy lifting of mounting tires in a final assembly plant.

In contrast, a younger worker's comparison might be with the ethereal labor of the information economy. Further, given what the young workers have seen happening to people in the airlines and steel industries, there is no certainty that their pensions and health benefits will be there when they retire, either as a result of the company entering bankruptcy or through a gradual whittling away just begun, as Curtis said. This, too, is an economic rationality equal in its logic to risk or portfolio management. In the portfolio made up of pension, Social Security, savings, and current wages, wages represent the least risky income stream.

Some older workers cited the appeal of the community of the shop floor as the main reason they didn't want to leave. Merle said he didn't want a buyout now, even though he will retire soon. "I don't know what I'll do away from all the good times and people here," he said of the plant. "Ford did so much for us poor southerners. . . . I wish the young people would appreciate the Ford family the way I do."

The third wave of buyouts was mostly an extension and expansion of the terms of the second: the same amounts of money offered for the same conditions of sale. These buyouts came as the once-certain transfer of operations to the Sylvania II plant was becoming uncertain. The number of workers going over, as reported in the rumor mill, had dwindled from "everybody" to 250 to 150. Those who had already gone over to Sylvania II from Sylvania had reported an ambivalent reception, and rumors—some from local newspapers—intimated that Sylvania II would soon be closed.

This wave of buyouts generated a reaction that had not accompanied previous offers, especially among younger workers—an explosion of anger.

One older shop-floor workers said of the buyouts, "They design these programs to play age against age, person against person." And that seemed largely true of the second buyout: younger workers turned against older workers in the plant and spoke of segmentation between the two groups. But what was different concerning the third buyout was that anger between workers was rarely expressed while anger toward the company flared up considerably. The idiom for expressing anger was surprisingly uniform: either "I will never buy a Ford car again" or "I [and others in my position] will never be able to afford a Ford car again." Given that buyouts are portrayed by many as "gifts" from the company, why would more "gifting" create resentment and anger, particularly of this form?

One answer might be that whereas the previous buyout had been accompanied by other ambiguous news that made settling on a final and certain future a moot project, this round of buyouts seemed to many to be the final word on the future—the company will be downsized. When considering the buyouts, shop-floor workers (other than the tendency to talk about the buyouts as $65,000 or $100,000, as discussed earlier) didn't really talk about going after the "big money"; instead, they discussed healthcare, their families, and the future. They talked about an imagined future trajectory, not market calculations. They talked about who they imagined being: if young and taking the buyout, about new and exciting identities; if not taking the buyout, statements such as "I like the work as much as any, given the pay" came up. Is this a calculation based in possessive individualism? No. It is a statement of what kind of occupational identity and place in the world is good enough. The buyouts, when the other option of keeping the union job with Ford still seemed tenable, left the future full of open possibilities.

The interesting and, frankly, sudden focus on Ford as an object of hostility could indicate a kind of collective realization of significant social change. The anger behind a vow to not buy another Ford, while understandable, has a different logic from that found in claims that the future will bring a situation in which those like me will no longer be able to afford a Ford (i.e., an end to the consumer capitalism heralded by Fordism). The latter contains a seed of thinking collectively about work and jobs, exactly the stuff out of which unionism is born.

What property the worker is giving up when coaxed into leaving can perhaps best be seen through a contrast with the rights and responsibilities of the next worker to do the task (e.g., makes starters as they do at Sylvania). That person will be on the second tier (no longer receiving a family wage), will likely have few health benefits and certainly no pension, and will probably be outside the union (so no rights to representation in the workplace).

As I edited this chapter in 2006, the announcement came that temporary workers would be brought in after the buyouts to replace the departed workers. Whereas the previous second-tier workers remained UAW members, these temporary workers will not be in the union (although they will work alongside UAW workers) and will have an even worse pay and benefits package than the second-tier workers. The jobs are being bought from the union and given to nonunion workers who come at a fraction of the cost and trouble to management.

Some say the union should oppose the buyouts if they mean a reduction in the UAW's total membership. Others criticize those in the union's leadership who oppose the buyouts, saying they are really only worried about keeping union dues flowing into their coffers. The head of a Detroit-area local did not allay these fears when he was quoted as complaining that his local's coffers would be down $12,000 a month if just fifty members took buyouts. He said buyouts would be acceptable only if Ford kept the membership rolls at the same levels by replacing bought-out workers with new ones: "Even if they were thinking of bringing them in at a lower pay scale or a two-tier pay system, I wouldn't have any problem with that" (*Detroit Free Press*, 2006). This unfortunate comment led to a long stream of criticism from UAW members on various union and autoworker message boards, decrying the aristocratic pretensions and arrogance of the union's leadership.

But even if the source of the comment was a local union officer, it is important to distinguish the local level of leadership from that of the International. Paul Durrenberger and Suzan Erem (2002) have shown that service workers in the Chicago area see their union representatives who operate above the local level as more like managers than themselves, and the same seems to be true of the UAW. The union local's leadership, while subordinate to that of the International, is distinct: when UAW members complain about fat cats and porkchoppers, they are usually talking about people who have appointments with the International—that is, persons who in a way could be said to have "tenure" in the union's hierarchy, meaning high pay for little work and even fewer results. While there are certainly people who have received cushy jobs in the local through family connections, the gravy doesn't really get thick and fat until you're part of the International.

Roy Hill told me of visiting the local's vice president, Frank Little. They were looking through old union meeting minutes in a back storage room of the local's hall. "Nineteen hundred people. That's how many used to be in this union local," Mike exclaimed as he looked through the local's history. "You wonder what happened to all those people and their families." The local's president joined them, and the three speculated on why this loss of community never made it into the press, why the press always portrayed the UAW (and by implication the union's locals) as only concerned with money and not with real people with real issues and real worries about their futures.

Conclusion

This chapter has described a local, path-dependent end to the rights earlier generations of UAW members fought for as they became property to be dispossessed by the current generation. This transformation of rights into property is in turn a central reason why the UAW has been unable to reproduce since the 1970s, to inculcate in arising generations the beliefs of unionism. Since that time, union rights have become a limited property—first to be hoarded by families, finally to be sold off by individuals. In the process, the transformation of rights to property has corrupted the union's officials and destroyed any sense of collective action.

As I have noted, treating a union job as individual property makes the most sense, and appeals the most, to those with the loosest social bonds to the job and the community of workers that is a union: young persons without responsibilities who still imagine an individual, personal future. Again, the contours of who took a buyout and who did not are best explained by the fact that the incentives were designed for economic individualists pursuing their own interests, not for those concerned about dependents, spouses, and other relations—including social relations on the shop floor.

But this process was in many ways ill-fated; for example, it could be seen as a long coming to fruition of the institutional forms demanded by Taft-Hartley and its framing of unions as collections of self-interested individuals. A union, to reproduce, must first be a unity of belief translating into practice, a unity built through the moral imagination of a group of situated people remembering the past and building the future through concerted action. The UAW has failed to actively create a future over the past few decades. The economic and governmental forces it stood against cannot be underestimated, but the one hope in that situation was to prevent fraction within the union. The pursuit of familial interests in the allocation of jobs—if we listen to the shop-floor membership—was a critical factor in undermining that unity of belief in the union's efficacy for all. Without this intervening phase of treating union jobs as family property, perhaps it would have been harder to convince workers that their jobs were individual property.

Kalb and Tak have noted of European neo-liberalism that "[t]he ideology of social rights . . . was slowly reduced to window dressing, except for those who practically 'owned' their rights" (2005:190). Is it better to think about the benefits of a union job as a kind of property, a kind of "effective property" at that, with solid, enshrined ownership rights? On the one hand, this would seem to give workers the illusion of a more level playing field when dealing with companies; on the other, the idea of a union job as property only really makes sense if there are jobs that are not union, if there are workers without union jobs who those with union jobs wish to exclude from the "property" of the union (such as the new temporary workers). Treating jobs as property allows the historical benefits of a union job to be assimilated with legal traditions, making those benefits and rights perhaps more defensible today, but at what price to one's soul? And at what price to the power of the union and the union movement as an instrument of economic democracy?

Strathern's goal, mentioned earlier, is obviously to redefine property in general by in-mixing Western and Melanesian categories. Against Strathern, weakening and expanding the category of property to make it more inclusive is not the right move. Instead, being precise about property and what property does serves the causes of freedom and moral clarity as well as the class interests of working people.

Notes

1. In this chapter I use "rights" in a sense borrowed from British Social Anthropology, where rights are always coupled with obligations and the balance of rights and obligations is part of a process of continual negotiation rather than given in theory. Recent critiques of how universal human rights have been used as part of neo-liberal global strategies do not apply here.

2. The past quarter-century has witnessed the slow decline of the old-guard unions that, through valiant effort, pushed open the door for unionism in the United States in the decade around World War II. Unions like the United Auto Workers (UAW) have struggled to maintain a role in the regulation and ruling of industrial production, a fact attested to by a decline in the UAW's membership from a high of 1.5 million in the 1970s to about 600,000 in 2006 (a figure the current round of

buyouts and layoffs riving the auto industry will only reduce further). I leave aside the admirable efforts of "new-guard" unions such as the Service Employees International Union to organize and represent, for example, hotel workers. My concern is with the lessons we can learn from the successes and failures of unions over time, particularly the question of what a union needs to be and do to reproduce.

3. I am aware of the ironies interconnecting the auto industry and oil, with oil the commodity most studied by Michael Watts as of late. Most auto workers would be happy making a better mode of transportation if their communities, wages, and benefits survived in basic form. I've encountered a kind of knee-jerk bigotry against autoworkers among academic leftists, punctuated with terms like "dinosaurs." Such attitudes remind me of Bertolt Brecht when he quipped during the revolt of East German workers in 1953 that "[t]he Party is not satisfied with its people, so it will replace them with a new people more supportive of its politics" (in Zizek, Labor Relations Board 2006).

4. I am focusing solely on the Ford/Visteon/ACH segment of the Big Three ("the crumbling two" for some wags). With all the alliances, it is almost impossible to say that the Big Three is as relevant a triad as it once was.

5. This is only for pensions; there is little legal recourse for healthcare promises and claims.

6. One second-tier worker told me of going to a Ford dealership and being denied credit, given his wages (his credit rating was fine), to buy even the most stripped down of Ford's cars. Henry Ford's notion, at the early heart of consumer capitalism, that a worker paid well would become the person who would consume his cars ends here in farce. I am not validating consumption as a measure of the good, but criticism of U.S. workers as spoiled or overpaid misses the point. Putting down U.S. workers is not a tenable path to support workers elsewhere and partakes suspiciously of anti-worker bigotry common to the U.S. left since at least the 1970s and the ascent of identity politics— a politics, I argue, that was always a class politics: that of the professional managerial class.

7. Paul Durrenberger, after reading a draft of this chapter, noted, "There's an older tradition that theorizes property as one aspect of states that maintain order in stratified social orders—along with concepts of law and the legitimate use of force— by this notion: property only exists in states as part of a control system in stratified societies and therefore of necessity is an artifact of class systems." This is in harmony with this chapter's thesis: that what counts as property and what does not must be considered from the perspective of class.

8. Strathern's rejoinder to Carrier and Miller is not convincing. She claims that Carrier assumes a distinction between form and practice that is illegitimate, reifying formal rules in the process. But she is doubly implicated in such a method. Her critique of Carrier continues: "Having located power and interest *outside* this model, he then attributes them to other 'forces'" (Strathern 1998:219). Strathern is among those who hold a commitment to a neo-Kantian vision in which discourse always

already models the world; in her criticism of Carrier, Strathern seems really to be saying that he is mistaken by calling upon something outside the model—that is, praxis (relations of production)—as a source of social relations.

9. Workers hired between 2000 and 2003 after Visteon took control of the plant were on a temporary second tier, rising to the higher tier of pay and benefits after being employed for a time. The contract that created a permanent second tier had a provision turning these temporary second-tier workers into full Ford employees with Ford benefits, including flow back to Ford plants should the Sylvania plant close—thereby guaranteeing that these workers would be motivated to vote yes on the contract.

10. Buyouts were shunned by most older workers in 2003 because they expected, or hoped for, flow-back rights instead. The agreement between Ford and the UAW that created Visteon promised workers at Ford-facilities-made-Visteon-facilities the right to return to a Ford plant and job should Visteon founder as a company (which it looked like it might do in 2003, posting heavy losses on paper).

11. Space requires that I leave aside here the special case of the skilled trades in the plants or to treat separately Ford/Visteon/ACH's later attempt to entice tradespeople to retire or otherwise leave.

12. With seniority as the bid, the sixty production workers who chose to bid and who had the highest seniority would get the buyouts in the plant. Some nuanced subsets of this offer were aimed at very small demographics.

13. Self-interest arguably is age-stage-specific rather than a global human condition, best representative of adolescence and adolescent fantasy (of a "[s]he who dies with the most toys wins" mentality).

References Cited

Aronowitz, Stanley

1973 Trade Unionism: Illusion and Reality. In *Theories of the Labor Movement*, ed. Simeon Larson and Bruce Nissen, pp. 117–130. Detroit, Michigan: Wayne State University Press.

Beynon, Huw

1973 *Working for Ford*. London: Allen Lane.

Briody, E., and M. L. Baba

1991 Explaining Differences in Repatriation Experiences: The Discovery of Coupled and Decoupled Systems. *American Anthropologist* 93(2): 322–344.

Brondo, Keri, Marietta Baba, Sengun Yeniyurt, and Janell Townsend

2005 Fertile Ground: Homegrown Loyalty Makes for Globally Competitive Industry. In *EPIC 2005*, 158–166. American Anthropological Association. Berkeley: University of California Press.

Burawoy, Michael

1979 *Manufacturing Consent: Changes in the Labor Process under Monopoly Capitalism.* Chicago: University of Chicago Press.

Carrier, James

1998 Property and Social Relations in Melanesian Anthropology. In *Property Relations: Renewing the Anthropological Tradition*, ed. C. M. Hann, 85–103. Cambridge: Cambridge University Press.

Carrier, James, and Daniel Miller, eds.

1998 *Virtualism: A New Political Economy.* New York: Berg.

Detroit Free Press

2006 Ford Buyout Plan Chills UAW Locals, August 23.

Doukas, Dimitra

2003 *Worked Over: The Corporate Sabotage of an American Community.* Ithaca: Cornell University Press.

Durrenberger, E. Paul, and Suzan Erem

1999a The Abstract, the Concrete, the Political, and the Academic: Anthropology and a Labor Union in the United States. *Human Organization* 58(3): 305–312

1999b The Weak Suffer What They Must: A Natural Experiment in Thought and Structure. *American Anthropologist* 101(4): 783–793.

2002 Structure, Thought, and Action: Stewards in Chicago Union Locals. *American Anthropologist* 104(1): 93–105.

2005a *Class Acts.* New York: Alta Mira.

2005b Staff, Stewards, and Strikes: Labor's Communication Gap. *Journal of Anthropological Research* 61(2): 179–200.

Fernandez-Kelly, Maria P.

1983 *For We Are Sold, I and My People: Women and Industry in Mexico's Frontier.* Albany: State University of New York Press.

Hallowell, A. I.

1967 *Culture and Experience.* New York: Schocken.

Harvey, David

2003 *The New Imperialism.* New York: Oxford.

Kalb, Don

1997 *Expanding Class: Power and Everyday Politics in Industrial Communities, The Netherlands, 1850–1950.* Durham, NC: Duke University Press.

Kalb, Don, and Herman Tak

2005 *Critical Junctions: Anthropology and History beyond the Cultural Turn.* New York: Berghahn Books.

Kerr, Clark

1948 *Causes of Industrial Peace under Collective Bargaining: Case Studies no. 1–9.* Washington, DC: National Planning Association.

Mayo, Elton

1933 *The Human Problems of an Industrial Civilization.* New York: Macmillan.

Ong, Aihwa

1987 *Spirits of Resistance and Capitalist Discipline.* SUNY Series in the Anthropology of Work. Albany: State University of New York Press.

Richardson, Peter

2007 Two-Tier Kin: Imagining and Contesting Familism in a UAW Local. *Journal of Anthropological Research* 63(1): 73–93.

Strathern, Marilyn

1998 Divisions of Interest and Languages of Ownership. In *Property Relations: Renewing the Anthropological Tradition*, ed. C. M. Hann, 214–232. Cambridge: Cambridge University Press.

Verdery, Katherine

1996 *What Was Socialism, and What Comes Next?* Princeton, NJ: Princeton University Press.

Watts, Michael J.

2006 Development and Global Neoliberalism. In *Culture and Development in a Globalising World,* ed. S. Radcliffe, 30–58. London: Routledge.

SIX

Approaching Industrial Democracy in Nonunion Mines: Lessons from Wyoming's Powder River Basin

Jessica M. Smith

In both popular and academic imaginations, the coal industry is often characterized by strong unions and dramatic strikes. In the decade after World War II, unionization rates in the coal mining industry exceeded 80 percent (Lichtenstein 2002:56). When the center of the U.S. coal industry shifted to western surface mines in the mid-1980s, however, most of the new operations were nonunion worksites.

The surface mines surrounding Gillette in northeastern Wyoming's Powder River Basin, which currently supply over a third of all coal burned in U.S power plants, played a key role in this shift.[1] The last major union drive in the basin took place at Black Thunder Mine—one of the largest mines in the country—in 1987, about ten years after most of the region's mines were first opened.

Based on ethnographic fieldwork and archival research in Gillette, this chapter traces the historical and cultural factors contributing to the region's nonunion status. After presenting the history of unionization in the basin,[2] it traces the debates surrounding job security and self-representation that contributed to the 1987 defeat of the United Mine Workers of America (UMWA) and its subsequent decline in regional influence. In particular, the chapter highlights the role western tropes of independent yet hardworking cowboys played in the community-wide debate. At the same time that many miners take pride in their nonunion status, he discussion also demonstrates that they have developed camaraderie-filled workplace relationships that resonate with the solidarity commonly prized by unionized workers and activists. Finally, the chapter argues that women miners in the basin have successfully integrated themselves into these family-like work relationships, countering the existing research on women miners that tends to emphasize the difficulties they face in the industry. The Gillette case thus provides a possible example of workers cultivating close-knit, dignified, and respectful work relationships with their peers and many managers without formalized union structures.

Most of the miners continue to be white, corresponding with demographic trends for the county and the state. According to the 2004 census, 97 percent of Campbell County residents identified themselves as white non-Hispanics, compared with 95 percent in Wyoming and 80 percent in the United States overall. Data available on-line at http://quickfacts.census.gov/qfd/states/56/56005.html.

Historical Precedents of Unionization in the Powder River Basin

Reeling from the Arab oil embargoes of the 1970s, major oil companies and government figures turned to the domestic coal reserves along the Rocky Mountains as an "All-American" solution to the national energy crisis. At the beginning of the boom in the Powder River Basin, an estimated 50 billion tons of low-sulfur coal lay in deposits that stretched for miles and approached 100 feet in height. In addition to their size and low levels of pollutants, these seams were desirable because they were located close to the surface and could be easily extracted with large machinery.

By the mid-1980s fifteen mines had begun major operations in the area, producing nearly 100 million tons of coal a year with a workforce that had more than doubled the town's population to approximately 20,000. The boom caught the attention of the national media not only because Gillette was touted as the nation's first modern boomtown but also because the mines were "union free," in the words of management, despite forceful campaigns by the UMWA. Establishing and keeping these mines union free comprised one branch of larger anti-union corporate strategies in the 1970s and 1980s (Durrenberger and Erem 1999; Lichtenstein 2002).

The establishment of the mines as nonunion began with the first efforts at recruitment. The oil companies operating the mines focused their efforts on traditionally nonunion areas such as the ranching regions of Wyoming and the farm belts of North and South Dakota. These corporations also hired miners from regions experiencing high unemployment, including Arizona's copper belt and Minnesota's taconite range. The biggest incentives for many of the workers were the unprecedented wages and benefits that surpassed the standards for comparable unionized workplaces. The *lowest* starting average hourly pay at the mines was two dollars an hour higher than the UMWA's average *highest* starting pay (Brown 1981:A2).

Along with high wages, companies offered unparalleled benefits that included full health, dental, and vision coverage for workers and their families, plus attractive pension plans and opportunities to invest in the corporations. They also offered grievance procedures taken directly from the union contracts with other energy companies, but they departed from those standards by eliminating specialized job titles and positions. In these mines, all hourly employees directly involved in coal processing and equipment maintenance would be classified as "technicians" hired and trained to be multi-skilled.[3]

These efforts were aimed at discouraging the new wave of miners from unionizing during the boom. Even though both Wyoming and labor historians have tended to focus on the Kemmerer, Rock Springs, and Sheridan areas in their studies of unionization, the only two Gillette mines in operation before the boom were both unionized. Employees at the Wyodak Mine and adjacent power plant, originally developed in 1924, voted to unionize in March 1973. All but 4 of the mine's qualified employees voted in the election, and they joined the International Brotherhood of Electrical Workers (IBEW) by a final tally of 139 to 86 (*The Gillette News-Record* 1973:5). In May 1984 Wyodak's miners voted to join the UMWA. Of the 53 workers, 32 cast ballots for the UMWA, 17 voted to stay with the IBEW, and 4 abstained. Power plant employees remained affiliated with the IBEW (Kolenc 1984:1). Two years later the 40 remaining workers at Wyodak voted to decertify, in part because they were earning an average of two to three dollars an hour less than their new, nonunion counterparts in the basin.

Belle Ayr, the region's first large-scale mine, was opened in 1972 by AMAX, a coal company based in Indianapolis. Steeped in traditions from the central and eastern U.S. coal regions, management initially tried to replicate many of its previous labor practices in Wyoming. For example, it required all miners to join a union even though many had never previously belonged to one and did not especially want to join. Yet miners were sufficiently committed to the union that in November 1974 they voted 45–3 to maintain their representation by the UMWA after the Progressive Mine Workers received permission from the National Labor Relations Board (NLRB) to hold an election.

A few months later, on January 12, 1975, Gillette's only major strike began when Belle Ayr miners walked off the job at the behest of the national UMWA leadership. At issue was the company's refusal to pay royalties into the union's welfare and retirement fund and to coordinate the contract of Belle Ayr miners with those in the eastern United States. By the end of March of that year, after months of stalled negotiations AMAX reopened the mine, announcing that it would take back any strikers who wanted to return but would also hire new workers if needed. By the beginning of April, 39 of the 52 striking workers opted to return to work given the conditions of the company's final offer, and the company hired an additional 6 new miners. Miners and their families continued picketing the mine through the summer and even traveled to New York in July to demonstrate outside an AMAX stockholders meeting. Throughout this time, the UMWA published full-page ads in the Gillette newspaper to drum up popular support for the strikers.

In December 1975 a labor organization called the North East Wyoming Affiliated Coal Mine Employees (NEWACME) filed a petition for certification at Belle Ayr with the support of 73 of the mine's 83 employees. Local UMWA officials publicly speculated that AMAX was behind the new union and urged their former coworkers not to join and lose the bargaining power that stemmed from affiliation with an established national union. The election was postponed because of existing negotiations between AMAX and the UMWA.

In January 1976 a settlement had still not been reached between AMAX and the UMWA, and a smaller group of miners continued the strike with the support of the national union. In the years that followed, NEWACME, UMWA, and the International Union of Operating Engineers engaged in a three-way battle until the NLRB allowed representational elections to take place in 1979. Of the 405 votes cast in the election, the unions collected only 33, 16 of which were contested ballots. In the end, the prolonged strike would be remembered in the community for producing or exacerbating tensions among the workforce without reaching its goals.

The next major drive did not take place until 1987, when a few Black Thunder Mine employees turned to the UMWA after becoming frustrated with decisions made by a management team undergoing personnel changes. Many miners were upset that they had been left out of decisions to change seniority policies and to move to twelve-hour shifts. They were also concerned that the mine's turn to contract labor in the midst of a soft coal market would put their jobs at risk. By September, union organizers had collected sufficient cards to order an election, and the entire community became embroiled in debates about the benefits and disadvantages of unionizing. The election was postponed until after the fall hunting season, which gave the company until November to present its position to the miners. When the votes were finally tallied, all but 11 of the 374 workers had participated in the election and had voted overwhelmingly against the UMWA, which was defeated by a 6-to-1 margin.

Although union organizers promised to stay in the community, organize other mines, and remain vigilant to ensure that mine managers keep the promises made during the election, the defeat effectively ended large-scale attempts to unionize Powder River Basin miners. Today, more than twenty years later, many miners continue to place stickers with a red strike through the initials UMWA on their hardhats and lunchboxes. Talk of unionization sometimes rumbles through the ranks when miners become frustrated with changes in healthcare, pension plans, or working conditions, but the majority of the workforce perceives these threats as strategies to get management's attention instead of serious calls for radical organization.

Job Security and Speaking for Oneself: Union Debates

Based on conversations during my fieldwork as well as a lively series of letters to the editor of the community newspaper, *The Gillette News-Record*, I suggest that the 1987 campaign boiled down to two key issues: job security and the politics of representation. Most Gillette miners were not completely opposed to the idea of unions. In fact, many continue to believe that in the earliest years of the mining industries, unions were necessary to counter the exploitative and unsafe working conditions endured by their fathers and grandfathers.

The 1914 massacre of miners, women, and children at Ludlow, Colorado, stands out for many as emblematic of this period.[4] During the 1987 drive, a supporter of the UMWA wrote: "The labor unions in this country have spent years fighting for the job benefits that all of us enjoy, like better and safer working conditions, shorter workdays, health benefits and paid holidays. There isn't a miner in this basin or a worker in this country for that matter that hasn't benefited from the legislation the unions have fought to pass" (Grant 1987:2). Even one of the drive's most vocal opponents of unionization wrote: "Eighty years ago there was a great need for labor reform. . . . And nobody can deny that fact, we do owe a lot to the unions. But because they had their place in this country's past and play an important part in this present time doesn't mean we owe them our allegiance and whole-hearted support for its organization attempt here in the Basin" (Ruiz 1987:4).

As this letter suggests, many miners also firmly believed the unions became obsolete once they developed their own bureaucracies. According to miners today, unions no longer help out the little guy but have turned into their own business, looking out for the interests of the national union staff as well as the corporations. These attitudes are emblematic of larger national shifts in public perceptions of unions as self-aggrandizing interest groups rather than levers for social change (Lichtenstein 2002:141). One of the key issues underlining the debates in the 1980s was thus whether the mining corporations or the unions would better protect workers' interests. Job security was a particular concern for miners, many of whom could trace with great detail the frequent boom-and-bust cycles that compelled multiple generations of their families to move around the state and the region in pursuit of work.

Union organizers tried convincing Gillette miners that unionizing was their best bet for job security by arguing that bargained contracts were superior to the handbooks offered by the companies. During the 1987 drive, however, this argument did not withstand the many testimonials of miners who had been fired from unionized workplaces. One worker who lost his job in Minnesota slyly remarked that unions simply prioritized the order in which people were fired, while another wrote that his experiences in Arizona's copper mines proved that job security came from the market since not even the unions could save their jobs in the midst of a downturn (Ruiz 1987:4).

Furthermore, the miners became convinced that instead of looking out for their jobs, the union was "just another business" that would actually threaten their jobs by decreasing the profitability of the mining corporation. One couple calculated that the dues from miners at Black Thunder would generate \$175,000 a year for the UMWA and concluded: "Sounds like a profitable business to me. And what do we get? Thunder Basin Coal Co. is here today in the Powder River Basin because they make a profit. The

UMW is knocking on our door to enhance their own profits. If we continue to support Thunder Basin Coal in their efforts to [be] profitable, then we all become winners" (Lucy and Lucy 1987:4).

Corporate officials also utilized this line of reasoning. Jim Herickhoff, the president of Thunder Basin Coal Company, publicly speculated that because more efficient nonunion operations were out-producing their unionized counterparts, the UMWA was in financial trouble and searching for new members. In an open letter published in the local newspaper during the campaign, he decried the high dues employees would have to pay to the UMWA and argued that "job security comes from one source and only one source: successful and profitable operations. Job security does not come from the union, nor is it guaranteed by a union contract" (ibid.:5).

Union organizers tried to counter these accusations by arguing that they could help prevent unfettered corporate greed. Keith Barnhart, the UMWA representative in Gillette, stated that his goal was to replace images of corrupt unions with "family-oriented workers who want to help other workers protect themselves from well-organized corporate greed" (quoted in Daly 1987:13; cf. Barnhart 1987:4). Community members were less persuaded by this argument; one person went so far as to write that it was the "duty of a company to make money" (Bennett 1987:2).

In fact, Gillette residents actually considered the possibility of strikes incurred by unionizing a greater threat to their job security than the corporation. For many people, discussions of unions spark memories of strikes that put family and friends out of work. Many miners and their spouses point to abandoned mines throughout the state and speak bitterly about high-ranking union officials "ordering" them to go on strike despite their own inclinations.

Financial liabilities coupled with their newfound earning power made the slightest possibility of a strike unacceptable for most miners (cf. Durrenberger and Erem 2005). The mine wages in Gillette provided many families with their first chance to "get ahead." Suddenly earning incomes they had never dreamed possible, many families immediately put money down for new homes as well as expensive cars, boats, and four-wheelers. One miner wrote that since the UMWA could not guarantee that strikes would not take place or that it would deliver on its promises to improve working conditions, unionizing would be a "high-risk investment. . . . We cannot put everything we have on the line for vague promises of a better return" (Olsen 1987:2).

Indeed, this evidence suggests that many miners came to think of the union rather than the corporation as the unnecessarily greedy party. The union organizer tried to portray the union as a family of regular coal miners, but the image of the union as just another business became powerful for many miners, who started reasoning that they did not need another boss. One miner wrote that when he had worked for union companies in the past, he had to pay dues regardless of whether his wages were good or he was on strike because of the "Boss Union": "I'm still paying my 'dues' for someone to talk for me. . . . Since my past farewells, I have decided I like to be my own individual. I like to talk 'Myself.' Yes, I still have a 'Boss Company' but they're promising me more than the other two put together" (Denton 1987:2).

Workers' view of unions as another source of power over them is a common concern in scholarship about unions in the West. For example, Janet Finn (1998) has shown that both miners and their wives in Butte, Montana, worried about getting "stuck in the middle" between unions and management. In these circumstances, the Gillette miners preferred to deal with local corporate officials whom they knew instead of unknown union officials based in the eastern United States. They spoke about trusting the people whose kids went to the same school as theirs more than they did "outsiders" who were believed to use their dues to make eastern coal operations more powerful than local ones.

Furthermore, the union's emphasis on distributing the spoils of corporate greed contradicted locally significant values of a fair day's wage. As one miner related to me: "My parents were hardworking people. I was raised that if you were paid for eight hours, you worked eight hours. Then there has got to be a certain amount of pride in what you do. To go out there and not give it your best, that's kind of a shameful thing, to not go out there and give them an honest day."

In his critique of the fragmentation and degradation of work through scientific management, Harry Braverman (1998:67) argued that the phrase is "inherently meaningless," since a worker's daily wage is not "fair" at all; it actually includes the surplus labor value appropriated by the capitalist through extending the working day beyond the labor time necessary to produce the value of the wages paid to workers.

Whatever its philosophical status in theory, the concept of a fair day's wage is locally meaningful for most miners.[5] This attitude about work ethic is couched in kinship relations and moral language about personal character and suggests one way workers have been able to make meaning out of potentially alienating labor conditions. Demonstrating an admirable work ethic is one way for miners to honor their parents and continue a family tradition of hard work (cf. Rodgers 1978 and Sennett 1988 for considerations of work ethic in the United States).[6]

Cowboys and Coal Miners: Debating Work, Personhood, and Workplace Relationships

While the crux of the 1987 debate over unionization appears to be the issues of job security and self-representation, I suggest that these debates were informed by very different conceptions of work, personhood, and workplace relationships that crystallized in the distinct imagery of cowboys and miners utilized by mine and union officials, respectively.

In speeches and letters, Herickhoff emphasized themes of trust and partnership, the proposed pillars of "new labor practices" at the mines, in comparison to the antagonism attributed to union operations. In his open letter to mine employees, he wrote:

> The people of Campbell County, the state of Wyoming, and the West have established a proud tradition of standing tall and then facing and beating whatever hardships might come their way. From the early days to now, Wyoming people still hold these values steadfastly and place a premium on dealing person to person, eyeball to eyeball and honoring a handshake which closes a deal. . . . We built into our employee programs opportunities for employees to grow and develop into the kind of person who stands on his/her own two feet and is proud of the ability to operate and repair some of the largest machinery in the world. (Herickhoff 1987:5)

He then argued that the solution to the problems at the mine could be found in their own history: "Proud Westerners have fiercely defended their right to deal straight on with a person when a problem develops—not through some third party who takes their money and really can't deliver."

The images painted by the company president accomplished two main things. First, he highlighted the technical aspects of operating and repairing heavy equipment, linking employees with the imagery of hardworking yet independent ranchers. In so doing, he encouraged the employees to identify with a specifically western heritage of hard work rather than a national heritage of mining.[7] In fact, in the letter he referred to the employees as technicians, *not* as miners, perhaps because the term is heavily associated with unionization and the Appalachian coal industry.

Second, he argued that western workers had no need for unions or any other mediating party to settle their problems because they were strong enough to do so themselves. He portrayed the miners as enjoying relationships of mutual trust and respect with the managers, with whom they can stand "eyeball to eyeball," which obviates the need for unions and contracts. The trope of the independent cowboy thus dovetails with the themes of trust and partnership, the proposed pillars of the "new" labor practices envisioned by corporate officials.

Likening Powder River Basin miners to ranchers had been a well-established management practice since the early years of the coal boom. As corporations began opening mines in the late 1970s and early 1980s, their representatives began publicly highlighting the distinctive "westernness" of the new operations. For example, a 1981 *Washington Post* article focused on the companies' efforts to "best unions at [the] benefits game." The author quoted E. H. Lovering, the employee relations manager of the Carter Mining Company, explaining why the nonunion approach was appropriate for the new workforce: "The individuals out here seem to be open, free, primarily rancher-types from small-town backgrounds. They've battled the elements all of their lives and survived. They don't take too kindly to being organized" (Brown 1981:A2).

What both the author of the *Post* article and the coal company president failed to mention is that company officials simply did not "find" these independent, cowboy-like workers already in Gillette, but they specifically recruited workers to move to the town from rural nonunion farming and ranching communities to decrease the chances that they would unionize. They also offered them higher wages and better benefit packages than the UMWA had established in its mines. Moreover, corporations did not just happen to find an "independent" workforce but actively created and encouraged it to meet their own business goals. As Lovering also explained in the article, "The union-free approach is a very practical thing. . . . For one thing, we don't have strikes or other work disruptions" (Brown 1981:A2). He also mentioned that with more flexible work rules, companies have better control over production, since they can move employees into the positions where they are needed most (cf. Gardner and Flores 1989:213).

Emphasizing the uniquely western characteristics of the new mines helped corporate officials downplay potential labor conflicts, since dominant popular portrayals of "the West" erase the class dynamics that give shape to it. Randall McGuire and Paul Reckner (2002:45) have argued that of all the relationships comprising western history, class struggles are the "most inimical" to the notion of the romantic West. Idealizations of western labor resonate more closely with cowboys rather than industrialized, wage-working miners.

In her foundational work critiquing western historiography, Patricia Limerick (1987:97) has argued that the type of labor popularly associated with the West emphasizes non-exploitative independence, in which people "simply gathered what nature produced. The laborer was to be self-employed, and the status of laborer was to be temporary, left behind when the profits made escape possible." The popularly imagined cowboy, not the miner, embodies this type of egalitarian labor. Donald Worster (1992:35–36) and David Igler (2004) draw on Limerick to suggest that associations of the West with open, sunny spaces have colored portrayals of ranching labor as relatively nonrepressive, especially since cowboys often worked outside in relative isolation. In many genres of Western novels and films, cowboys are portrayed as hopelessly independent, working free from both government regulations and capitalist business pressures. "The mythical cowboy is not always a working cowboy in the sense of herding cattle. . . . The 'cowboy' of the myth is defined by his strength, honor and independence, his wilderness identity, not by his job" (Wright 2001:6).

Class dynamics have animated the cattle industry since its beginnings but are tellingly absent from the most popular representations of mythic cowboys. As Igler (2004:93) has written, "The Marlboro Man works precisely because Philip Morris situates him in a landscape free from the big cattle companies and daily wages that structured the lives of real cowboys." Contemporary popular and scholarly portrayals of the ranching industry (e.g., Starrs 1998) have tended to strip it of its exploitative class dynamics, collapsing actors as diverse as big cattle barons to hired hands into the figure of the independent middle-class rancher (Merrill 2002). Bonnie Christensen (2002:112) locates the power of this trope in its the fusion of the cowboy's romanticized free outdoor work with the responsibilities and independence of capitalist land ownership.

These depictions obscure the "cowboy proletariat" responsible for the daily functioning of ranch life. Zeese Papanikolas (1995:75) has written that without his horse, the cowboy was "but one more seasonal worker attached to the industrial world by railroads that led to Chicago stockyards and ranches owned as often as not by Eastern bankers or Scottish investors." These cowboys sometimes organized formal protests against their working conditions, including an 1883 strike in Texas (McGuire and Reckner 2002:49) and an 1885 strike in Wyoming's Sweetwater County (Papanikolas 1995:75). Recent historical research details the hierarchical, capitalist labor relations that shaped the cattle industry from its inception (Igler 2001; Merrill 2002; Sheridan 2007) and provides a corrective for these romanticized images that continue to permeate many contemporary scholarly and popular accounts of ranchers and the cattle industry.

The social processes that have encouraged and shaped popular imaginations of freedom-loving cowboys are the same ones that have contributed to particular exclusions and inclusions in the history of western mining. These romanticized myths of western labor arose as eastern urbanized Americans imagined escapes from increasing industrialization and its concomitant social ills (Cronon 1995; Limerick 1987; Papanikolas 1995; Worster 1992). "Westerns primarily appealed to people in the urban East, where factories and cities had long replaced any sense of a wild frontier. The cowboy became popular as America became industrial" (Wright 2001:7).

Coal mining in Wyoming does not fit easily into such narratives because the industry industrialized early and quickly, setting limits on the possibility that rank-and-file miners might strike it rich—the narrative organizing dominant histories of the industry. Limerick (1987) has noted in western history an enduring fascination with the relatively brief period of speculation mining exemplified in the Black Hills and California gold rushes. Windfall mining fits well into these dominant narratives because of its association with labor that is a temporary, egalitarian, and non-exploitative gathering of nature's bounty: prospecting and panning were done outside, with miners searching for precious metals among equals who conceivably all had a chance at striking it rich. Limerick (1987:108) suggests that industrial mining practices were left out of most western histories because "this version of life in the Wild West did not strike the imagination of the time or appeal later to the novelists or moviemakers: the scene made it too clear that the West was hardly a refuge from industrialism."[8]

In the 1987 union drive, corporate imagery of miners as independent ranchers contrasted starkly with the common tropes union advocates utilized in their speeches and letters. They most often emphasized the image of "union brothers and brotherhood," in which men would work together to achieve common goals in the face of oppression from management (see Richardson

2007 for a recent discussion of union sibling-ship). Barnhart saw his role in the community as educational, stripping away the image of unions as corrupt strongmen and replacing it with images of family-oriented workers who wanted to help others protect themselves against corporate greed. He was quoted in a newspaper article at the beginning of the campaign as saying, "We're going to be here. We've made that commitment. The coal companies have the Wyoming Mining Association, and the miners will sooner or later realize they need us. It's a matter of unity" (Daly 1987:13).

Very few miners adopted this language of mutual assistance and brotherhood, even though they simultaneously spoke about their coworkers as a second family. Instead, the miners believed the potential strikes they thought would accompany unionizing would take away their ability to provide for their families, a key component of their identities as breadwinners (cf. Broughton and Walton 2006; Townsend 2002). Union organizers made little effort to engage this language in their communications with miners, choosing instead to continue emphasizing images of mutual assistance and brotherhood (cf. Durrenberger and Erem 2005 on union communication gaps).

Even though many miners adopted ranching idioms in talking about their own work, mine management did not control this western imagery so much as make use of it. These images of cowboys and ranchers were meaningful for many of the miners with ranching experience. Before the first oil boom in the 1960s, Campbell County was primarily a ranching area, and Gillette was a small town where families could buy supplies and socialize. Although many new mine employees in the 1970s and 1980s were recent arrivals to Gillette, a significant number were local ranchers who had sought employment to keep the family ranch afloat during lean years. Many others intended to use their earnings to finally buy a ranch of their own, including those who had previously worked as ranch hands or grown up knowing ranching families. Even those with no ranch experience came to embrace this idealized image of independence after moving to the region, so much so that local ranchers often joked about wearing sneakers to distinguish themselves from the "wannabe cowboys" (see Tauxe 1993 for a similar discussion of the idealized image of the heartland farmer in a North Dakota mining and farming community). A 1977 article in the Sheridan newspaper makes the link between ranching and coal mining explicit. Entitled "Independent, Hard-Working, They're Called New Cowboys," the article examined the similarities between mine and ranch work and then explored the miners' memories of the past and dreams of future ranch lifestyles (Temple 1977).

The miners' adoption of ranching symbolism also points to their own complex class identities. In the campaign, the organizer tried to argue that the coal miners rightfully belonged to a larger group: the working class. Throughout his speeches in Gillette, Barnhart referred to the miners as *laborers*, a term the miners had not previously used to describe themselves, and he urged them to take their rightful place alongside the rest of the American working class. This language contradicted most miners' firm resistance to being considered working class, a label they associated with poorer and more exploited workers who needed unions to represent their interests. Most continue to prefer to speak of themselves simply as *workers*. Even though miners view their work as qualitatively different from the kind undertaken by managers because theirs is productive and physically demanding (cf. Halle 1984), they sometimes speak of themselves as middle class because of their sizable incomes. It is telling that most anti-union letters to the editor from miners have emphasized not just their high wages but also their stock options in the company. Portraying themselves as stockholders further distances the miners from their understanding of the working class.

The resistance of most miners to include themselves among the ranks of the working class prompted some union supporters to insinuate that they were willing agents of corporate capitalism. In explaining their choice not to unionize, most highlighted their own decisions informed by their life experiences (cf. Metzgar 2000 on speaking from experience). One miner wrote that he and his coworkers' decisions not to unionize did not make them "mindless machines that are intimidated and manipulated by company officials and their policies." Another wrote:

> UMW, you insult my intelligence, then you turn around and say, "I'm not going to take a defensive stance to their [miners'] ignorance and misinformation!" I, for one, am not an "apple polisher" and I don't consider my letter to be a "shiny apple on the company desk." I am not just siding with the company, either. I believe in what I am saying here. I am an educated, intelligent person who has been exposed to many circumstances of employment in my life. (Whetstone 1987:2)

Following some labor theorists, including Michael Burawoy (1985), one could argue that the miners' local "culture" and the apparent coordination of interests between the miners and capital are actually products of capitalist hegemony that further disadvantage the worker. In "Wage Labor and Capital," Karl Marx (1978:210–211) cast doubt on the benefits accruing to workers through capitalist profiting: "To say that the worker has an interest in the rapid growth of capital is only to say that the more rapidly the worker increases the wealth of others, the richer will be the crumbs that fall to him, the greater is the number of workers that can be employed and called into existence, the more can the mass of slaves dependent on capital be increased."

In a similar vein, scholars like John Alt (1976) have suggested that rising standards of living and consumption patterns make work more tolerable for employees, thus discouraging organizing. Although the real value of national blue-collar wages has actually decreased since the late 1980s, in the basin it remained relatively constant during that period, an insight that sheds some light on the situation in Gillette. "In defense of mining," said one longtime miner during an interview, "it has always paid the bills. I have never missed a paycheck for twenty years."

In crafting their life histories, many miners have emphasized the values of hard work and perseverance in ways that could appear to echo the psychology of meritocratic individualism, in which success and failure are viewed as the results of individual effort and ability (Dudley 1994; Newman 1988). At the same time, however, most miners draw on their own everyday experiences to maintain a sophisticated understanding of the structural class dynamics at work in the coal industry. Having critically assessed their options to bring about change, they have simply chosen to work within that structure rather than to organize against it. In many ways, these efforts have resulted in the miners creating working places and relationships they value. Labor theorists should not discount the significance of these creative efforts by miners to improve their everyday working lives, especially since they might shed light on strategies for workers to achieve the ideals held by union supporters.

Approaching Industrial Democracy

Labor historian Nelson Lichtenstein (2002:30–31) commends the unionism following the New Deal for striving to attain the democracy that was sorely lacking in workplaces despite its popularity within a political culture that celebrated free speech, democratic participation, and autonomy. Industrial democracy was supposed to generate informed and willing consent and to bring women and minorities into labor movements, but these efforts stalled as individualistic, rights-based goals gradually replaced pluralist group ones (Lichtenstein 2002:177, 181). Government policy contributed to this shift, particularly in the form of the 1947 Taft-Hartley amendments to the 1935 Wagner Act, which changed the structure and nature of unions into legalistic bureaucracies forced to focus their efforts on handling grievance cases (Durrenberger and Erem 2005). This section explores the extent to which the Gillette miners have been able to approach the ideals of industrial democracy articulated by labor advocates.

Perhaps the biggest lesson learned by the coal companies after the 1987 union drive was that they had to include miners in major decision-making processes. To this end, most mines have developed formal procedures for employees to make concrete proposals for improving workplace practices and relationships. These suggestions can be brought up to crew supervisors casually in conversations or more formally at start-up and safety meetings, and they can also be submitted anonymously through written comments. Managers especially value the miners' input to identify and remedy safety hazards and often keep their doors open to encourage employees to approach them with concerns.

The most respected managers and front-line supervisors are those who actively solicit input from their employees. One miner warmly remembered a supervisor who epitomized this quality. On his first night as their boss, he sat down with the crew and said he was going to rely on them to explain what they needed him to do to help them accomplish the goals they had set for themselves. This boss was highly regarded not simply because he was honest and displayed integrity but also because he respected the crew's knowledge and utilized their input.

Management teams routinely hold meetings to receive feedback about major proposed changes such as altering shift schedules. To be sure, the miners' abilities to resist major changes are often limited, and they become frustrated when their suggestions are not integrated into the workplace. For example, when one of the last mines in the basin switched from ten- to twelve-hour shifts, many of the most experienced miners complained bitterly about the long night shifts they would have to endure. While some eagerly anticipated the larger number of days off built into the twelve-hour shift schedule, very few relished the thought of trying to stay alert while working night shifts that stretched from six in the evening to six in the morning. They had also appreciated the fact that ten-hour shifts let them "have a life" when they were done with work rather than being forced to eat a quick meal and immediately go to bed once they came home from a twelve-hour workday plus commute. Many miners took advantage of crew meetings to voice these concerns, and while they were unable to stop the change, they appreciated that they "at least had been listened to."

This feeling of appreciation also played a major role in the 1987 drive, when many miners considered managements' efforts reasonable enough to decline union representation, as one miner articulated:

> I believe the mine manager is sincere in trying to help the employees regain a higher morale and an improved workplace. I am thankful for having a job that not only pays good wages, but has a superb benefit program, and especially so in these economic times. I have been able to voice my opinions to management in the past, and I will continue to do so. I may not get everything I want, but I have been listened to, and some results were achieved. As long as management will respect my opinions, and me as an employee, I will respect management. Therefore I do not feel the need for a union here at this time. (Whetstone 1987:2)

This issue of management listening to employees and taking their concerns seriously seems central to debates about union representation in the basin. In an interview during my fieldwork, one miner remembered that whenever his coworkers started talking about unionization and putting UMWA stickers on their hardhats and lunchboxes, management "stepped up to the plate and started listening to the concerns people had. . . . They took more of an involved approach. I think things did get better. Before, you couldn't hardly get anybody to listen to you if you came up with an idea." This notion of "listening" to employees is one of the hallmarks of the new type of management-worker relations the companies ideally support. It seems that the threat of unionization remains a powerful tool for miners' to shape the contours of their everyday work practices.

Miners also retain some ability to oppose the policies they consider disrespectful or dangerous. When speaking about notorious supervisors or ridiculous disciplinary policies, many miners relished memories of entire crews expressing their discontent through "laying down," or slowing production to a standstill while remaining within official company policy. One of the ways miners accomplish this is by following safety rules to the letter. This work-to-rule strategy, a common theme in labor history, is effective in the Powder River Basin mines because of their emphasis on production. If a crew is unhappy with a new supervisor, for example, dramatically decreasing production numbers has proven to be one way to force upper-level management to reconsider its selection. Low production numbers reflect badly on the supervisor, but the miners protect themselves from incurring punishment because they are officially upholding company policy.

This tactic of "laying down" often translates into managers and supervisors making efforts to cater to their employees' wishes within the bounds of productivity. During my fieldwork, for example, a manager at one mine decided to take away the microwave from the pit break room because it could encourage the workers to return late from lunch. The crew members were upset because they felt professionally and personally insulted; they were rarely late, and every other area of the mine had a microwave for hot lunches. After the manager took the microwave to the office, the crew's unofficial leader drove to the onsite warehouse, obtained another one, and took it back to the lunch shack. A week later the same manager found the new microwave during rounds and threatened the entire crew with locking up the break room (which also had their coffee machine and water cooler) and making them eat lunch by themselves on their equipment if he found a microwave there again. The next day, an unnamed person showed up to work early and posted signs around the office that said "When microwaves are outlawed, only outlaws will have microwaves"—a clever play on the National Rifle Association slogan.

Needless to say, the signs were quickly taken down, and managers interpreted the joke as one of insubordination and bad attitudes rather than a legitimate critique of workplace policies. The manager threatened to put whoever had posted the signs on "step," a disciplinary technique. But after the pit crews expressed their frustration by intentionally following every safety rule to the letter and thus slowing down production for two weeks, the manager quietly let it be known that he would no longer be stopping by the break room during his rounds. The microwave was just as quietly replaced, and the crews returned to their normal levels of production and microwaved lunches.

To be effective, entire crews must engage in work-to-rule actions together, demonstrating a solidarity that is often translated into miners' frequent statements that their crews become family. The basin's women miners have been integrated into these close relationships, prompting a reconsideration of the existing literature on women's experiences in male-dominated blue-collar workplaces.

Women and Workplace Families

Although mining is often considered one of the masculinized industries (Campbell 1984; Duke 2002; Lahiri-Dutt and Macintyre 2006), women have played a major role in the Powder River Basin mines as both the kin of male miners and as miners themselves. During the initial coal boom, companies hired large numbers of women to work in production in the pits, plants, and maintenance shops. Many adjusted easily to their new work because they had grown up around heavy equipment on the region's farms and ranches, but even those with no previous experience found ample opportunity for training and advancement. Many of the original employees continue to work in the mines along with younger women just beginning their adult working lives. On average, women make up 20 percent of production crews in the basin. In addition to providing the means to support their families, most women miners point to close relationships with their "crew families" as their primary reason they enjoy their work.[9] For most women miners, this solidarity is evident in the support they receive during times of crisis and in the positive joking relationships they have crafted with coworkers.

One of the most respected shovel operators on her crew began as a temporary employee. When her parents died during this probationary period, she had to take time off to take care of their estate. Since temporary workers do not receive any company leave, she would have struggled to make ends meet without her bimonthly paycheck of $900. Even though she had worked with them for only a few months, her crew members collected money to support her during her absence. "They collected enough for me to eat and keep my house," she said during an interview. "We help each other." Throughout the years, members of her crew and their families also helped insulate and put trim around her house, as well as fix her car and computer. In return, she took them out for dinner and helped them with home improvement projects for other coworkers.

At another mine, when the son of a couple who both worked in production was seriously injured in a car accident, the entire crew came together to collect their personal money and to convince management to match and then donate their production bonuses to the family. Instead of receiving submarine sandwiches or pizza for meeting their production goals, as was customary, the crew requested that the mine donate the money for the food plus matching funds directly to the couple in need. Every single person in the pit worked through lunch to keep a steady stream of money flowing to their coworkers while they cared for their son.

Women and men also craft camaraderie in the mines by participating in both practical and verbal jokes. For many women, these jokes constitute the favorite part of their day. One woman who has been operating equipment in the mines since the 1990s considers her closest coworkers those who she can "joke around with." Her memory of her last day of work before transferring to a new mine highlights the importance of jokes in constituting relationships. One of her favorite things about her old crew was something they called "Sing and String." Whereas truck drivers are expected to back up completely to the berm so their loads of overburden fall over the side, "stringing" refers to the practice of leaving the dirt in long strips on the top of the dump. This causes extra work for the dump's dozer operator, so the act can be interpreted as either malicious or funny depending on the strength of the relationship between the dozer and truck operators. This woman's crew had turned stringing almost completely into a joke. Operators make up a song that can be silly or that tells a story about the dozer operator and sing it over the radio while stringing dirt everywhere. "It was fun," she said during an interview. "I would just laugh so hard when someone did that to me." On her last day with the crew, she knew she had to Sing and String. "So I made a nice little song and everybody was in tears and then all I could do was say 'Okay' and then string out a little smiley face on the dump. And it was just fun. It was just a good time." She intended for her joke to leave her coworkers with a sense of close friendship and camaraderie.

These practices prompt a closer analysis of the distinction between enjoyable sexualized banter and harassment. During an interview, a longtime equipment operator aptly explained how she distinguished between sexual harassment and joking:

> Camaraderie. I love that word because of what it builds. It's more friendly, building a trust, because they know that I'm not going to go to HR [human relations]. . . . You have to know the person first, then you build and you can say whatever you want—body humor, sexual jokes, whatever—because you know each other.[10]

Here the miner suggests that engaging in behaviors that could possibly be interpreted negatively actually fosters trust under the right conditions. A much younger woman expressed a similar sentiment during an interview:

> I really liked all of the guys. They all gave me a hard time, but that's what I like. They'd always make nicknames for me. They were always trying to

> tease me or make fun of me or pull a practical joke on me. But that was their way of, you know, interacting with me. At first they didn't know. They feel you out to know if you're going to laugh or if you're going to turn them in or if you're not funny. They need to know that.

In fact, the only time during my research that someone labeled behavior harassment instead of good-natured joking involved a situation that threatened the camaraderie of the entire crew. Before the start of a shift, a male equipment operator said, "Women should mind their men." The only woman present to hear the comment interpreted it as an insult to her skills and a statement that she did not belong on the crew. For her, the comment was particularly hurtful because she took pride in her good work reputation and thought that others recognized it as well. The other men on the crew also took offense to the statement, especially since it fit into larger patterns of that worker "running off his mouth" and "trash talking" his coworkers. In fact, the men were the ones who eventually reported the incident to their supervisor to support the female colleague and to encourage their male coworker to change his behavior more generally. At his supervisor's prompting, the man apologized to the entire crew, an action appreciated by his male and female coworkers alike for restoring good feelings throughout the entire crew (Smith 2008).

Thus even the few studies of women miners have tended to focus on the sexual harassment and discrimination they experience (Tallichet 1998, 2006; Yount 1991, 2005), I suggest that these joking practices actually facilitate rank-and-file solidarity among men and women in the basin. This research calls attention to the importance of fine-grained ethnographic analysis for better understanding workplace relationships.

Conclusion

This chapter has traced the historical and cultural factors contributing to the decision of a group of miners not to unionize in the last major union drive in the Powder River Basin. Whereas union representatives insinuated that these decisions stemmed from the miners' alleged ignorance in supporting corporate interests, I have argued that their decision was actually based on concerns about job security and self-representation. In particular, I suggested that the union's emphasis on interdependent brotherhood contradicted the conceptions of appropriate work, personhood, and workplace relationships intertwined with the western ranching imagery utilized by mine management and the miners. Finally, I have shown that with few exceptions, the miners have been able to craft camaraderie-filled workplace relationships and dignified working conditions that approach the ideals of industrial democracy. Even though the current research surrounding women miners tends to highlight their exclusion from these relationships, I have drawn attention to the ways in which women in the Powder River Basin have successfully integrated themselves into the mines' crew families.

Many of my academic colleagues and personal acquaintances are surprised to hear that the coal miners I know in Wyoming are not unionized. These reactions point to both popular and academic tendencies to associate the industry with unionization, despite the fact that as of 2005, only 11 percent of America's 108,000 coal miners were unionized—a number that corresponds to the national average for all workers. For an industry that once boasted union membership levels exceeding 80 percent, this decline is dramatic (Cook 2006). These numbers are the direct result of corporate strategies seeking to rid their workplaces of unions, as well as a few key missteps made by the most bureaucratized labor unions (Lichtenstein 2002; Metzgar 2000).

Many observers fear that these trends increasingly endanger miners' safety and their ability to confront dangerous corporate cost-cutting strategies. The most sobering lessons in this regard came from the January 2006 disaster at West Virginia's nonunion Sago Mine and the August 2007 tragedy at Utah's Crandall Canyon Mine, believed by many to have been prompted by business profit pressures and lax government regulation.

As the country tried to come to grips with these tragedies, many public intellectuals and journalists attributed the dangerous working conditions to the miners' nonunion status. Scholars and activists should remain vigilant in monitoring these developments and preventing similar disasters, but they should also be careful in generalizing about nonunion workplaces, especially considering the arguably more positive experiences of miners in Gillette. While no one would argue that the men and women in Gillette have not endured hardships, they have also worked together to create some of the safest mines in the country and the types of workplaces they value.

Notes

1. In 2006, the approximately 4,000 full-time miners in the Powder River Basin produced 431 million tons of coal. That same year, unionized mines in the United

States produced 220 million tons of coal, while their nonunionized counterparts produced 941 million tons. Statistics are available on-line from the federal Energy Information Administration: http://www.eia.doe.gov/fuelcoal.html.

2. I focus on the history of unions in the Powder River Basin because it is rarely mentioned in the more general overviews of labor politics in Wyoming and the West. For more detailed accounts of larger trends in Wyoming labor history, see Gardner and Dudley (1989); Long (1989); Wolff (2003).

3. These developments correspond with larger neo-liberal demands that entrepreneuring subjects prudently and independently navigate increasingly "flexible" and insecure domains as diverse as the market, workplaces, family life, and citizenship (Dunn 2004; Freeman 2007; Martin 1994; Ong 1999).

4. For discussions of the Colorado Coalfield Wars and the Ludlow massacre, see Long (1989); McGovern and Guttridge (1972); McGuire and Reckner (2002); Papanikolas (1995); Saitta (2004); Wolff (2003).

5. Of course, some miners in Gillette do not share these views and even try to negate them in their everyday practice by slacking off on the job. They would often comment to me that it was their way of "getting back" at the company. Not surprisingly, tensions between miners who espouse these differing views sometimes erupt into conflicts at the worksite. Despite these differences, in 1987 some of the miners still opposed unionization because it potentially protected "lazy workers" from losing their jobs (see Metzgar 2000 for a critique of this stereotype and an analysis of the high productivity of union workplaces).

6. Thanks to Tom Fricke for these references.

7. Thanks to Paul Durrenberger and Karaleah Reichart for bringing this point to my attention.

8. Historians and archaeologists have recently begun reintegrating the capitalist class processes of extractive industries into western history (e.g., Gregory 2004; Jameson 1998; McGuire and Reckner 2002; Saitta 2004; Wolff 2003), but more work remains to be done on integrating a rich body of western labor history with the new western history.

9. In Smith (2008) I offer a more in-depth analysis of the challenges women miners face, primarily in managing home and work responsibilities while working a rotating shift schedule.

10. These positive experiences support the efforts by scholars to distinguish pleasurable sexualized workplace interactions from harassment (Anderson 2006:300; Williams, Guiffre, and Dillinger 1999:77).

References

Alt, John

1976 Beyond Class: The Decline of Industrial Labor and Leisure. *Telos* 28: 55–80.

Anderson, Elizabeth
2006 Recent Thinking about Sexual Harassment: A Review Essay. *Philosophy and Public Affairs* 34: 284–311.

Barnhart, Keith
1987 Coal Miners Still Need Union. *The Gillette News-Record*, September 16, 4.

Bennett, Jacqueline
1987 ARCO Miners Have It Good. *The Gillette News-Record*, October 15, 2.

Braverman, Harry
1998 [1974] *Labor and Monopoly Capital.* New York: Monthly Review Press.

Broughton, Chad, and Tom Walton
2006 Downsizing Masculinity: Gender, Family and Fatherhood in Post-Industrial America. *Anthropology of Work Review* 27(1): 1–12.

Brown, Warren
1981 Powder River Basin Mines Try to Best Unions at Benefits Game. *The Washington Post*, July 1, A2.

Burawoy, Michael
1985 *The Politics of Production.* New York: Verso.

Campbell, Bea
1984 *Wigan Pier Revisited: Poverty and Politics in the Eighties.* London: Verso.

Christensen, Bonnie
2002 *Red Lodge and the Mythic West: Coal Miners to Cowboys.* Durham, NC: Duke University Press.

Cook, Christopher D.
2006 Coal Miners Slaughter. *In These Times,* January *25, www.inthesetimes.com/article/2478/ (accessed July 1, 2008).*

Cronon, William
1995 The Trouble with Wilderness; or, Getting Back to the Wrong Nature. In *Uncommon Ground: Toward Reinventing Nature,* 69–90. New York: W. W. Norton.

Daly, Dan
1987 Fight to Unionize in the Basin Continues. *The Gillette News-Record*, August 16, 1, 13.

Denton, Ernie
1987 Union Just Another "Boss." *The Gillette News-Record,* September 17, 2.

Dudley, Kathryn Marie
1994 *The End of the Line: Lost Jobs, New Lives in Postindustrial America.* Chicago: University of Chicago Press.

Duke, David C.

2002 *Writers and Miners: Activism and Imagery in America.* Lexington: University Press of Kentucky.

Dunn, Elizabeth

2004 *Privatizing Poland: Baby Food, Big Business, and the Remaking of Labor.* Ithaca: Cornell University Press.

Durrenberger, E. Paul, and Suzan Erem

1999 The Abstract, the Concrete, the Political and the Academic: Anthropology and a Labor Union in the United States. *Human Organization* 58(3): 305–313.

2005 Staff, Stewards and Strikes: Labor's Communication Gap. *Journal of Anthropological Research* 51(1): 179–200.

Ferguson, James

1999 *Expectations of Modernity: Myths and Meanings of Urban Life on the Zambian Copper Belt.* Berkeley: University of California Press.

Finn, Janet

1998 *Tracing the Veins: Of Copper, Culture and Community from Butte to Chuquicamata.* Berkeley: University of California Press.

Freeman, Carla

2007 The "Reputation" of Neoliberalism. *American Ethnologist* 34(2): 252–267.

Gardner, A. Dudley, and Verla R. Flores

1989 *Forgotten Frontier: A History of Wyoming Coal Mining.* San Francisco: Westview.

Gillette News-Record, The

1973 Wyodak Unionized. March 29, 5.

Grant, Bob

1987 Unions Have Benefited All. *The Gillette News-Record,* September 17, 2.

Gregory, James N.

2004 The West and Its Workers, 1870–1930. In *A Companion to the American West,* ed. W. Deverell, 240–255. London: Blackwell.

Halle, David

1984 *America's Working Man.* Chicago: University of Chicago Press.

Herickhoff, Jim

1987 Open Letter to All TBCC Employees and the Powder River Basin Community. *The Gillette News-Record,* October 28, 5.

Igler, David

2004 Engineering the Elephant: Industrialism and the Environment in the Greater West. In *A Companion to the American West,* ed. W. Deverell, 93–111. London: Blackwell.

Jameson, Elizabeth
1998 *All That Glitters: Class, Conflict, and Community in Cripple Creek*. Urbana: University of Illinois Press.

Kolenc, Vic
1984 UMW Wins Coal Miners' Vote. *The Gillette News-Record*, May 24. 1.

Lahiri-Dutt, Kuntala, and Martha Macintyre
2006 Introduction: Where Life Is in the Pits (and Elsewhere) and Gendered. In *Women Miners in Developing Countries: Pit Women and Others*, ed. Kuntala Lahiri-Dutt and Martha Macintyre, 1–22. Burlington, VT: Ashgate.

Lichtenstein, Nelson
2002 *State of the Union: A Century of American Labor*. Princeton: Princeton University Press.

Limerick, Patricia
1987 *The Legacy of Conquest: The Unbroken Past of the American West*. New York: Norton.

Long, Priscilla
1989 *Where the Sun Never Shines: A History of America's Bloody Coal Industry*. New York: Paragon House.

Lucy, Michael, and Debbie Lucy
1987 UMW Wants Your Money. *The Gillette News-Record*, October 2, 4.

Martin, Emily
1994 *Flexible Bodies: The Role of Immunity in American Culture from the Days of Polio to the Age of AIDS*. Boston: Beacon.

Marx, Karl
1978 [1849] Wage Labor and Capital. In *The Marx-Engels Reader*, 2nd ed., ed. R. C. Tucker, 203–217. New York: W. W. Norton.

McGovern, George, and Leonard Guttridge
1972 *The Great Coalfield War*. Boston: Houghton Mifflin.

McGuire, Randall H., and Paul Reckner
2002 The Unromantic West: Labor, Capital, and Struggle. *Historical Archaeology* 36(3): 44–58.

Merrill, Karen R.
2002 *Public Lands and Political Meaning: Ranchers, the Government and the Property between Them*. Berkeley: University of California Press.

Metzgar, Jack
2000 *Striking Steel: Solidarity Remembered*. Philadelphia: Temple University Press.

Newman, Katherine
1988 *Falling from Grace: Downward Mobility in the Age of Affluence.* Berkeley: University of California Press.

Olsen, Ralph
1987 UMW Offers Empty Promises. *The Gillette News-Record,* October 29, 2.

Ong, Aihwa
1999 *Flexible Citizenship: The Cultural Logics of Transnationalism.* Durham, NC: Duke University Press.

Papanikolas, Zeese
1995 Cowboys, Wobblies and the Myth of the West. In *Trickster in the Land of Dreams,* 73–91. Lincoln: University of Nebraska Press.

Richardson, Peter
2007 Two-Tier Kin: Imagining and Contesting Familism in a UAW Local. *Journal of Anthropological Research* 63(1): 73–94.

Rodgers, Daniel T.
1978 *The Work Ethic in Industrial America.* Chicago: University of Chicago Press.

Ruiz, Sal
1987 Unions Have Had Their Day. *The Gillette News-Record,* September 24, 4.

Saitta, Dean
2004 Labor and Class in the American West. In *North American Archaeology,* ed. T. Pauketat and D. Loren, 359–385. Blackwell Studies in Global Archaeology. London: Blackwell.

Sennett, Richard
1988 *The Corrosion of Character: The Personal Consequences of Work in the New Capitalism.* New York: W. W. Norton.

Sheridan, Thomas E.
2007 Embattled Ranchers, Endangered Species and Urban Sprawl: The Political Ecology of the New American West. *Annual Review of Anthropology* 36: 121–138.

Smith, Jessica M.
2008 Crafting Kinship at Home and Work: Women Miners in Wyoming. Theme issue, Women and Work, *WorkingUSA* 11(4): 439–458.

Starrs, Paul F.
1998 *Let the Cowboy Ride: Cattle Ranching in the American West.* Baltimore: Johns Hopkins University Press.

Tallichet, Susan
1998 Moving Up Down in the Mine: The Preservation of Male Privilege Underground. In *More Than Class: Studying Power in U.S. Workplaces,* ed. A. Kingsolver, 124–147. Albany: State University of New York Press.

2006 *Daughters of the Mountain: Women Coal Miners in Central Appalachia.* University Park: Pennsylvania State University Press.

Tauxe, Caroline

1993 *Farms, Mines, and Main Streets: Uneven Development in a Dakota County.* Philadelphia: Temple University Press.

Temple, Kerry

1977 Independent, Hard-Working, They're Called New Cowboys. *The Sheridan Press,* October 11, 1.

Townsend, Nicholas

2002 *The Package Deal: Marriage, Work, and Fatherhood in Men's Lives.* Philadelphia: Temple University Press.

Whetstone, Nancy

1987 Union Insults Worker, She'll Vote No. *The Gillette News-Record,* October 30, 2.

Williams, Christine, Patti Guiffre, and Kirsten Dillinger

1999 Sexuality in the Workplace: Organizational Control, Sexual Harassment and the Pursuit of Pleasure. *Annual Review of Sociology* 25: 73–93.

Wolff, David A.

2003 *Industrializing the Rockies: Growth, Competition and Turmoil in the Coalfields of Colorado and Wyoming, 1868–1914.* Boulder: University Press of Colorado.

Worster, Donald

1992 *Under Western Skies: Nature and History in the American West.* New York: Oxford University Press.

Wright, Will

2001 *The Wild West: The Mythical Cowboy and Social Theory.* London: Sage.

Yount, Kristen

1991 Ladies, Flirts and Tomboys: Strategies for Managing Sexual Harassment in an Underground Coal Mine. *Journal of Contemporary Ethnography* 19(4): 396–422.

2005 Sexualization of Work Roles among Men Miners: Structural and Gender-Based Origins of "Harazzment." In *In the Company of Men: Male Dominance and Sexual Harassment,* ed. J. Gruber and P. Morgan, 65–91. Boston: Northeastern University Press.

SEVEN

Small Places, Close to Home: The Importance of Place in Organizing Workers

Lydia Savage

> In small places, close to home—so close and small they cannot be seen on any maps of the world. . . . [T]hey are the world of the individual persons; the neighborhood . . . the school or college . . . the factory, farm, or office. . . . Such are the places where every man, woman, and child seeks equal justice, equal opportunity, equal dignity without discrimination. Unless these rights have meaning there, they have little meaning anywhere.
>
> —ELEANOR ROOSEVELT (1958)[1]

The challenges unions in the United States face in organizing workers are enormous and should not be underestimated. Recent changes at the national and international levels, such as the Change to Win coalition departing from the American Federation of Labor–Congress of Industrial Organization (AFL-CIO), are indicative of philosophical and strategic differences within the U.S. labor movement. While much of the focus is now on organizing, efforts and resources seem to be concentrated on a speedy certification election and building union membership density. In this chapter I argue that workers choose unionization based on their own lived experiences in "small places, close to home." I suggest that a single-minded focus on density can easily lead unions away from building deep roots in workplaces and communities. If unions are to organize for the long term and to rebuild the labor movement, it is not enough to understand the relationship between workplace variables and union election outcomes; organizers must also understand how workers' experiences in their community, workplace, and home affect their decisions.[2]

To talk about the importance of place and local context for organizing and representing workers, I draw upon research carried out since 1992 on the State Healthcare and Research Employees (SHARE).[3] SHARE ran an organizing campaign at the University of Massachusetts Medical Center (UMass Medical) in Worcester, Massachusetts, from 1990 to 1997 when it successfully won a certification election. Since 1997, SHARE has represented workers with innovative contracts that provide for flexibility, work redesign, benefits for part-time workers, worker education projects, and expansive work security.

In this chapter I first outline the background of the organizing campaign, then discuss obstacles to organizing including previous organizing attempts, and finally present the challenges and possibilities in organizing a diverse group of workers in an industry that is under tremendous financial pressure. In doing so, particular attention is paid to ways in which "small places, close to home" inform workers and organizers in their efforts to build a strong union.

Worcester and UMass Medical

In 1990 several clerical and technical workers from UMass Medical independently contacted the Harvard Union of Clerical and Technical Workers (HUCTW) about organizing their workplace. HUCTW had received much publicity for winning a seventeen-year campaign at Harvard to represent 3,700 workers. Two organizers from HUCTW—Elisabeth Szanto and Jean Lafferty—began exploring the possibility of organizing at UMass Medical. They had both been laid off from HUCTW after the first contract was settled with Harvard University and were looking for a place to start organizing again. UMass Medical offered the HUCTW organizers a chance to test their model of one-on-one organizing and their belief in building deep roots within a workplace in a city less than fifty miles away. HUCTW and SHARE represent nearly 8,000 workers, and the sister unions are affiliated with the American Federation of State, County, and Municipal Employees (AFSCME).[4]

Kris Rondeau, the team leader, explained that the organizers are committed to the idea that the union should have a relationship with every one of its members, with the overall goals of creating community and changing the experience of work.[5] The guiding principle is that without relationships in the workplace between organizers and workers as well as among the workers, the union and workers cannot create change. The relationships built during and after the organizing campaigns allow the union to build leadership and negotiation skills among members.

Rondeau has identified four areas that HUCTW and SHARE view as key pieces of their work. They first seek as much participation from members as possible through a variety of activities such as work redesign, joint committees, joint education projects, and problem solving.

Second, the unions promote the importance of learning, negotiate for education funds, and urge members to take advantage of educational opportunities at their workplaces so they can gain new skills and increase their career mobility.

Third, the unions promote community building, both in and out of the workplace. For example, the unions have vigorously fought for and won benefits for part-time workers. Part of their argument is that part-time work with benefits is an important "societal glue" that allows workers to maintain a standard of living and contribute to the community by raising their families, volunteering, and performing other services. Finally, they negotiate everyday standard-of-living issues to build a middle class within the service sector. In the process of implementing their philosophy in the organizing campaigns at both Harvard and UMass Medical, the unions learned a great deal about how the geographic context of an employer and its employees affects the organization and representation of workers.

Worcester, Massachusetts, is in many ways an ideal location for examining the ways local context mediates union organizing, particularly in light of economic restructuring and the rise of the service sector. Worcester's history as a city of manufacturing is reflected in both the landscape and the personal histories of individuals.[6] Worcester has not remained unscathed by national economic trends, as manufacturing jobs have disappeared and service jobs have grown dramatically—all of which has implications for workers and households. Almost everyone I interviewed spoke of factories in which a relative or friend had worked and then, almost immediately, said the factory had closed.

Manufacturing employment for the city of Worcester was at its peak in 1960, when 46 percent of workers had manufacturing jobs. By 2005, only 28 percent of the city's labor force worked in manufacturing or a related sector. Services accounted for less than 15 percent of the Worcester area's jobs in 1960 but had risen to 72 percent by 2005 (U.S. Bureau of the Census 2005). The increase in the service sector has been fueled in part by the growth of UMass Medical. Susan Hanson and Geraldine Pratt (1995:36) have argued that the area's economy "received a major boost when, in the early 1970's, the state launched the University of Massachusetts Medical Center and Hospital."

Since its opening, UMass Medical has become the largest employer in Worcester and central Massachusetts and has locations scattered across the central part of the state. Further growth came when, following SHARE's union certification election, a 1998 merger between Memorial Hospital (a private hospital) and UMass Medical resulted in the creation of a private-sector institution called the University of Massachusetts Memorial Medical Center (UMass Memorial) and retained UMass Medical School as a separate, public-sector entity.

While UMass Medical School currently employs 6,200 workers and UMass Memorial is the largest healthcare facility in the area, employing roughly 12,500 workers, the two facilities are among many hospitals in the area, as healthcare is an important sector of the Worcester area's economy. Whereas in 2005 healthcare and social assistance employed 14 percent of all workers in the United States and 16 percent of workers in Massachusetts, 19 percent of workers in Worcester County worked in healthcare (U.S. Bureau of the Census 2005).

Organizing at UMass Medical: 1990–1997

UMass Medical has long been a place where people actively seek to work because it has enjoyed a reputation of paying competitive wages, offering a good benefits package for both full-time and part-time workers, and offering a choice of shifts for clerical and technical workers. Several of the workers I interviewed had pursued a job for years at UMass Medical before finally being hired. Others started as temporary workers and were eventually hired permanently. One worker was collecting unemployment when she was directly hired through the unemployment office. She recognizes her situation of being "handed a job at UMass" as unusual because, as she said, people "try to get UMass for years and years."

These repeated efforts at "trying to get UMass for years and years" emphasize the role of UMass Medical as a good employer within the local Worcester labor market. Hanson and Pratt (1995:194) found that "people in Worcester tend to 'fall into' jobs, discovering them through personal networks and chance encounters." Almost every worker I interviewed explained that it was difficult to get a job at UMass Medical unless you "knew somebody." The difficulty in getting a job there results in part from the low turnover.

The clerical and technical workers organized by SHARE at UMass Medical constituted the largest group of workers who were eligible for unionization but were not unionized within the statewide University of Massachusetts system. Unions represented most employees within the multi-campus university system and had brokered a "master agreement" with an alliance of unions that represent workers throughout the system, mainly locals affiliated with the Service Employees International Union (SEIU) and the AFSCME. Wages and working conditions are set for all unionized employees system-wide through the master agreement.

Closer to home, there *were* unions at UMass Medical; in fact, the only unrepresented workers were the clerical and technical workers. Skilled-trades people and custodians in Environmental Building Services numbered around 250 and had been represented by AFSCME, Local 2616, since 1974. The Massachusetts Nurses Association had organized nurses in 1980, and the National Association of Government Employees represented the campus police force.

In theory, organizing a group of public-sector workers who work alongside union members should be relatively less difficult than organizing private-sector workers, for two reasons. First, public-sector employers rarely engage in the anti-union campaigns run by private employers, and in many places, state employers are banned from spending state funds on anti-union consultants or campaigns. To specifically address this issue and in direct response to complaints made by unions trying to organize at UMass Medical, an amendment was added to the Massachusetts state budget in 1980 that made it illegal for state money to be spent on anti-union activity.

Second, research has shown that union organizing campaigns are more successful if unions are already present in the workplace. Kate Bronfenbrenner (1993:312) found that unions enjoyed an average win rate of 49 percent in certification elections in workplaces where other unions were present, compared with an average of only 38 percent when no other unions were present. John Delaney's (1981) research on healthcare units demonstrated that unions perform significantly better in certification elections in larger hospitals, and unions win more elections in hospitals with other unionized bargaining units.

Delaney also found a "positive and significant" relationship between a prior election and election outcomes. These patterns did not hold in Worcester, however. UMass Medical's clerical and technical workers had the opportunity to vote for union representation in 1986, but SHARE's success seems to have occurred despite, rather than because of, the 1986 election. The election was not a positive experience for most workers, and the outcome was not close.[7]

In the early 1980s Jane Dube, a clerical worker at UMass Medical, began organizing an independent union called the Massachusetts Association of Service and Health Care (MASH) to represent clerical, technical, and service employees. In 1985 MASH petitioned the State Labor Relations Commission for permission to represent a group of approximately 1,300 nonprofessional employees as a single bargaining unit.[8] To petition for representation rights, a union must submit cards of support from 30 percent of the workers in the potential bargaining unit. Almost immediately, three other unions—Teamsters Local 170, AFSCME District 93, and the Office and Professional Employees International Union (OPEIU)—filed for the right to be accepted as interveners and were granted that status. Such status is hugely beneficial because to intervene, a union must submit cards of support from only 10 percent of the bargaining unit; if a union election is subsequently held, the interveners appear on the ballot along with the original petitioner (MASH in this case).

In the spring of 1985, the State Labor Relations Commission began hearings to determine the appropriate bargaining unit for nonprofessional UMass Medical workers. UMass Medical management and MASH agreed on the need for one "wall-to-wall" bargaining unit; AFSCME wanted four, and the Teamsters wanted two. Hearings concluded on July 29, 1985, and that fall the State Labor Relations Board decided that one bargaining unit would represent the1,300 employees.

A certification election was held in May 1986. With a turnout of almost 90 percent, the vote overwhelmingly favored no union representation. The nonunion choice received 830 of the 1,415 votes cast (57 percent). AFSCME, Council 93, received 163 votes; MASH received 154 votes; OPEIU had 41 votes; and Teamsters Local 170 received 28 votes. The four unions combined lost the vote by more than a 2-to-1 margin. (Nearly 200 votes were set aside after being challenged, and 1 vote was voided; as a result, 1,214 votes were counted.)

Workers remember the 1986 election as an unmitigated disaster, regardless of how they voted. Of the thirty workers I interviewed in 1994 and 1995, thirteen had been working at UMass Medical at the time of the 1986 election; eight had voted for union representation, but five had voted against it. Seven workers who voted for union representation could not recall what union they voted for. The five workers who voted against union representation remembered that they did not vote against union representation per se but rather against the specific unions that were vying for their vote and the tactics they employed.

Many workers, including some who voted for a union, remembered the organizing campaigns as hostile both to UMass Medical as the employer and to the competing unions. One worker called the hostility among unions "a union catfight." Each union made claims about what it could accomplish for employees and denied that the other unions could win anything for workers. Leaflets littered cafeteria tables and workers' mailboxes as the unions attacked their employer. Many workers remembered that they found this tactic personally offensive. "If things were so bad, did they think I was stupid enough to stick around for it?" asked one worker.

Some workers recalled that the campaigns followed them home. One worker lived very close to UMass Medical, on the same street as several other employees, and remembered being visited repeatedly at home. She would look out her window and see "these gray suits coming down the street, going door-to-door. It was an intrusion into my personal life" (quoted in Keough 1995:11). Another worker said that workers couldn't walk into the cafeteria without "being accosted by Guido and Luigi." (Guido and Luigi were nicknames several workers used in reference to the two male Teamster organizers remembered for wearing suits.) This worker avoided the hospital cafeteria, but she was still bothered by the flood of literature from the four unions.

Among the pro-union workers, the presence of four unions created more tension. MASH supporters felt the three unions that were granted intervener status were raiding territory they had already claimed. MASH had been started by a group of UMass Medical employees who felt "outsiders" were trying to take over an essentially independent, internal organizing effort. AFSCME supporters saw logic in having another local of a union that was already present and represented a bargaining unit at UMass Medical. One employee remembered that "everyone was angry at everyone."

"We've Been Driving to Worcester Ever Since": SHARE at UMass Medical

When SHARE organizers arrived at UMass Medical in 1990, the election was still a vividly remembered part of many workers' experiences and the workplace history. Jean Lafferty recalled that the 1986 election entered her early conversations with workers at UMass Medical because there was "a living memory of that disaster [the election] in the minds of everyone who had been here and some people who had not been here but had heard about it, and we came to feel almost like we had been here because the stories were so vivid. . . . We had a lot to overcome, a lot to get over." Elisabeth Szanto observed, "I think that the first three years of our organizing drive were to undo the bad taste that the election had left in everybody's mouth. You know, we would sort of walk up to people and say, 'Hi I'm Elisabeth, and we're talking about forming a union—not at all like what happened in 1986.' "

Initially, Elisabeth recalled, they spent the first year "commuting organizing"; they drove to Worcester to meet with workers but did not have an office. As she remarked, "We've been driving to Worcester ever since." Early in the drive, they often met a worker during a morning coffee break and would not have another meeting until lunch or dinner. Jean remembered that they sometimes went back to Cambridge between appointments because they were not yet organizing in the building and, as mentioned, had no office in which they could spend time. Elisabeth and Jean began with a handful of names and a self-designed rule that "we would never call anybody unless we had a reference." Organizers contacted the first 1,000 workers at UMass Medical (out of a total of nearly 2,200) using personal references. Eventually, a UMass Medical worker named the nascent effort SHARE. Funding from AFSCME was secured in 1991, more organizers were hired, and SHARE opened an office down the road from UMass Medical and began to add organizers. The group also began to organize "in the building."

In their conversations with workers, organizers emphasized the role of having voice in a workplace rather than wages and benefits. Within the local context of Worcester, workers at UMass Medical were well-paid and had good benefits ranging from medical care to educational benefits; even part-time workers qualified for most benefits. As an administrator for the hospital said, "This is not a West Virginia coal mine" (quoted in Keough 1995:10). Workers agreed that UMass Medical was a relatively good employer, but they wanted an even better employer and a better work experience.

UMass Medical's reputation for providing good, stable jobs and the availability of a wide array of shifts means that workers come from all over central Massachusetts. Only a few workers I interviewed had neighbors who worked at UMass Medical, and, not surprisingly, those workers lived within a ten-minute drive of work. When asked if she ever socialized with coworkers, one woman replied no, she lived too far away, but she added that "some of them [coworkers] live quite a distance, too. One of them lives in Brookfield, one in Southbridge [both thirty to forty minutes away]. . . . It's not like everyone lives in Worcester."

The residential dispersion of workers has implications for organizers. Neighborhood networks that connect workers to each other and that could be used by organizers simply do not exist for most workers. In addition, home visits, typically seen as a tactic that works well in organizing workers, are not feasible. The distances workers live from UMass Medical make home visits a logistical problem and would be an inefficient use of organizers' time. More important, however, the increased journey-to-work time adds to workers' space-time constraints when combined with their family responsibilities.

"We Know Their Lives"

> In terms of people's time . . . it is much more difficult to get people to come to meetings. People have kids that need to be picked up from one relative or another, or another relative who needs to go to the doctor. . . . People's commitments outside of work are much greater and a lot more people work second jobs [than is the case at Harvard].
>
> —ORGANIZER

Early in the research I asked several organizers for statistics on UMass Medical workers, and one of the organizers simply stated, "We don't know the statistics [off the top of our heads], we know their lives." SHARE organizers viewed their job as one of building relationships with the workers. This means that when organizers drop by work and visit with someone or talk to the person on the phone, they often do not mention the union. They talk about "different things with different workers," ranging from kids to vacations to night classes to hobbies. The recognition of workers' multiple roles and responsibilities allows organizers to learn what is important to workers and why.

Two-thirds of the UMass Medical workers interviewed were married, and almost all of those interviewed were mothers. Aside from their immediate families, many workers have extended family in the area that they use as a resource, but extended families also represent another set of responsibilities. Women workers' home responsibilities are frequently assumed to be a barrier to organizing, but as one worker said, "We have huge responsibilities at home, and we know how to have huge responsibilities at work." Many workers' home responsibilities were growing, and this affected their views of the importance of their work.

Most workers interviewed felt fairly secure about their jobs; they did not see their jobs disappearing. At the same time, they worried about changes in pay and benefits because their jobs were increasingly important to their household economies. One of the "classic" workers at UMass Medical was a woman who went to work there for the health and welfare benefits because her husband was a construction worker. He had been laid off, and her job had become the sole source of economic support of her family. Five of the women interviewed who had children were divorced, a life event that meant balancing home and work without the emotional or financial help of a partner.

Nearly one-third of the workers interviewed had families affected by recent layoffs, and many families were not just two-job households but had three jobs. As a result of layoffs or plant closures, several workers held down more than one job themselves, and several more had partners with more than one job. One worker operated a home childcare business during the day and worked part-time at UMass Medical at night while her husband tried to start a business after he was laid off from an electronics firm. Why UMass Medical, a forty-minute commute? She needed to work somewhere that offered benefits so her family would have health insurance. UMass Medical was a logical, if distant, choice because she could work only part-time and still receive benefits.

One worker was expecting her second child at the time of the interview, and her husband had just been laid off from an electronics firm. She became instantly responsible for the financial support of the family, and he became responsible for childcare. All of this occurred as UMass Medical changed its pay structure and eliminated step increases. Many workers expressed a belief that a union may not help them get back what they had lost, but they saw a union as providing some protection against further changes. An organizer explained that at UMass Medical, "People are longer term, people are working because that's what you do. . . . [The workers] have families, they have responsibilities—even the young people."

Family Responsibilities

> They [workers] work evenings for a reason. It's because "my husband works during the day and I take care of the kids, and then I go to work and he takes care of them." And they can't come to a potluck, and they can't come in early, and they can't stay late.
>
> —ORGANIZER

As mentioned earlier, the combination of competitive wages and benefits, along with the considerable flexibility in shift choices, results in the fact that UMass Medical workers are very residentially dispersed. The range of choices in shifts also means many workers can use sequential scheduling with their partners as a form of childcare. Several of the women I interviewed commuted more than thirty minutes each way to work so they could work the second or third shift.

One woman and her husband arranged their days by using sequential scheduling to meet their childcare needs. She explained:

> So what I do now is I leave here [at 7:30 a.m. from a town forty minutes from UMass Medical] and drop Connor [her son] off with Jack [at his workplace in a town between home and UMass Medical at 7:50 a.m.]. We meet in the parking lot, and then I go on to work, and they turn around and come home. Luckily he [Connor] sleeps four hours during the day so . . . Jack puts him in and then he goes to bed. He sleeps as long as Connor does, gets up, makes dinner, has it on the table when I get in the door [at 5:45 p.m.], and then he goes back to bed. He gets up at like 10:30 [p.m.] and goes to work.

This arrangement is not unusual and demonstrates the intricate time ballet many parents dance.

This childcare arrangement of sequential scheduling is common in Worcester. In their representative sample, Hanson and Pratt (1995:136) found that 29 percent of all dual-earner households with children under age thirteen used sequential scheduling. The use of sequential scheduling influences the types of employment chosen by both women and men and emphasizes the importance of UMass Medical's range of shifts for workers. Hanson and Pratt (1995:136) cited a woman who worked as a bartender. She explained her choice of work: "I can't be a secretary and work 9 to 5. My kids come first so I have to work around their schedules." Another woman said, "I love doing office work, running an office. Nothing like that is available in the evenings" (Hanson and Pratt 1995:136).

UMass Medical was an unusual employer in the particular local context of Worcester; it offered both the types of jobs and the choice of hours many women wanted but did not typically find available in their job search.[9] Many sequential schedulers cited the combination of the type of work and the hours they wanted as the reason they were willing to travel longer distances to work and had stayed at UMass Medical for so long.

Sequential scheduling has important implications for organizers. Meeting with workers before or after work, even for a few minutes, is nearly impossible because it throws off a delicate balancing act. In addition, many workers who had an hour for their lunch break used the time to run errands or to go for a walk because that break is, literally, the only time they have for themselves. Trying to schedule meetings with workers during their breaks often means joining them on their walks or not being able to meet with them at all.

Workers' ability to participate in union activities is made difficult by the space-time constraints of their days. The two main reasons women gave for not participating in union activities as much as they would have liked were a lack of time and a lack of knowledge. The women who used sequential scheduling commented on the difference between the time they spent with their children and the time their partners spent with their children. The women noted that their partners helped by watching the children, but much of the responsibility for organizing everything and performing the "work" of raising children fell to the women (shopping, preparing meals, doing laundry, and similar tasks). As a result, they had little time at home to even speak on the phone to organizers, let alone to coworkers.

Aside from sequential scheduling, other forms of family childcare were widely used by workers at UMass Medical. Parents, siblings, and older children were childcare providers for several workers; only three of the nineteen mothers I interviewed used day-care facilities. One woman actually moved into the neighborhood where her ex-husband's family (his parents and a sibling) lived so her son could be "looked after by family." These findings resonate with the findings of Hanson and Pratt (1995), who cited family childcare as a widespread practice in Worcester.

Sequential scheduling, combined with the widespread practice of using family members for childcare, means that onsite day care—one of the biggest issues in the Harvard campaign—was much less of an issue at UMass Medical. Only two of the workers I interviewed expressed an interest in onsite day care, but all of them expressed the need for flexibility in their schedules in relation to their childcare arrangements. Workers cited a need for supervisors and administrators to recognize that sometimes childcare arrangements fall apart, school is canceled because of snow, and kids get sick.

One worker's daughter had just broken her arm. Her supervisor told her she could not go upstairs to the orthopedics department while her daughter's arm was put into a cast. The worker responded by going upstairs with her daughter and telling her supervisor that she came in early every day, left late, and rarely took breaks so, at the very least, the department owed her an hour. She also told the supervisor that there was a late appointment the supervisor would have to deal with because she was no longer willing to stay late. This issue was raised repeatedly in similar campaigns; many times clerical work seems tied to a notion of flexibility on the part of the worker, not the supervisor.

Some workers who were taking care of older relatives also needed flexible schedules. One worker was responsible for her bedridden widowed mother. She was often about fifteen minutes late for work because the home healthcare assistant who stayed with her mother during the day was late. She also occasionally needed to take time during her workday to take her mother to doctor's appointments. Her supervisor was unsympathetic even though she worked in an office situation where continuous coverage was less critical than in patient care areas. He told her she would have to make other arrangements for her mother or make a choice between caring for her mother and her work. It did not escape the worker's attention that when childcare arrangements fell apart for the male supervisor, he brought his children to work.

This worker responsible for her mother's care was single. Like many people who live and work in Worcester, she had as many family responsibilities as married workers did. In fact, she had lived in another state but returned home as her parents aged so she could care for them. Hanson and Pratt (1995:154) found in their representative sample that one out of four single women and men reported that they regularly took care of someone other than a child or a partner. One worker, despite working more than one job, cited his single status as the reason he spent time with his parents. His parents did not need elder care, but the worker both enjoyed spending time with them and felt the family responsibility fell to him since he was single and "had more time."

The family responsibilities of married and single people are embedded in the social networks and practices of Worcester's local context and limited the amount of time workers had for union activities. In contrast, many workers at Harvard were not originally from the area, so few of them had family connections there; as a result, few had routines involving family obligations and commitments. As one organizers said, "They had a lot of time for activism."

The inability to contact all workers in the workplace, to visit workers at home, and to meet with workers before or after work because of time constraints combined to cause organizers to modify the one-on-one organizing strategy used at Harvard in the UMass Medical context. Telephoning workers at home became a large part of SHARE's organizing strategy.

Ma Bell, Gender, and Organizing

> The telephone is symptom, possibility, weapon, companion, tool, and lifeline.
>
> —RANKOW (1992:154)

As a result of the residential dispersion, neighborhood networks that could be used in organizing do not exist for UMass Medical workers, and home visits—an increasingly common and successful tactic for organizing—are not feasible. These factors, combined with less than complete access to workers at UMass Medical and the workers' family obligations, have caused organizers to develop the skill of organizing by phone.

Contacting workers by telephone is done frequently when they already belong to a union. For example, HUCTW talks to workers at Harvard by telephone. As one organizer reported, however, speaking to each worker in person was so ingrained that for a long time she would walk across campus to talk to someone and then realize she could have simply picked up the phone.

Organizing workers they had never met by phoning them was a somewhat new strategy but one SHARE organizers found worked well, even though the use of the telephone in union organizing drives is generally seen as undesirable and ineffective. Bronfenbrenner (1993) reported from her analysis of organizing successes that use of the telephone resulted in fewer wins (40 percent) than did campaigns where no phone calls were used (53 percent). The assumption that use of the telephone is ineffective should be explored, however, because Bronfenbrenner's analysis lacks an examination of the gender mix within the bargaining unit as well as the occupations being organized.

Lana Rankow conducted an ethnographic field study focusing on the gendered use of the telephone in a small midwestern community she called "Prospect." She wrote that "use of the telephone by women is both gendered work—work delegated to women—and gender work—work that confirms the community's beliefs about what are women's natural tendencies and abilities" (1992:33). She argued that although the telephone has the technological ability to level social hierarchies and transcend time and space, the technological possibilities have never become social practice, in part because the telephone was introduced into a gendered world. The telephone has become embedded and is a "site at which gender relations are organized, experienced, and accomplished in both the family and the larger community and political world" (1992:154). Rankow observed that men and women use the phone differently and for different reasons:

> Women's actual and perceived use of the telephone in Prospect is not only related to the different form, style, and content of talk that is considered appropriate and natural for women, but it is also integral to the gendered work that women accomplish in the community. Women organize significant community activities, perform work for their husbands, maintain relationships among family and friends, and perform time-consuming and little-recognized care-giving roles via the telephone. (1992:53)

"Telephone talk" is not a skill that can only be learned by women but rather is a skill women learn more frequently than men do. In the workplace, clerical and office workers conduct much of their work over the phone and are also more likely to be women. At home, once again women are more likely than men to use the phone to maintain networks of family and friends. The persistence of both occupational segregation and socially constructed gender roles means "telephone talk" is a skill women are more likely than men to have developed. This recognition of telephone talk as a skill resonates with my discussions with organizers. One organizer remarked, "Frankly it's a better tool for time reasons . . . if you can learn how to talk on the phone."

Organizers recognized the need to use the phone, but they also emphasized the need to have an in-person conversation with each worker at some point during the drive. As one organizer commented, "Home phoning has been good, it's been efficient, but we use it to set goals for meeting people." The organizers felt the telephone had been valuable and timesaving, but it can only be one part of the overall strategy to reach workers.

Organizers never phoned a worker at home without her permission and still continued to visit workers at UMass Medical and to meet them during lunch or other breaks when schedules could be arranged. In addition, organizers had small potlucks and information meetings for interested workers, usually at a worker's home but sometimes at a local restaurant. These small meetings were successful, and workers told me they found them useful and enjoyable. Similar meetings were not used at Harvard, largely because access was not a problem there and workers could spend lunch hours together. One organizer reflected that differences between work cultures at Harvard and UMass Medical made potlucks successful at the latter. She believed that for workers at Harvard, going to lectures and large meetings was much more a part of people's everyday lives. At UMass Medical, she suggested, there "isn't as much of a sense that going to a meeting in a room either onsite or offsite is a normal thing, but going to someone's house is a normal thing." Organizers also felt that having potlucks created a "safe space for people to talk about the union."

Personal conversations (in person or over the phone) between organizers and workers are central to the way SHARE organizes. While the local context of UMass Medical challenged organizers to incorporate different ways to contact workers (i.e., telephone, potlucks), local context also led organizers to recognize the need to change the conversations from drive to drive. One organizer explained, "In every drive you learn something new. You just strip it down to basically what does it take to build a relationship with people."

Identity, Organizing, and Place

Organizing women who work in the service sector is frequently discussed in terms of the many perceived "cultural" barriers to organizing stemming from women's lack of experience with unions, the different class identities service workers are perceived to have, and the emphasis service workers—particularly women—place on "social" issues over economic issues. These issues may be true for some women and men in the service sector, but they are highly dependent on local context and work cultures.

One organizer explained, "The workers at UMass Medical are older, they have families, they have bigger responsibilities, and they see themselves as workers." Another organizer cited a much more realistic sense of work at UMass Medical: "This is my job. This is what I do because I have to feed my children. I have to pay my bills. I have to have health insurance." The same organizer reflected on her own work life and recalled that there came a point when "I was ready to think of myself as a worker, not as someone who was trying to figure out who I was going to be when I grew up."

Organizers estimated worker turnover at UMass Medical to be about 15 percent. The commitment to the workplace "makes the stakes slightly higher, but it's easier to catch their [workers'] attention." One organizer remarked that "if you're in a workplace to work, the conversation is different. . . . Here [UMass Medical] I think we say essentially the same things [as workers do at Harvard], but it isn't necessary to label it as being about being women. You can say to people here, this is about power."

Gender does make a difference, organizers indicated, but class and family roles make a bigger difference at UMass Medical. One worker told an organizer: "Yeah, well, we're a lot smarter than men. We know that we don't need to beat up management to get what we want." Another organizer reflected that women's ages mattered as well. UMass Medical workers, she said, "seem to be more used to representing themselves. I like UMass workers because they're feisty."

UMass Medical workers also tend to have extended families and partners who work in manufacturing or construction, reflecting Worcester's economy. These family connections to manufacturing are also related to the widespread use of sequential scheduling as a form of childcare. Hanson and Pratt (1995) found that sequential scheduling is most common in households in which the male partner does manual labor. Shift work is more easily adapted to sequential scheduling than are typical business hours.

All the organizers commented that workers at UMass Medical had significant experience with unions, despite Worcester's anti-union reputation. According to one organizer, responses from workers were as varied as their experiences with unions: "Oh no, my husband lost his job because of the union . . . or yeah, I was with the union the last place I worked, I'll sign right up. That's kind of a problem, too, because you want to tell them about the kind of union you want to build, and they can't hear that because they have an idea already."

About one-third of the workers interviewed had previous personal experience with unions. Several workers had been employed by other state employers and had belonged to a service-sector union. Several others had worked in the manufacturing sector before they came to UMass Medical. One worker had been a shop steward for United Steelworkers, while another had gone on strike and picketed her former employer. For many workers, family and friends' positive experience with unions was important in making their decision.

One worker's husband worked at the same factory that had employed her father. Both men were very active in the union; they attended meetings and held various steward positions. She had no personal previous experience with a union but was pro-union. When asked why, she explained that when the factory that had employed her husband closed five years ago, the union "did right by my husband." Her husband has found another job, but it does not pay well and provides no benefits. Her benefits at UMass Medical protect her family, and she can use her educational benefits to send her children to college.

Reflecting the local economy, union experiences were often with male-dominated, blue-collar unions such as the Teamsters and United Steelworkers. Organizers have found in their conversations with workers that "many people think unions are about rules and deciding for the union is deciding for rules." One organizer explained, "Eight generations of relatives in the carpenters' [union] seem to have made it impossible to convince people that we really are about flexibility." One woman was concerned that by emphasizing voice and participation for workers rather than work rules and union rallies, the "union's [SHARE] going to be too soft."

Another worker, however, was pleased that the union was going to be "too soft" in comparison to the Teamsters. She said: "Most of us haven't been exposed to unions. If we have, they're . . . you know, the Teamster's union and everybody has this picture in their mind of these unions going around breaking people's arms and legs. Unions aren't that way . . . anymore."

The failed 1986 union election left some workers with a bad impression of unions generally. The one-on-one organizing model has helped people get past the bad experience. One worker said: "When I first heard union, I went 'Oh God, don't let this happen again.' . . . Talking to them [the organizers], I knew they weren't going to be like that. Your impression of them matters to your impression of the union. They handle themselves well, which is not easy to do when you've got somebody jumping down your throat." This worker felt that if the organizers could deal with the workers that effectively, she wanted them in the room with management too. Union organizers needed to be able "to keep their cool and state the facts calmly."

An organizer reflected on how perceptions of unions affect organizing: "I think that people have an idea that when you say unions, it's about wages and benefits and that sort of stuff. I think what I want them to know first is that it's about representing themselves in the workplace—having a voice and values. If you get that, then you understand how you can deal with a broad range of issues once they come up."

In 1997 a union certification election for the nearly 2,200 eligible workers at UMass Medical was held, and SHARE won the election with 63 percent of the vote and an 85 percent turnout. The organizers immediately set to work negotiating the first contract and continued to organize workers, new and old. SHARE continues to refer to its entire staff as organizers, and many organizers such as Elisabeth and Jean have been with SHARE since the beginning of the effort.

SHARE Today

Organizers have not only had to negotiate a contract but also to contend with a merger between the private-sector Memorial Hospital and UMass Medical that began to be implemented in 1998. Deep roots within the community of workers led to a strong first contract and additional new members once the merger was complete and SHARE successfully organized former Memorial Hospital workers. The merger created two SHARE locals, with one representing private-sector hospital workers and the other representing public-sector medical school workers.

SHARE currently represents about 2,600 workers (around 85% of whom are women) at UMass Memorial Medical Center, with about half of the members in clerical roles and the other half involved with patient care. SHARE also represents workers at UMass Medical School, where it has 500 members (approximately 75% women) including research technicians and library and clerical staff.

The knowledge of the workers' lived experiences and needs organizers gained during the campaign allows for strength and flexibility in representation. Contracts are largely without rules and regulations governing issues such as hours worked, but they have provisions for processes such as problem solving at the department level.

Workers are coached in negotiation skills because rather than a traditional grievance procedure, HUCTW and SHARE use a system they call problem solving. Problem solving takes the adversarial nature out of the process, is not limited to issues spelled out in the contract, and emphasizes union and management working together to solve the problem. If a worker has a problem, she can arrange a meeting with a member of the problem-solving team (an organizer or a trained coworker) and sit down with a supervisor; together, they work out a solution. If the problem-solving process does not work, the contract spells out that workers have the right to mediation followed by arbitration as the final step, if necessary.

SHARE is currently engaged in joint projects with management on issues of patient care. It argues that workers are committed to patients and that, by listening to workers who are constantly engaged with patients and their families, the hospital not only improves patient care but also improves the quality of both work and life for everyone.

The union uses the deep roots and skills it has created in the workplace to argue for flexibility. For example, management purports that "fairness" is a set of shared rules that govern all employees, but the organizers argue that fairness entails achieving the most important issues for each member, whether that means creating a job-sharing situation or adjusting work hours by fifteen minutes so a mother can drop her kids off at school before beginning her workday. Management agrees to such concessions with the caveat that doing so does not set a precedent. Elisabeth reflected that the organizers have agreed to the concessions because they have no doubt that they can get them again; in fact, they have done so repeatedly because they understand the complexities of workers' lives and have given workers the skills to argue for a workplace that honors that complexity.

In their efforts to organize workers, labor unions must always plan for the long term. As one worker said, "They've tried to talk to everybody, which is a must. If the union gets in, it'll be because people wanted it, and if they don't get in, people will still feel good about it [the experience]." The importance of creating good experiences with unions—win or lose—must be underscored. The failed 1986 election at UMass Medical demonstrates that short-term outlooks on the part of unions can be damaging. Many workers who voted against the union in 1986 voted for SHARE, but workers and organizers alike explained that it took a long time and a lot of talking to get past the history of that election. Unions do not have that kind of time to spend.

Conclusion

Organizing is clearly on the mainstream labor movement's agenda, and it is critical that it succeed. If unions fail to organize new members after declaring that to be their primary goal, they will be seen as obsolete. If unions devote resources, organizers, and training to the problem of declining union density and the problem still doesn't go away, they will be seen as unwanted by workers and society. Can the world survive without unions? Yes, but then the question changes to, is that the kind of world we want?

Beyond understanding how the "small places, close to home" affect organizing efforts, we must heed Eleanor Roosevelt's warning that unless "equal justice, equal opportunity, equal dignity without discrimination . . . have meaning there, they have little meaning anywhere." While it is critical that the labor movement makes a commitment to international solidarity and organizing across borders, unions must also make themselves relevant to people's everyday lives. As unions attempt to build ties at regional, national, and international levels, the labor movement must connect workers to each other and show them why they need to care about other people's issues both in their own workplaces and in other places.

Labor unions hold enormous potential for creating a democratic and a just society. Union supporters often look back to the CIO unionism of the 1930s with great nostalgia as a time when labor unions talked about values and justice as well as wages and benefits. We must remember, however, that it was certain kinds of justice for certain kinds of workers. Unions cannot rightfully reclaim their role as the voice of workers without rebuilding American unions to represent all kinds of workers and fighting for all kinds of justice. The issues on which the labor movement must refocus its attention are economic and social justice, notions of which vary from place to place.

Can unions organize workers without recognizing the complexities of their lives? Once again the answer is yes, but the question becomes, would that be the kind of labor movement we want? While it is possible for labor unions to survive as undemocratic institutions that represent a narrow group of workers in a limited number of occupations, it seems unlikely that the U.S. labor movement could survive in that form. People will not support a movement that does not represent them.

Unions must create many new models of unionism and recognize many types of work as activism—hosting a potluck, giving organizers names and phone numbers of potential members, taking a coworker to lunch. If unions continue to rely on counting attendance at rallies as the only measure of strength and militancy, they will leave out many, many people who have neither the time nor the desire to participate in "traditional" union actions.

Notes

1. Cited in Cook (1992:18).

2. The relatively new field of labor geography has argued for the importance of place and workers' lived experiences in shaping economic landscapes. Researchers are careful not to focus on the idiosyncratic nature of place but rather to document patterns and processes to make connections across scales (e.g., local, regional, national). See Aguiar and Herod (2006); Berman (1998); Castree et al. (2004); Hanson and Pratt (1988, 1991, 1992, 1995); Herod (1998, 2001); Johns (1998); Johns and Virayla (2000); Savage (1998, 2004, 2006, 2007); Savage and Wills (2004); Tufts (1998); Walsh (2000); Wills (1996, 1998a, 1998b, 2001).

3. I began this research project when I was a student in the Graduate School of Geography at Clark University in Worcester only about a year after the organizers began their campaign. I eventually wrote my dissertation on the organizing effort and have since returned many times to the union offices and the workplace to meet with, shadow, and interview organizers and workers.

4. John Hoerr's (1997) excellent and very readable book, *We Can't Eat Prestige: The Women Who Organized Harvard*, is a comprehensive history of HUCTW's beginnings. Other researchers have documented various aspects of the ways HUCTW and SHARE are representing workers in service workplaces (see, e.g., Clawson 2003; Cobble 1993, 2007; Eaton 1996; Hurd 1993; Oppenheim 1991; Savage 1998, 2007).

5. This section draws from Cobble (2007:181–216). I am grateful to Sue Cobble for giving me the rare opportunity to publish an edited transcription of a conversation with six of the organizers from HUCTW and SHARE.

6. In 1994–1995, I conducted lengthy semi-structured interviews with thirty workers and the eight organizers who worked full-time on the campaign from 1994 to 1996 (Samantha Erickson, Nicholas Killick, Jean Lafferty, Laurie Peterson, Martha Robb, Elisabeth Szanto [lead organizer], Stephanie Tournas, and Janet Wilder). Additional information was gathered from time spent at the Cambridge office of HUCTW with Kris Rondeau and Tom Canel, a UMass Medical tour with Janet Wilder, and numerous informal conversations with all the organizers. I deeply appreciate the time the workers and organizers have spent and continue to spend with me.

7. Much of the information discussed in this section on the 1986 election is from interviews with organizers and UMass Medical workers, but the information

was confirmed through newspaper articles in *The Worcester Telegram* and *The Evening Gazette* (Worcester).

8. The National Labor Relations Board is the relevant body for unions attempting to organize private-sector workers, but each state has its own laws governing the unionization of public-sector workers. As a result, in Massachusetts the State Labor Relations Commission oversees unionization efforts in the public sector.

9. Another layer of the importance of shifts and hours is UMass Medical's role as a state employer. Most workers at UMass Medical have state and federal holidays off. Since these holidays coincide with their children's school holidays, they do not have to scramble for childcare coverage on those days.

References Cited

Aguiar, L.L.M., and A. Herod, editors
2006 *The Dirty Work of Neoliberalism: Cleaners in the Global Economy*. Oxford: Basil Blackwell.

Berman, L.
1998 In Your Face, in Your Space: Spatial Strategies in Organizing Clerical Workers at Yale. In *Organizing the Landscape: Geographical Perspectives on Labor Unionism*, ed. A. Herod, 203–224. Minneapolis: University of Minnesota Press.

Bronfenbrenner, K.
1993 Seeds of Resurgence: Successful Union Strategies for Winning Certification Elections and First Contracts in the 1980's and Beyond. PhD dissertation, Cornell University, Ithaca, NY.

Castree, N., N. M. Coe, K. Ward, and M. Samers
2004 *Spaces of Work: Global Capitalism and Geographies of Labour*. London: Sage.

Clawson, D.
2003 *The Next Upsurge: Labor and the New Social Movements*. Ithaca: Cornell University Press.

Cobble, D. S., editor
1993 *Women and Unions: Forging a Partnership*. Ithaca: ILR Press.
2007 *The Sex of Class: Women and America's New Labor Movements*. Ithaca: Cornell University Press.

Cook, B. W.
1992 *Eleanor Roosevelt, Vol. One: 1884–1933*. New York: Viking.

Delaney, J. T.
1981 Unions' Success in Hospital Representation Elections. *Industrial Relations* 10: 149–161.

Eaton, S. C.

1996 The Customer Is Always Interesting: Unionized Harvard Clericals Renegotiate Working Relationships. In *Working in the Service Society*, ed. C. Macdonald and C. Sirianni, 291–332. Philadelphia: Temple University Press.

Hanson, S., and G. Pratt

1988 Reconceptualizing the Links between Home and Work in Geography. *Economic Geography* 64: 299–321.

1991 Job Search and the Occupational Segregation of Women. *Annals of the Association of American Geographers* 81(2): 229–253.

1992 Dynamic Dependencies: A Geographic Investigation of Local Labor Markets. *Economic Geography* 68: 373–405.

1995 *Gender, Work, and Space*. New York: Routledge.

Herod, A.

1998 *Organizing the Landscape: Geographical Perspectives on Labor Unionism.* Minneapolis: University of Minnesota Press.

2001 *Labor Geographies: Workers and the Landscapes of Capitalism*. New York: Guilford.

Hoerr, J.

1997 *We Can't Eat Prestige: The Women Who Organized Harvard.* Philadelphia: Temple University Press.

Hurd, R.

1993 Organizing and Representing Clerical Workers: The Harvard Model. In *Women and Unions: Forging a Partnership*, ed. D. S. Cobble, 316–336. Ithaca: ILR Press.

Johns, R.

1998 Bridging the Gap between Class and Space: US Worker Solidarity with Guatemala. *Economic Geography* 74(3): 252–271.

Johns, R., and L. Virayla

2000 Class, Geography and the Consumerist Turn: UNITE and the Stop Sweatshops Campaign. *Environment and Planning A* 32: 1193–1213.

Keough, R.

1995 Union Label for UMass? *The Worcester Phoenix*, July 28, 10–11.

Oppenheim, L., editor

1991 Women's Ways of Organizing: A Conversation with AFSCME Organizers Kris Rondeau and Gladys McKenzie. *Labor Research Review*, No. 18. Chicago: Midwest Center for Labor Research.

Rankow, L. F.

1992 *Gender on the Line: Women, the Telephone, and Community Life*. Urbana: University of Illinois Press.

Savage, L.
1998 Geographies of Organizing: Justice for Janitors in Los Angeles. In *Organizing the Landscape: Geographical Perspectives on Labor Unionism*, ed. A. Herod, 225–252. Minneapolis: University of Minnesota Press.
2004 Public Sector Unions Shaping Hospital Privatization: The Creation of Boston Medical Center. *Environment and Planning A* 36(3): 547–568.
2006 Justice for Janitors: Scales of Organizing and Representing Workers. *Antipode* 38(3): 648–667.
2007 Work Redesign and Labor Forms of Flexibility: A Conversation with HUCTW and SHARE Organizers. In *The Sex of Class: Women and America's New Labor Movements*, ed. D. S. Cobble, 181–216. Ithaca: Cornell University Press.

Savage, L., and J. Wills, editors
2004 New Geographies of Trade Unionism. Themed issue of *Geoforum* 35(1).

Tufts, S.
1998 Community Unionism in Canada and Labor's Re(organization) of Space. *Antipode* 30(3): 227–250.

U.S. Bureau of the Census
2005 *County Business Patterns, 2005, Massachusetts.* Washington, DC: U.S. Government Printing Office.

Walsh, J.
2000 Organizing the Scale of Labor Regulation in the United States: Service Sector Activism in the City. *Environment and Planning A* 32(1): 1593–1610.

Wills, J.
1996 Geographies of Trade Unionism: Translating Traditions across Space and Time. *Antipode* 28: 352–378.
1998a Taking on the Cosmocorps: Experiments in Transnational Labor Organization. *Economic Geography* 74: 111–130.
1998b Space, Place and Tradition in Working-Class Organization. In *Organizing the Landscape: Geographical Perspectives on Labor Unionism,* ed. A. Herod, 129–158. Minneapolis: University of Minnesota Press.
2001 Community Unionism and Trade Union Renewal in the UK: Moving beyond the Fragments at Last? *Transactions of the Institute of British Geographers* 26(4): 465–483.

EIGHT

Economic Globalization and Changing Capital-Labor Relations in Baja California's Fresh-Produce Industry

Christian Zlolniski

The fresh-produce industry, within which transnational corporations organize production in developing countries that lack strong labor unions employing indigenous and other vulnerable segments of the workforce, raises the question of how economic globalization in this growing industrial sector affects workers' ability to organize. It also raises the issue of whether the labor exploitation of indigenous and immigrant workers in Mexico and other Latin American countries fuels alternative forms of labor organization not based on class consciousness alone. This chapter explores these and other related questions from the vantage point of the San Quintín Valley (SQV), a region that specializes in the production of tomatoes and other horticultural products for export to the United States and other international markets.

Over the past few decades the fresh-produce industry has served as a primary vehicle for developing nations to expand their presence in global trade and become key players in international commodity chains (Alvarez 2006). In Latin America particularly, the export of fresh fruits and vegetables has become one of the fastest-growing agricultural sectors, often employing migrant indigenous workers connected through transnational social networks (Alvarez 2006; Echánove 2001; Lara 1996; Llambi 1994; Loker

1999; Reynolds 1994). In Mexico the fresh-produce industry has increased dramatically because of the combined effect of foreign demand for fresh vegetables; the expansion of U.S. agribusinesses south of the border attracted by access to land, soft environmental regulations, and cheap labor; and national agrarian policies that have reduced government subsidies for traditional crops, privatized *ejido* lands, and promoted export agriculture along free-trade agreements such as the North America Free Trade Agreement (NAFTA) (Alvarez 2005; Echánove 2001; Echánove and Steffen 2005; Marsh and Runsten 1988; Sanderson 1986; Weaver 2001). In addition to increasing the country's economic competitiveness, the Mexican government has supported neo-liberal agrarian policies in hopes of reducing poverty, labor migration of rural workers to the United States, and the potential for social and political instability—especially among indigenous workers. After all, indigenous political rebellions in Mexico since the mid-1990s have shown the ability of marginalized workers to respond to the state's neo-liberal projects (Nash 2001).

Yet scholarship on the fresh-produce industry has focused mainly on the macro forces driving the new international division of labor in agriculture, ignoring the question of how such forces shape the working conditions of farm laborers employed in this sector and their opportunities to organize. Based on grounded ethnographic studies, anthropologists are in a privileged position to document the effects of the globalization of food production on different locales, its impact on farmworkers' labor and working conditions, and their ability to mobilize to defend their labor rights. Ethnographic studies can also challenge the premise of globalization as a homogenizing force, showing that rather than social fragmentation and disruption of local institutions and communities, globalization can also lead to collective responses that challenge these forces (Nash 2007).

This chapter builds upon this approach by focusing on the SQV as a recent product of the increasing penetration of U.S. agribusiness corporations south of the border. Its local economy is based on contract agriculture, an export-oriented system in which foreign agribusiness corporations supply capital and technology and control key decisions in the production process, while local growers provide land and labor and manage production on the site (Martínez Novo 2004; Runsten and Griffith 1996; Zabin 1997). Local growers have developed close commercial links with U.S. distributing firms to market their products. Since 1994, NAFTA has provided additional opportunities to California growers to expand production in the SQV and other regions in Mexico. In addition, the 1992 reform of Article 27 of the Mexican Constitution to allow the privatization of communal *ejido* lands made it easier for U.S. companies to buy or lease land in the region and to invest in infrastructure and technology. Because of these elements, the SQV is a natural laboratory to examine the economic and social effects of the developing fresh-produce industry and neo-liberal economic policies at a regional level. In contrast to rural communities in Central and Western Mexico, where structural adjustment policies implemented since the 1980s have led to economic decline, labor out-migration, and the loss of private and state investment, the SQV has received heavy capital investment from the private sector and experienced explosive economic and demographic growth. Also, the strength of ethnic-based organizations led by indigenous activists makes this region an ideal case to examine the circumstances under which social movements organized around ethnic rather than class identity tend to emerge, as well as the advantages and limitations of such movements.

Previous studies have characterized the SQV as a region of environmental degradation, high economic inequality, labor exploitation, poverty, and health problems related to the unsanitary working and living conditions of thousands of indigenous migrants employed in commercial agriculture (Garduño, García, and Morán 1989; Grammont and Lara 2004; Martínez Novo 2004, 2006; Velasco Ortiz 2005; Wright 1990). Commercial agriculture has also fueled labor migration to the United States because of geographical proximity, contributing to lower wages for farmworkers in California and greater difficulty organizing them into unions (Zabin and Hughes 1995). Other authors have presented a more positive picture, highlighting the collective responses of Mixtec and other indigenous workers in Mexico and the United States who have forged transnational and pan-ethnic forms of identity and political organization to fight for labor and civil rights (Kearney 1996; Stephen 2007; Velasco Ortiz 2005). Like other studies on Latin America, these findings reveal how globalization contributes to the re-indigenization of ethnic groups that help segment the labor force along ethnic lines while, at the same time, indigenous workers use ethnicity as a weapon to defend their labor and human rights (Jackson and Warren 2005; Kearney 1996; Lewellen 2002).

Building upon this discussion, I argue that the effects of economic globalization in this region are complex and uneven, including some unexpected benefits as well as expected hardships and unintended consequences. As growers in the SQV have strengthened their links with large U.S. shippers and partners, the balance of power between producers and workers in the local community has shifted in favor of the growers. Intensification of production has increased labor control and productivity, which has translated into more stable employment and better wages for indigenous farm laborers. Working and living conditions have also improved as the result of market forces and stricter government regulations. Yet the intensification of production has also led to stricter forms of labor control and exploitation. In light of weak and ineffective labor unions and a history of labor exploitation in the region, independent ethnic organizations have emerged to protect workers' labor, civil, and human rights—a new form of social movement mobilization with a strong ethnic component. Yet these ethnic organizations' fragmented nature and instability make them vulnerable vis-à-vis growers and their trade associations. This outcome is not the result of global economic forces alone; rather, the state plays a key role in shaping the power struggle between local growers and independent ethnic organizations seeking to ensure the neo-liberal project of export agriculture while keeping the possibility of labor and ethnic unrest at bay.

First, I outline the major stages of the history of commercial agriculture in the SQV. In the chapter's second section, I discuss how the restructuring of the fresh-produce industry has affected the organization of the work process, the sources of labor, and the forms of labor recruitment and control. In the next sections I focus on wages and forms of payment, benefits, and working conditions for indigenous farm laborers in the region. The responses by labor unions and independent labor and ethnic organizations to channel workers' grievances and the ways government policies shape what demands these organizations can effectively pursue are discussed next. In the conclusion I reflect on the positive and negative effects globalization has brought to field workers in this region and ethnic organizations' potential and limitations in confronting local growers who operate in a transnational arena.[1]

The Development of Commercial Agriculture in the San Quintín Valley

Surrounded by the Pacific Ocean to the west and arid lands to the east, the nearly 37,000 km^2 valley of San Quintín is located in the state of Baja California about 300 kilometers south of the U.S. border at San Diego (Velasco 2005:45). The combination of good climate, access to underground water resources, geographical proximity to the U.S. market, government support, and a large labor supply have made of this region an ideal location for commercial agriculture.

This development first started when the Mexican government gave large tracts in Baja California to growers in Michoacán and Western Mexico whose lands had been expropriated as part of the agrarian reform during the Cardenas administration in the mid-1930s. During this initial phase, growers produced potatoes for Mexican markets with seed imported from the United States, and the region started to populate rather sparsely. In 1973 a proto-globalization phase started with the construction of the trans-peninsular highway that connected the region with the Tijuana–San Diego border, which opened new opportunities to export produce in a more efficient and timely manner and transformed the valley into one of the most rapidly growing agricultural regions in Northern Mexico. Agricultural production shifted from potatoes for domestic markets to horticultural products, especially tomatoes, for export to the United States. The expansion of commercial agriculture increased the demand for labor, and local growers started to recruit workers from outside Baja California—especially indigenous Mixtecs from Oaxaca who were housed in labor camps in the SQV during the harvest season in a pattern of cyclic labor migration (Lara 2000).

The third agro-industrial stage began in the early 1980s when the volume of agricultural production skyrocketed triggered by the arrival of ABC Farm, one of the largest companies growing and exporting tomatoes to the United States that had financial and marketing arrangements with Castle and Cook, a U.S. multinational agribusiness corporation (Kistner quoted in Wright 2005:41). To survive, other growers also had to dramatically expand their operations and establish new alliances with commercial distributing partners in California to capitalize the renovation of their infrastructure facilities. The intensification of production put increasing pressure on the limited water supply as growers pumped higher volumes every year to irrigate new lands, while labor demand also dramatically increased and a massive system of labor recruitment of indigenous workers expanded into further, remote areas in rural Oaxaca.

By the late 1990s this system of high-volume agricultural production reached its limit and entered a period of economic slowdown. Unrestricted growth led to salinity problems in the aquifer and many water wells were abandoned, while a severe drought that lasted several years exacerbated the water shortage. Also, starting in the mid-1980s and continuing through the late 1990s, the SQV went through intense episodes of labor conflict and social unrest as thousands of farm laborers mobilized against their employers to protest the dreadful working conditions they had endured for years at the hands of local growers (Martínez Novo 2006; Velasco Ortiz 2005).

In one such episode, workers blocked the trans-peninsular highway. Looting several offices and shops in town and burning municipal, state, and federal cars, several hundred workers protested to the management of the Santa Anita Ranch in the summer of 1996 because they had not been paid wages for several weeks (Martínez Novo 2006:30–31). In response to the increasing climate of social tension and violence, the Mexican government started developing diverse assistance programs to alleviate poverty, address basic public health problems, and mediate between growers and workers who organized in diverse ethnic and civic organizations.[2]

In response to the economic and social crisis, a restructuring process began in the early 2000s as the fresh-produce industry began shifting from high-volume production with large amounts of irrigation water to high-quality production based on technological changes. Using capital investment from their U.S partners, between 2001 and 2005 local growers built about twenty desalinization plants of different sizes with technology imported from Spain. A second technological response was the gradual shift from open-field cultivation to plasticulture and greenhouse production to reduce water consumption and increase yields.

By 2006 the SQV was at the cutting edge of horticultural production technology in Mexico and the second-largest exporter of tomatoes in the country. Combining technologies from Spain, Belgium, Israel, and the United States, the region illustrates the global nature of the fresh-produce industry and its strategic location on the Mexico-U.S. border to reach international markets. Growers also diversified production by expanding other prime crops through commercial agreements with partners in California, including strawberries, cucumbers, zucchinis, green onions, and onions, among others. Thus, according to figures from the Ministry of Agriculture, Livestock, Rural Development, Fisheries and Food, the percentage of land dedicated to tomato production decreased from about 50 percent in 1996 to 25 percent in 2003. Also, strawberry production increased from about 10,000 tons in 1992 to about 30,000 tons in 2003, mostly fueled by giant U.S. companies like Driscoll, which have invested heavily south of the border to expand production and reduce labor and other costs.

As a result of these changes, today there are three types of growers in the region. At the top, about eight agribusiness companies dominate production.

For example, companies like Los Pinos and San Vicente Camalú cultivate 2,000 and 1,200 hectares, respectively. Los Pinos has grown dramatically over the past few years, increasingly shifting to shade-house and greenhouse production and operating a state-of-the art packing plant for tomatoes and other fresh produce destined for international markets.

The company's rapid growth is the result of the direct investment of U.S. partners. While capital investment and commercial links with U.S. growers have a long tradition in the modern history of the SQV, both NAFTA and the *ejido* reform have facilitated and further encouraged private investment in lands and technology since the mid-1990s, which in turn has contributed to the concentration of land and power among a few companies in the region.

A second layer of midsize growers cultivates about 100 hectares of land and has distribution contracts with partner companies in the United States. Many of these growers have had a hard time adapting to the changes in the structure of the industry and to technological innovations that have taken place since the early 2000s. Thus some have been displaced from the market, while others have become further indebted to foreign partners to finance desalinization plants and nurseries.

A third and thinner layer of small-scale growers or *rancheros* (ranchers) produces for domestic markets. Their number has shrunk considerably since the early 1990s, and only a small handful remain to produce for domestic markets. Unlike large growers, these ranchers employ smaller, temporary work crews only during the harvest season.

As noted by Robert Alvarez (2006), NAFTA and the implementation of the certification of fresh produce imported to the United States from Mexico have prompted Mexican growers to create private institutions to help them adapt to such regulations and promote their exports. To obtain certification requires complying with a variety of phyto-sanitary processes of the U.S. Department of Agriculture (USDA) as well as regulations from the U.S. Food and Drug Administration (FDA) regarding the use of clean water, weeding and cleaning fields, portable sanitary facilities, and other conditions that vary from crop to crop. In addition, all packing plants must have food safety certification, which is usually performed for the FDA by certified laboratories.[3] To adapt to these requirements and keep labor costs down, growers in the SQV maintain close ties with local associations into which they are organized.

Five grower associations in the region are organized by locality, the largest of which—the Asociación de Productores de San Quintín (San Quintin

Growers' Association)—includes sixteen local producers. All of these local associations fall under the umbrella of the Unión Agrícola de Baja California (Agricultural Association of Baja California), which integrates growers in the SQV and the Maneadero Valley south of Ensenada. The Unión Agrícola is in charge of negotiating labor contracts with the two labor unions that represent farmworkers in the SQV. It also negotiates with Mexican government institutions and authorities, including the Mexican secretary of agriculture, about issues such as Social Security regulations for fieldworkers, fiscal benefits, loans, subsidy packages, and other government programs for growers in Baja California.

More recently, the Consejo Agrícola, a new growers' association, was formed in the SQV. Unlike the producers' Unión, the Consejo is integrated solely by local producers in the SQV, and its main purpose is to help growers negotiate the terms of export for their commodities with Mexican and U.S. government officials. Local rumors portray the Consejo as the stepchild of the right-wing PAN (Partido de Acción Nacional) government, which is aligned with the interests of entrepreneurs and advocates neo-liberal economic reforms. Despite the rivalry between the two organizations, most local growers belong to both, as they feel this gives them more leverage and ability to represent their interests and lobby federal and state government officials and institutions.

The economic growth from the fresh-produce industry has fueled explosive demographic growth. Between 1990 and 2000 alone, the population in the SQV increased from 38,151 to 74,427 inhabitants, while in the summer during the harvest season it is estimated that it is close to 100,000 inhabitants (Coubès, Velasco, and Zlolniski 2009). This demographic growth has been accompanied by a shift from labor camps, where workers lived temporarily while employed in agricultural tasks, to *colonias*—local subdivisions of house lots often obtained through squatter invasion—where farm laborers, as a result of the availability of year-round employment opportunities, have settled down with their families and children. While the number of labor camps has decreased, there has been a proliferation of new squatter settlements where workers and their families live today. In the years 1996 to 1999, the number of squatter settlements in the valley went from sixteen to forty-three (Coubès, Velasco, and Zlolniski 2009:31). The number of people living in these *colonias* increased from 8,120 in 1989 to 20,800 in 1999 (Velasco Ortiz 2005:50), while the proportion of farm laborers residing in labor camps during the tomato harvest season decreased from two-thirds to one-third in the same period (Instituto Nacional Indigenista and Pronjag [Programa Nacional de Jornaleros Agricolas], cited by Velasco Ortiz 2002:71).

Labor Changes within the Agribusiness Industry

The intensification of production in San Quintín has led to important changes in the sources of labor, forms of labor recruitment, and organization of the work process. The first change has been a major shift from seasonal circular labor migration to a more permanent workforce made up of indigenous workers from Oaxaca, Guerrero, and other neighboring states (Velasco Ortiz 2005). The oldest source of indigenous labor is Mixtec workers who migrated from Sinaloa or rural communities in Oaxaca and returned to their hometowns after the harvest. The intensification of production eventually led local growers to recruit workers from other ethnic groups in Oaxaca, producing a more ethnically diverse labor pool. Zapotec workers started migrating to the SQV in the 1980s and, like Mixtecs, have established strong roots in local squatter settlements. Triquis are the most recent ethnic group that has migrated and settled in the area. They are clustered in their own *colonias* and, over time, have developed their own ethnic organizations to defend their labor, civic, and human rights (Camargo 2005).

Not surprisingly, agricultural employment in the SQV is segmented along ethnic and gender lines. Mestizo women from Sinaloa tend to be employed in packing plants where the fresh produce is sorted and packed before it is transported to San Diego. Many of these women have established residence in the region since the late 1980s, while others still come to work temporarily during the packing season from July to November. Meanwhile, Mixtec, Zapotec, and Triqui indigenous workers make up the bulk of the labor employed in field tasks associated with the preparation, cultivation, and harvesting of tomatoes and other fresh vegetables—the most labor-intensive and harshest jobs. Men and women participate almost equally in labor tasks in the fields, including planting and harvesting. Yet men tend to specialize in the hardest manual tasks such as placing poles in the tomato fields, placing the plastic sheets that cover the furrows, removing and carrying them out after the harvest, placing threads that guide the tomato plants, and unraveling them at the end of the season. Women tend to be employed in labor-intensive but less strenuous physical tasks such as pruning, weeding, and cleaning the plants.

The recent proliferation of nurseries for tomatoes, strawberries, and other produce has further contributed to the division of labor by gender. Indigenous women are selectively hired to work in these occupations because of what growers call their "natural ability" to carefully handle the prime crops grown in greenhouses and their "more hygienic habits" compared with men. Meanwhile, male workers are mostly employed in the fields because of their reputed higher tolerance for working under the sun. The discourse of local growers on this issue resonates with that used in the 1980s in the maquila industry on the Mexico-U.S. border, this time adapted to the agro-export industry. This folk explanation does not take into account the fact that both the temperature and the humidity under which women work in the greenhouses are often considerably higher than they are outside.

Forms of labor recruitment have also changed as production has intensified. Throughout the mid-1980s when agricultural employment was temporary, local growers worked with *enganchadores*, labor contractors with whom they have long-established relationships, in places like Oaxaca and Sinaloa to recruit workers during the busiest season of the summer. To anchor a seasonal labor force through the end of the season, growers provided housing in labor camps for migrant workers and their families and allowed workers to bring their children, who were often employed in the harvest (Martínez Novo 2006; Velasco Ortiz 2005). Living conditions in the camps were poor, with insufficient and inadequate water supplies, a few restrooms for hundreds of workers, and unsanitary rooms—all of which earned this region a negative public image in the local and national Mexican media.

As employment became steadier throughout the year, a second form of labor recruitment developed in which growers used local labor contractors to hire workers who had settled in the *colonias* with their families. Unlike independent labor contractors in California (Krissman 1995), in San Quintín local labor recruiters are part-time, as they normally work as regular laborers for their employers during the slow season and are then employed as supervisors and labor recruiters during the harvest season.

Foremen are typically responsible for recruiting fieldworkers for their crews, which they do by word of mouth in the *colonias* where their *paisanos* live. Foremen are paid a bonus for each worker they bring to the field, and their success depends on their ability to capitalize on their social networks to maintain and replenish the workforce—a challenging task given the high labor turnover that characterizes agricultural employment. The growth of an internal market for labor recruitment has significantly reduced local growers' costs associated with the hiring, transporting, and housing of crews and shifted these costs to the supervisors who work as labor recruiters and to farmworkers themselves. It has also diluted growers' responsibilities toward their workers and made contractual labor agreements more difficult than they were in the past (Velasco Ortiz 2005:48).

The third way to recruit labor is to hire temporary workers at day laborer sites. Especially during the summer harvest, growers who are short of workers recruit day laborers through this informal system. The expansion of this system provides further evidence of the casualization of labor that has resulted from the intensification of production. This source of casual labor is partially made up of recently arrived migrants who lack the social connections with local growers or foremen to find more stable employment. However, some local residents, especially women, prefer to work as day laborers because they are typically paid twenty pesos more per day than those who are more regularly employed and they often work less. They are paid in cash every day rather than with a check once a week, and they can decide when to work, which offers them more flexibility to attend to their family and household chores that fall on their shoulders.

The intensification of production in the agribusiness industry has been also fueled by the introduction of new forms of labor control similar to those used north of the border. For example, one producer who grows strawberries for Driscoll replaced the traditional system of punch cards with electronic cards to keep track of the number of harvested trays. Workers used to keep one copy of their cards every day they went to work, but in the new system only the employer can read the information recorded on the digital cards, while workers have to write it down on their own or memorize it. Farmworkers complain that electronic cards do not always properly record the number of trays they harvest and, more important, that they have lost the ability to check their accuracy. As Teresa Figueroa (2004) has shown, this is a sophisticated tracking system commonly used in the strawberry industry in California as a mechanism of labor control and discipline that helps growers monitor workers' productivity and the quality of their work. This trend clearly speaks of a process of convergence of local growers with agribusiness in California and the global fresh-produce industry Carol Zabin (1997) identified in the early 1990s. A corollary of this process is that as labor control has tightened, it has contributed to widening the power gap between growers and farmworkers in the region.

Wages and Forms of Payment

A front on which farm laborers in the SQV have experienced some gains is wages. The rising demand for labor along with the increase in productivity fueled by both technological innovations and the intensification of labor has led to a significant rise in wages since the 1990s. According to one estimate, fieldworkers in San Quintín were paid between 25 and 35 Mexican pesos (between $3.00 and $4.50 U.S) for an eight-hour day in the 1990s (Martínez Novo 2006:34), while by 2005 a day's wages oscillated between 80 and 90 pesos ($7.20 and $8.10 U.S. at the going exchange rate). This wage increase, however, does not take into account the high rate of inflation in Mexico since the mid-1990s, especially following the devaluation of the peso in 1994. Moreover, with the shift from labor camps to *colonias*, housing and living costs in the SQV have significantly increased. To confront these costs, many workers have opted to migrate to California.

Men especially have developed extensive transnational connections that allow them to pursue employment opportunities on both sides of the border and send remittances from work in California agriculture back to their families in San Quintín. By 2003, an estimated 8 percent of the people in the region, mostly men, were working in the United States (Velasco Ortiz 2005:50). As the SQV continues its technological transition to intense production in greenhouses, labor demand for women will likely increase while work opportunities for men may not, further increasing the pressure on them to migrate north of the border.

Along with raising wages, major changes in forms of payment have also led to a sharp rise in the intensification of labor. Thus producers are seeking to stimulate labor productivity by different means. Day wages, the most common form of remuneration in the past, have been largely replaced by piece-rate and task systems.

The piece rate is most commonly used for harvests of strawberries and tomatoes. Because it depends on workers' productivity, it varies significantly. For example, in 2005, according to fieldwork data I collected, fieldworkers employed in the tomato industry usually earned between 80 and 100 pesos a day (between $7.20 and $9.00 dollars U.S.) for eight hours of work, but during the harvest, when they are paid by piece rate, the more productive laborers could make around $180 pesos ($16.20). I was told that the fastest workers at the peak of the season could fill about ninety buckets each day, making 270 pesos a day.

Strawberry workers can make significantly more than those in the tomato industry, but the work is more labor-intensive because they have to sort and carefully pack strawberries in plastic trays to pass rigorous quality controls in the field. As in the case of the strawberry industry in Santa Maria, California, studied by Teresa Figueroa (2004), this means that only production time is paid, while dead time spent sorting and discarding bad strawberries and packing is not. Despite this, during the harvest season workers can make about 285 pesos a day ($25.67 U.S. approximately). Workers employed by small ranchers usually earn higher wages than those who work for large companies, but they are employed for shorter periods. Because of the differential in wages, many farm laborers shift among picking tomatoes, strawberries, and other crops according to the season to maximize their incomes, fueling the high labor turnover that characterizes this industry.

A third common form of remuneration is the task system in which workers are paid an established amount per activity, usually planting, pruning, and cleaning plants. Tasks are often measured by the number of furrows completed. Each task is commonly remunerated with one day's wages, so the higher the number of completed tasks, the higher the income workers can bring home—provided they complete the tasks within the time frame established by their employers.

The task system most often involves crews of several workers at a time. The foreman recruits a crew, coordinates workers in the field, and pays them. This system allows growers to keep labor costs down during the slow season when time is less pressing a factor than it is during the harvest season. It also allows them to retain part of their workforce in the winter and reduce the time and costs involved in recruiting new workers when the work pace picks up again in the spring.

Most laborers prefer the piece rate over the task system because they have better control over their earnings and do not depend on workmates. Yet they prefer working for tasks over the day-wage system because it allows them to bring home a higher income and gives them the opportunity to complete the tasks in less than a full day. Women seem to particularly like the task system because they can go home in the early afternoon to cook and attend to their families.

In short, growers have shifted from the previous day-wage system to the piece-rate and task systems to increase labor productivity, which, as Sutti Ortiz (2002:404) has pointed out, is accomplished by the intensification of labor. Growers in the SQV are well aware of this principle. According to the president of a local growers' association, the shift from day wages to piece rate has led to significant increases in labor productivity in his company as today thirty-five workers can do the job equivalent to eighty *jornales*—the wages paid to eighty workers—performing the same work only a few years ago.

Benefits and Labor Conditions

Until recently, most farmworkers in the SQV were officially regarded as *jornaleros,* that is, day laborers who had no long-term relationship with any particular grower. According to Mexican labor law, *jornaleros* are casual, temporary migrant workers who follow the crops from one region to the next, working for many different employers throughout the year. Because of this, field laborers in the SQV were not included in the legal regime of the Social Security system; as a result, they did not qualify for job security, health coverage, pensions, unemployment compensation, sick leave, or maternal coverage.

Only a small fraction of workers—usually administrative workers, engineers, technicians, machine operators, and a few crew leaders—are legally considered *trabajadores de planta*, regular employees entitled to fringe benefits. If they are laid off even for a few weeks or switch employers during the year, farmworkers are classified as casual employees, regardless of how long they have been working in the region. As a result, workers employed by the same growers for fifteen or more years do not receive any pensions when they retire because their employers did not register them in the Social Security system. Given that most farm laborers employed in the agricultural sector are indigenous workers, they are by far the least protected and most vulnerable segment of the working population. They have weak legal and union protection, have no job security, and are hired and laid off continually according to their employers' changing needs (Velasco Ortiz 2005:48).

As farmworkers settled in the SQV in response to the demand for a stable labor force, it became more difficult to keep treating them as migrant day laborers. As explained earlier, a large proportion of farm laborers in the region are no longer migrants but are permanently settled workers employed year-round in different agricultural tasks, often by the same employer. This, along with the rapid growth of agricultural wage laborers that has resulted from neo-liberal agrarian reforms in Mexico, led the federal government to reform the old law that excluded farm laborers from the Social Security system. In April 2005, after years of negotiation with powerful growers' associations who had stalled implementation, the Mexican government finally decided to apply a new law to include agricultural workers in the nation's Social Security system. According to this law, fieldworkers employed by the same company for ninety days or longer are to be considered regular employees and hence are entitled to the basic labor rights and benefits established by the Mexican Federal Labor Law. The new legislation also establishes that children under age sixteen can only be employed four hours a day, and their employment should be compatible with attending school (Gaceta Parlamentaria 2005). The impact of this change on the labor conditions and benefits of farmworkers in the SQV remains to be seen.

The employment of farm laborers as casual workers with no benefits for many decades is one of the key factors explaining the poor health conditions of the region's working population. The lack of health coverage is one of the most important problems fieldworkers confront; as a result, the SQV has historically been plagued by serious health epidemics and high infant mortality rates. When workers fall sick at work, most employers provide medical passes so they can visit public health facilities run by the state. Rather than considering it a basic labor right, employers often use this privilege as a weapon of labor control, further reinforcing the patron-client relations that are common in the region (Martínez Novo 2006:37). Some companies have opted to have their own private clinics, which contributes to tighter control over their workers and allows them to underreport the number of people they employ, thus reducing payments to the national health system.

The lack of benefits is largely responsible for the high labor turnover that has traditionally predominated in the SQV, as workers have little incentive other than wages to stay with the same employer. As explained earlier, farm laborers often switch employers when they have the opportunity to increase their earnings, especially during harvest seasons. Others prefer to stick with the same employer to avoid having to search for work in the winter during the slow season.

Ironically, growers often express concern about the high labor turnover, blaming workers for lacking loyalty and other employers for "stealing" their employees. In the end, farmworkers are treated as temporary laborers, which dilutes employers' legal and contractual responsibilities toward them and enhances labor flexibility. The ultimate effect of this system is the creation of a labor pool, made up of permanent "temporary" workers with no strong legal ties to any particular employer, that provides a reliable yet cheap and flexible source of labor. This situation is similar to the case of African immigrant workers employed in the fresh-vegetable industry in El Ejido in the province of Almería, Spain (Martínez Veiga 2001), which speaks to a common feature brought by about the globalization of this sector.

Despite the casualization of labor, some working conditions have improved since the early 2000s, which illustrates the uneven effects of commercial agriculture in the region. For example, most large growers have installed portable bathrooms in the fields. They also provide clean drinking water and have considerably improved the living conditions in their camps. Many camps have now running water and electricity, better sanitary facilities, and childcare centers for workers' infants. Many of these changes are the result of the requirements associated with the certification process and stricter enforcement of basic labor regulations by the Mexican government that seeks to ensure the commercial success of export agriculture.

A case in point is child labor, a controversial practice with a long tradition in the SQV. Child labor was so common for many decades, especially during the harvest season, that some old-timers who worked as foremen specialized in the supervision of child work crews. Since the early 2000s, however, the use of child labor has considerably decreased and has become less visible than in the past. This change is most noticeable among large growers who try to avoid being caught breaking the law so as not to jeopardize their ability to export produce to the United States. The Mexican government has also stepped in to more closely monitor the ban of child labor, especially since PAN won the presidential elections in 2000. This party, which has controlled the state government in Baja California since 1989, favors neo-liberal economic policies aimed at promoting exports and encourages growers to comply with international trade regulations, especially with the United States. In addition, compulsory schooling, required of a more settled population, has contributed to less child labor.

While it has declined, child labor has not disappeared. Because they are less likely to be monitored than large agribusiness companies, medium-sized growers still employ children between ages ten and fourteen in significant numbers, along with their parents. Yet even large companies still employ children during the harvests, especially in the summer when they are out of school. While acknowledging the use of child labor, local growers portray it as a "cultural problem," the result of a well-entrenched tradition among indigenous migrant worker parents who come to this region, rather than a practice of employers recruiting children. This can be seen as a political strategy that seeks to shift the responsibility for the use of children in agriculture to the workers themselves, a political discourse with deep roots in Mexico and elsewhere in Latin America that portrays indigenous peoples and their culture as an obstacle to modernization, progress, and civilization (Martínez Novo 2006).[4]

Labor Unions, Independent Organizations, and Ethnic Leaders

How have field laborers in the SQV responded to the new challenges brought about by the intensification of labor in the local agribusiness industry? How do indigenous workers voice and push for their labor demands given their economic and legal vulnerability? Are there signs of new forms of labor and political organizing that can serve as a counterbalance to the otherwise powerful economic interests of local growers and their U.S. partners? As explained earlier, the increasing convergence of local growers with agribusiness in California fueled by NAFTA has lead to a widening power gap between growers and farmworkers. As a response and in light of weak, state-controlled labor unions, indigenous farm laborers have organized around independent unions and ethnic organizations to defend their labor, civil, and political rights. While providing an alternative outlet to channel workers' labor demands, ethnic organizations are rather fragmented and lack the leverage power to negotiate with and confront powerful growers and their trade associations.

The Mexican government has authorized two labor unions to represent farmworkers in the SQV. The larger and more important by far is the Sindicato Nacional de Trabajadores, Obreros de Industria y Asalariados del Campo (National Union of Industrial and Wage Agricultural Workers; SINTOIAC), a branch of the Confederación de Trabajadores de México (Confederation of Mexican Workers; CTM), while the second and significantly smaller one is the Confederación Regional de Obreros Mexicanos (Regional Confederation of Mexican Workers; CROM). The CTM is an old union historically associated with the corporatist political structure of the

Partido Revolucionario Institucional (Institutional Party of the Revolution; PRI) that dominated Mexican politics for over seventy years until the victory of the right-wing opposition National Action Party (PAN) in 2000.

This corporatist structure was originally developed by the Mexican government as a political-institutional framework to control labor unrest and support the model of import-substitution industrialization that characterized Mexico's economy until the shift to neo-liberal economic policies in the 1980s (Samstad and Collier 1995). In the SQV, the CTM has almost a monopoly right to represent fieldworkers and negotiate their labor contracts with the Unión Agrícola, which represents the growers. Historically associated with the PRI, the CTM has a long history of working closely with local growers to defend their interests and guarantee political and labor stability. Thus, according to several of the local growers I interviewed, the most important political role of the CTM is to prevent the formation of independent unions that could fuel labor unrest in the region. Because of this, the CTM has little credibility among farmworkers, many of whom do not even know that this union represents them, while others openly express their distrust and portray the CTM as a corrupt union aligned with the interests of employers rather than workers.

The failure of the CTM to address workers' concerns has prompted the emergence of several independent unions and ethnic-based organizations that have sought to mobilize agricultural workers. A number of these groups have emerged as the result of grassroots political organizing by indigenous leaders and labor activists. The most important and influential independent labor union is the Central Independiente de Obreros Agrícolas y Campesinos (Independent Union of Agrarian Workers and Peasants; CIOAC), a national independent union that first emerged in 1975 in the state of Sinaloa—Mexico's largest agricultural export region—to organize day laborers (Velasco Ortiz 2005; Zabin 1997) and that is sympathetic to the left-wing Mexican opposition party Partido de la Revolución Democrática (Party of the Democratic Revolution; PRD).

As an independent union, CIOAC's initial goal was to provide a long overdue response to the demands of thousands of indigenous workers employed by local growers. It started by denouncing the harsh working conditions that prevailed in the agricultural sector, the exploitation and mistreatment of mostly indigenous fieldworkers, the use of child labor, and the corruption of the CTM, which maintained close links with the most important growers.

From the beginning, growers, government authorities, and officers of the CTM alike perceived CIOAC as a threat to the status quo, and it never obtained legal recognition from the Mexican government to represent field-workers in the SQV. Despite its lack of legal status to represent farmworkers, since the mid-1970s and especially throughout the 1990s CIOAC played an active and militant role in promoting labor rights of farmworkers by organizing strikes and work stoppages, shutting down harvesting for short periods, blocking roads, taking over local government offices, and organizing rallies and marches to protest the inhumane working and living conditions thousands of indigenous workers endured in both the fields and labor camps (Velasco Ortiz 2005). Because of this, powerful growers, or caciques, and government officials severely repressed CIOAC, especially in the 1980s when some of its leaders were tortured and assassinated (Martínez Novo 2006).

With time, as farm laborers settled down in the SQV, CIOAC started to shift its agenda away from labor confrontations and demands to issues related to housing and access to public services such as water, electricity, pavement, and schools in the newly formed *colonias* where many fieldworkers had been living since the 1980s (Martínez Novo 2006:25; Velasco Ortiz 2005:120–122). The workers' need to demand their rights as local residents rather than "migrant workers," as they are often portrayed by growers and government officials to escape responsibility toward them, was an important reason for this shift (Velasco Ortiz 2005:122).

Rather than confront agricultural employers, CIOAC gradually evolved from a labor union that tried to unite Mixtec, Triqui, and Zapotec workers based on their shared class identity and interests into a broader urban-like social movement with a multipurpose agenda that seeks to negotiate with government authorities to push for demands related to poor living conditions in the *colonias* (Martínez Novo 2006:25). At the same time, since 2000, the year PAN ascended to the national government, CIOAC has experienced further political and judicial pressure from the state. Under accusations of corruption, the state government has confiscated much of the land from which this independent union obtained most of its local funds by renting to shop owners. Today, CIOAC's influence has dramatically declined to the point that is now a union in bankruptcy.[5]

Largely in response to the repression of independent labor unions, ethnic-based organizations have emerged as an alternative form of organization to defend indigenous labor and civil rights, and they are much more popular than unions. Most appeal to the ethnic or pan-ethnic identity of the indigenous workers and families who live in the region. As documented by Laura Velasco Ortiz (2005), San Quintín has a long tradition of this type of ethnic organization—most founded by Mixtecs, Zapotecs, and Triquis—including some pan-ethnic groups such as the Frente Indígena Oaxaqueño Binacional (Binational Mixtec Indigenous Front; FIOB) and the Movimiento de Unificación de Jornaleros Independientes (Movement for the Unification of Independent Day Laborers; MUJI). Several of these organizations were founded by male indigenous activists in the *colonias* where their co-ethnics settled and have multipurpose political agendas to address problems such as housing, access to health care, sexual harassment, labor exploitation, and other issues indigenous workers confront.

An example is the Frente Indígena de Lucha Triqui (Triqui Indigenous Front; FILT), founded in 1998 by a former farmworker who started mobilizing to improve living conditions in Nuevo San Juan Copala. This is a squatter settlement located on land donated by the state government, where hundreds of Triqui families relocated after living for several years in a rundown labor camp owned by one of the largest local growers in San Quintín (Camargo 2005; Velasco Ortiz 2005:50). FILT's political activities focus on demands related to housing, public services, and infrastructure for the *colonia*, as well as social discrimination and human rights violations of Triquis, with labor demands often occupying second place. Many of these organizations maintain connections with indigenous activists and migrant workers across the border through dense social networks, promoting ethnic and cultural identity as well as mobilization around labor, residential, human rights, and cultural issues (Stephen 2007; Velasco Ortiz 2005:126).

Despite the important role ethnic organizations have historically played in the SQV in mobilizing indigenous workers, some limits have curtailed their political power, especially when dealing with labor demands. First, ethnic-based organizations have traditionally been rather unstable and prone to internal conflicts, leading to constant splits and fragmentation and thus undermining indigenous peoples' political power (Velasco Ortiz 2005). Also, as Martínez Novo (2006) has shown, these organizations often lack a large grassroots base, and their leaders have ties to state institutions and government-supported programs, which limits their ability to act independently and promote actions to address labor demands and confront growers. A third limiting factor involves state policies toward civil society. Starting with the shift to neo-liberal policies in Mexico and especially since the right-wing PAN seized control of the federal government, state policies have clearly shifted toward independent unions, as well as ethnic and civic organizations. Support for independent organizations that employed a radical political discourse and focused on class struggle, used as a tool for political control and co-optation by the PRI, has been dramatically reduced. Instead, PAN has taken an open, harsh approach to such unions and civic organizations using legalistic means to undermine their strength and insulate them, especially independent unions and indigenous organizations with a defiant class discourse.

In addition to ethnic organizations, there are independent activists and community leaders who often act on behalf of the agricultural workers' labor demands. Popularly known as "leaders," they are individuals who have charisma and public recognition to act as brokers between indigenous peoples and government authorities, growers, or both. Often, these leaders are the heads of independent ethnic organizations, while others are independent activists who enjoy the recognition and respect of their countrymen.

In San Quintín, dozens of these community leaders are present at any time, although only a few have public recognition in the entire region. Indigenous leaders often bring political experience from their home communities, translating and adapting this knowledge to address the needs of their co-ethnics in the SQV. Many are acknowledged by government authorities as legitimate interlocutors and are called whenever an important matter is to be discussed, serving as transmission links for top-down government programs that target indigenous groups (Velasco Ortiz 2006). For example, when federal and state officials arrived in the SQV in the summer of 2005 to introduce the new legislation regarding labor rights for farmworkers, they called a meeting with the leaders of some ethnic organizations as well as recognized independent ethnic and community leaders rather than with the leaders of the unions who officially represent farm laborers in the region.

Ethnic leaders are also often called upon to intervene and mediate when labor conflicts between farmworkers and growers arise. For example, in cases of work stoppages initiated by workers to protest work conditions or demand higher wages, indigenous leaders might intervene to negotiate on behalf of their co-ethnics with their employer. Because of their role as labor and political brokers, leaders are both feared and despised by growers, who publicly portray them as corrupt figures who take advantage of their own people for personal gain. Growers complain that the government gives too much recognition to indigenous ethnic leaders and demand that public officials crack down on, rather than negotiate with, them. To local growers, ethnic leaders represent a threat—albeit a small one—to their otherwise almost complete power monopoly over labor in the region.

In the end, the lack of a legal framework for independent organizations to represent workers' labor interests critically contributes to the unstable position and limited power of ethnic leaders and organizations. Some leaders fall short of enjoying public esteem because they acquire a stigma as corrupt individuals who take advantage of their position as cultural brokers at the expense of their own people. In the absence of a strong and independent labor union to represent farmworkers' interests, the effect of this dynamic has been the fragmentation and weakening of indigenous organizations, thereby increasing the power inequality between capital and labor.

Conclusion

Neo-liberal economic policies in Mexico have contributed to the uprooting of traditional peasant communities, leaving many rural people with few employment opportunities and transforming them into rural proletarians—thus creating a large pool of cheap, flexible migrant labor used in large-scale commercial, export-oriented agriculture in the northern part of the country. The expansion of commercial agriculture in San Quintín reflects this shift in Mexico's rural economic policies from import-substitution to export-oriented production, which gained full support in the 1980s with the implementation of a neo-liberal economic agenda. As shown here, the globalization of horticultural production in the SQV has led to a major restructuring process characterized by heavy capital investment in new production technologies, a shift from quantity to quality fresh produce, the use of sophisticated methods of labor control to enhance productivity and labor flexibility, and a change from temporary migrant labor to a settled immigrant workforce. Globalization has further increased the interdependence between local growers and their commercial partners in California, many of whom have become integrated into a single vertical production system in which they share the same sources of capital, production technologies, and a common pool of labor across the U.S.-Mexico border (Zabin 1997).

The articulation of San Quintín's regional economy with the global fresh-produce industry is not just the product of international market forces but has been made possible by its historical socio-political configuration as a self-contained region with sharp power inequalities between a small elite of mestizo growers and a large mass of indigenous workers segmented along ethnic and gender lines. As Miriam Wells (1996) has shown in her study of the strawberry industry in California's central coast, the region's particular political economy plays a key role in shaping capital-labor relations at the local level. In the SQV, transnational corporations that forge commercial ventures with local growers under the system of contract agriculture have capitalized on the historical features of the region's political economy to organize production and manage labor to export to international markets at competitive rates.

But the globalization of food production in the SQV has also had unexpected consequences that have contributed to the improvement of some working and living conditions. Most notably, the certification process growers have to meet to export their produce has contributed to improved worker health and sanitary conditions in both the fields and the remaining labor camps. Child labor has also declined as growers have learned about the international political sensitivity toward labor and indigenous workers' human rights issues. This shows that, as Marc Edelman and Angelique Haugerud (2005) have argued, the effects of economic globalization are not uniformly negative but often double-edged, including unexpected outcomes.

Other changes have come about as a result of the political mobilization of indigenous workers, often through ethnic-based organizations rather than labor unions. Improvements in the squatter settlements, especially in housing, are the result of farmworker grassroots movements to pressure government officials to deliver public services and invest in infrastructure in their *colonias*. After living for several generations as itinerant migrant workers in overcrowded and unsanitary labor camps, settling down in local *colonias* and living in their own homes represents a considerable improvement for thousands of indigenous farmworkers as well as a vehicle for economic mobility. While modest, these squatter settlements give fieldworkers the opportunity to raise their families in a more spacious, pleasant, independent, and stable environment while also becoming homeowners. As in the Coachella Valley north of the border, where agriculture is also based on the production of prime-value crops (Du Bry 2007), the intensification of agricultural production and the consequent settlement of farm laborers in local squatter settlements have opened new work and economic opportunities for many workers—some of whom have been able to leave harsh jobs in agriculture and start their own small family businesses, often as local merchants. Fieldworkers have also been able to send their children to school, as the government has built numerous schools to accommodate the needs of the thousands of children who have settled in the valley with their families.

Despite these improvements, the modernization of horticultural production in the SQV has exacerbated the power gap between growers and workers, a common feature in other world regions that specialize in export-oriented agriculture (Martínez Novo 2004, 2006). San Quintín's largest growers have gradually become true transnational capitalist actors, as structural forces have integrated them into the international agribusiness market and they have learned to move at ease on both sides of the Mexico-U.S. border. Meanwhile, leaders of independent labor organizations such as CIOAC have no such transnational connections, and their political strategies of local labor protests and confrontations lack the international savvy needed to confront powerful companies that operate in the international arena. Moreover, since the early 1980s, as the Mexican government and international monetary institutions pushed to replace the old import-substitution economy with an export-oriented model, the corporatist structure of state-controlled unions in the rural sector has changed little, and independent unions such as CIOAC have been under attack by the state.

The state thus plays a central role in shaping the outcome of capital-labor power relations within the context of neo-liberal market policies. In the SQV, the government has developed public assistance policies to combat poverty and diffuse social conflict after decades of "free-market" policies to fuel economic growth. Rather than deregulation, as expected from the neo-liberal paradigm, a re-regulation approach has taken place in which the state sets up basic environmental, labor, and civil laws to address the ills of unchecked free-market forces. To be sure, this can be seen as fulfilling the state's role in a region where the federal and state governments traditionally had a weak presence until the 1980s. Yet the government has developed populist policies that seek to contain the social ills provoked by a model of economic growth with limited labor protections to secure the establishment of a stable working-class population necessary to feed the labor needs of the agribusiness industry. At the same time, it has systematically repressed any independent unions and organizations focused on labor issues and a class-oriented approach while accommodating ethnic-based organizations that focus on the social, human, and cultural rights of the different ethnic groups in the region as long as they do not seriously challenge growers and the local power structure (Martínez Novo 2006).

The fact that economic globalization in regions like the SQV contributes to the regeneration of ethnic and pan-ethnic organizations raises the question on whether ethnic identity can serve as a vehicle for the political mobilization of workers' labor rights. Some authors have portrayed ethnic organizations as a grassroots response to the forces of globalization and the trans-nationalization of labor in which indigenous workers coalesce around a renewed sense of ethnic identity to struggle for their labor, civil, political, and human rights (Kearney 1996). Others have argued that ethnicity as the basis for political mobilization contributes to fragmenting workers' political power and undermines their ability to form strong labor unions (Martínez Novo 2006).

The evidence presented in this chapter shows that these outcomes are not necessarily incompatible but instead suggests two sides of the same coin. Ethnic-based organizations have emerged largely because of the ineffectiveness of state-controlled labor unions and in response to high levels of exploitation and abuse of indigenous workers that have prevailed in the region for several decades. They have played a critical role in both improving indigenous workers' labor conditions and negotiating with state authorities to access lots to build their homes and bring much-needed material and social infrastructure to the *colonias* in which they have settled (Velasco Ortiz 2005).

On the other hand, ethnic-based organizations are not solely the product of social mobilization from below but are often supported by the state from above as an instrument for political control and co-optation and for diffusing social conflict around labor-related issues designed to prevent the formation of independent labor unions (Martínez Novo 2006). Also, organizations based on ethnic identity seem to contribute to the reinforcement of ethnic boundaries, particularly between mestizos and indigenous workers, thus facilitating rather than challenging the ethnic segmentation of labor that has historically prevailed in the SQV (Martínez Novo 2006).

What, then, is the future of labor organizing in communities like the SQV that are deeply integrated into the global economy through the fresh-produce industry? Three lessons can be learned from the case study presented here. First, rather than uncritically assuming that economic globalization necessarily leads to the decline of the state's power to regulate what goes on within its boundaries, there is the need to recognize the central role state policies play in shaping the institutional and legal framework in which labor unions operate within national boundaries. In Mexico the government's institutional control over nationwide labor unions such as the CTM has been the key factor preventing the organization of millions of Mexican workers employed in commercial agriculture in regions like the SQV. Without legal and political reform to allow the formation of independent unions and associations, farm laborers will have a difficult time defending their labor rights against increasingly powerful growers.

Second, while ethnic organizations provide a political space for workers to mobilize for labor issues in a context where there are no strong unions, they also face important limitations confronting growers who have links to transnational corporations. While ethnic organizations tend to be unstable and fragmented, local growers have gained political muscle by getting together in powerful trade associations and establishing commercial links with partners north of the border.

Rather than privileging ethnicity over class identity as the basis for collective mobilization, both areas need to be integrated because they are deeply interwoven in the social lives of most fieldworkers. Based on my experience, most indigenous farmworkers in the SQV tend to self-identify first in occupational and class terms and second in terms of ethnicity. Their stated goals are those of the working class: they want job security and economic stability, the opportunity to provide for their children's educational and occupational mobility, and the chance to integrate into the local community as residents with full rights. This is not surprising given the long history of social stigmatization they have experienced as indigenous migrants, in which their real or attributed cultural traditions have been used to set them apart from the mestizo population. In my view, independent labor unions that capitalize on fieldworkers' potential to mobilize for basic citizenship rights including labor, civil, political, and ethnic-related demands—reflecting the multifaceted reality for these workers and their families—offer the best promise to directly address and confront the power inequalities between capital and labor that have historically characterized this region.

Third, while economic globalization has forced local growers in the SQV to become players in the international arena, independent labor unions and leaders have not caught up with these changes and often approach labor struggles using local political strategies in which many were trained in the 1960s. While local strikes and mobilizations were somehow successful in the past, this political approach is out of synch with today's global scenario in which local growers have become international actors and are less vulnerable to localized labor struggles. In fact, even today, local companies seek to contain labor disputes within the confines of the region, where growers have considerable political clout, and to avoid labor disputes that reach the international arena, where they feel more vulnerable to negative public campaigns. Just as growers have organized into transnational associations, so, too, workers and independent union organizations need to forge collaborative links with their counterparts in the United States to gain leverage power to confront and negotiate with local employers and their commercial partners. By the same token, labor unions representing farmworkers in California and elsewhere in the United States need to create alliances with independent organizations south of the border to avoid loosing further ground as more U.S. agribusinesses relocate to Northern Mexico, where organized labor has a weak presence (Griffith 2009). Only by establishing such coalitions and orchestrating public campaigns that connect producers and consumers of the fresh-produce industry on both sides of the border and by strategically exploiting the vulnerability of transnational corporations that move flexibly across international borders will labor unions that represent farm laborers in Northern Mexico and the United States have a chance to break away from their current disadvantaged power position.[6]

Notes

1. This chapter is based on preliminary findings of an ongoing study and fieldwork conducted in the SQV in 2005. The study is part of an interdisciplinary project with two research faculty at El Colegio de la Frontera Norte (COLEF) in Mexico: Dr. Marie-Laure Coubès, a demographer, and Dr. Laura Velasco, a sociologist. I am solely responsible for any errors of fact or interpretation.

2. In light of the production crisis and labor tensions, several growers moved their operations to Vizcaino, farther south in Baja California, where water resources were more readily available and there was no history of labor unrest.

3. Alvarez (2006) has maintained that although requirements are needed to control the danger of contaminated food crops, they also use the leverage power of the United States to manipulate the market in its favor. Thus, while NAFTA and neo-liberal policies project the image of openness, free trade, and markets, they have also instituted a coercive system to favor the interests of U.S. producers.

4. The controversial political nature of child labor and its economic ramifications are illustrated by the case of Los Pinos, one of the largest tomato growers in the region. In 2003 a U.S. television news report denounced the use of child labor by this company in the SQV. The company vehemently rejected the accusation, arguing that the report was a fabrication by U.S. growers who were loosing market share to Los Pinos. The news caused a backlash for the company, as several of its U.S. buyers stopped their orders, including large supermarket chains. As a result, the company suffered important economic losses, and the report provoked a political storm in the

valley where local growers became even more suspicious of outside scrutiny—including by academics—than they had been in the past.

5. The deterioration of CIOAC was such that when I interviewed its leaders in the summer of 2005, the office had no phone or electricity because it could not pay the bills.

6. While agriculture has followed the flexible production model that characterizes other industries in today's global economy (Friedland 1994; Reynolds 1994; Sanderson 1986), the fact that it still requires more long-term investment and infrastructure than do other, more mobile industries (e.g., garment and textile production) seems to provide more economic opportunities and stability for workers than the latter industries offer. In San Quintín this has not translated into organized labor capitalizing on the political opportunities of this situation.

References Cited

Alvarez, Robert R.

2005 *Mangos, Chiles, and Truckers: The Business of Transnationalism*. Minneapolis: University of Minnesota Press.

2006 The Transnational State and Empire: U.S. Certification in the Mexican Mango and Persian Lime Industries. *Human Organization* 65(1): 35–45.

Camargo, Abbdel

2005 Etnografía de Una Colonia Triqui en Baja California: Nuevo San Juan Copala. Unpublished report. Tijuana, BC: El Colegio de la Frontera Norte, México.

Coubès, Marie L., Laura Velasco, and Christian Zlolniski

2009 Asentamiento residencial y movilidad en el valle de San Quintín. Reflexión metodológica sobre una investigación interdisciplinaria. In *Encuentros disciplinarios y debates metodológicos. La práctica de la investigación sobre migraciones y movilidades,* ed. Liliana Rivera Sánchez and Fernando Lozano Ascencio. México, DF: Miguel Angel Porrúa Librero Editor y Universidad Nacional Autónama de México (CRIM).

Du Bry, Travis Anthony

2007 *Immigrants, Settlers, and Laborers: The Socioeconomic Transformation of a Farming Community*. New York: LFB Scholarly Publishing.

Echánove, Flavia H.

2001 Working under Contract for the Vegetable Agroindustry in Mexico: A Means of Survival. *Culture and Agriculture* 23(3): 13–23.

Echánove, Flavia H., and Cristina Steffen

2005 Agribusiness and Farmers in Mexico: The Importance of Contractual Relations. *Geographical Journal* 171(2): 166–176.

Edelman, Marc, and Angelique Hauderud
2005 Introduction: The Anthropology of Development and Globalization. In *The Anthropology of Development and Globalization: From Classical Political Economy to Contemporary Neoliberalism*, ed. Marc Edelman and Angelique Hauderud, 1–74. Malden, MA: Blackwell.

Figueroa, Teresa
2004 Mexican Farm Workers and the Reorganization of Labor in the California Strawberry Industry. Unpublished manuscript, Department of Anthropology, University of California, Santa Barbara.

Friedland, William H.
1994 The New Globalization: The Case of Fresh Produce. In *From Columbus to ConAgra: The Globalization of Agriculture and Food,* ed. Alessandro Bonanno, Lawrence Busch, William H. Friedland, Lourdes Gouveis, and Enzo Mingione, 210–231. Lawrence: University of Kansas Press.

Gaceta Parlamentaria
2005 No. 106. Martes 12 de abril. Senado de la República. Cuidad de México, Mexico.

Garduño, Everardo, Efrain García, and Patricia Morán
1989 *Mixtecos en Baja California: El Caso de San Quintín*. Mexicali, BC: Universidad Autónoma de Baja California (UABC).

Grammont, Hubert C. de, and Sara Lara
2004 *Encuesta a hogares de jornaleros migrantes en regiones hortícolas de México: Sinaloa, Sonora, Baja California Sur y Jalisco*. México, DF: Instituto de Investigaciones Sociales–Universidad Nacional Autónoma de México (UNAM).

Griffith, David
2009 Unions without Borders: Organizing and Enlightening Immigrant Farm Workers. *Anthropology of Work Review* 30(2): 54–66.

Jackson, Jean, and Kay B. Warren
2005 Indigenous Movements in Latin America, 1992–2004: Controversies, Ironies, New Directions. *Annual Review of Anthropology* 34: 549–573.

Kearney, Michael
1996 *Reconceptualizing the Peasantry: Anthropology in Global Perspective*. Boulder: Westview.

Krissman, Fred
1995 Farm Labor Contractors: The Process of New Immigrant Labor from Mexico and Californian Agribusiness. *Agriculture and Human Values* 12(4): 18–46.

Lara, Sara

1996 Mercado de Trabajo Rural y Organización Laboral en el Campo Mexicano. In *Neoliberalismo y Organización Social en el Campo Mexicano*, ed. Hubert C. de Grammont, 69–112. Mexico, DF: Universidad Nacional Autónoma de México (UNAM), Plaza y Valdes.

2005 Características de las migraciones rurales hacia regiones hortícolas en el noroeste de México. In *Los actores sociales frente al desarrollo rural*, ed. Yolanda Massieu Trigo, Michelle Chauvet Sánchez, and Rodolfo García Zamora, vol. 2, 109–126. México, DF: Asociación Mexicana de Estudios Rurales/Ed. Praxis.

Lewellen, Ted C.

2002 *The Anthropology of Globalization: Cultural Anthropology Enters the 21st Century*. Westport, CT: Bergin and Garvey.

Llambi, Luis

1994 Comparative Advantages and Disadvantages in Latin American Nontraditional Fruit and Vegetable Exports. In *The Global Restructuring of Agro-Food Systems*, ed. Philip McMichael, 190–212. Ithaca: Cornell University Press.

Loker, William M.

1999 Grit in the Prosperity Machine: Globalization and the Rural Poor in Latin America. In *Globalization and the Rural Poor in Latin America*, ed. William M. Loker, 9–39. Boulder: Lynne Rienner.

Marsh, Robin R., and David Runsten

1988 Smallholder Fruit and Vegetable Production in Mexico: Barriers and Opportunities. In *The Transformation of Rural Mexico: Reforming the Ejido Sector*, ed. Wayne A. Cornelius and David Myhre, 277–306. San Diego: Center for U.S.-Mexican Studies.

Martínez Novo, Carmen

2004 The Making of Vulnerabilities: Indigenous Day Laborers in Mexico's Neoliberal Agriculture. *Identities: Global Studies in Culture and Power* 11: 215–239.

2006 *Who Defines Indigenous? Identities, Development, Intellectuals and the State in Northern Mexico*. New Brunswick, NJ: Rutgers University Press.

Martínez Veiga, Ubaldo

2001 *El Ejido: Discriminación, exclusión social y racismo*. Madrid: Libros de la Catarata.

Nash, June

2001 *Mayan Visions: The Quest for Autonomy in an Age of Globalization*. New York: Routledge.

2007 *Practicing Ethnography in a Globalizing World: An Anthropological Odyssey*. Lanham, MD: Altamira.

Ortiz, Sutti
2002 Laboring in the Factories and in the Fields. *Annual Review of Anthropology* 31: 395–417.

Reynolds, Laura
1994 Institutionalizing Flexibility: A Comparative Analysis of Fordist and Post-Fordist Models of Third-World Agro-Export Production. In *Commodity Chains and Global Capitalism*, ed. Gary Gereffi and Miguel Korzeniewicz, 143–162. Westport, CT: Greenwood.

Runsten, David, and David Griffith
1996 Labor in the Tomato Industry: A Comparative Discussion of California and Florida. In *Immigration Reform and U.S. Agriculture*, ed. Philip L. Martin, Wallace Huffman, Robert Emerson, J. Edward Taylor, and Refugio I. Rochin, 355–378. Oakland: University of California, Division of Agriculture and Natural Resources.

Samstad, James G., and Ruth Berins Collier
1995 Mexican Labor and Structural Reform under Salinas: New Unionism or Old Stalemate? In *The Challenge of Institutional Reform in Mexico*, ed. Riordan Roett, 9–37. Boulder: Lynne Rienner.

Sanderson, Steven
1986 *The Transformation of Mexican Agriculture: International Structure and the Politics of Rural Change*. Princeton: Princeton University Press.

Stephen, Lynn
2007 *Transborder Lives: Indigenous Oaxacans in Mexico, California, and Oregon*. Durham, NC: Duke University Press.

Velasco Ortiz, Laura
2002 *El Regreso de la Comunidad: Migración Indígena y Agentes Étnicos. Los Mixtecos en la Frontera México-Estados Unidos*. México, DF: El Colegio de México and El Colegio de la Frontera Norte.
2005 *Mixtec Transnational Identity*. Tucson: University of Arizona Press.

Weaver, Thomas
2001 Time, Space, and Articulation in the Economic Development of the U.S.-Mexico Border Region from 1940 to 2000. *Human Organization* 60(2): 105–120.

Wells, Miriam J.
1996 *Strawberry Fields: Politics, Class, and Work in California Agriculture*. Ithaca: Cornell University Press.

Wright, Angus

2005 *The Death of Ramón Gonzalez: The Modern Agricultural Dilemma*. Austin: University of Texas Press.

Zabin, Carol

1997 U.S.-Mexico Economic Integration: Labor Relations and the Organization of Work in California and Baja California Agriculture. *Economic Geography* 73(3): 337–355.

Zabin, Carol, and Sallie Hughes

1995 Economic Integration and Labor Flows: Stage Migration in Farm Labor Markets in Mexico and the United States. *International Migration Review* 29(2): 395–422.

NINE

The Tobacco Trap: Obstacles to Trade Unionism in Malawi

Marty Otañez

Based on ethnographic data on tobacco farmworkers and trade unionists in Malawi, this chapter analyzes child labor and labor organizing in Malawi's tobacco sector. Malawi is economically reliant on tobacco growing and experiences high levels of child labor on tobacco farms. Men and women with little or no access to land or wage work agree to contracts with farm owners to grow and sell tobacco on land the owners provide to them.

Black Malawians own virtually all of the country's tobacco farms and sell at auctions to U.S.-based leaf-buying companies that have prearranged contracts with Philip Morris, British American Tobacco, and other global cigarette manufacturers. Men and women send their children to the fields instead of to school so they can cultivate enough leaf to satisfy contracts. Children and their parents employed in tobacco farming become trapped in a downward cycle of poverty as tobacco farm owners and tobacco companies earn profits from leaf produced with child labor.

Union organizers in Malawi struggle to eliminate child labor and improve the livelihoods of tobacco farmworkers. However, organizers encounter obstacles in the global political economy of tobacco, where the Malawian government promotes tobacco growing and health policy-makers seek to decrease it. Both sides present daunting challenges to labor organizers.

Political Economy of Tobacco in Malawi

Beginning in 1981, structural adjustment programs (renamed Poverty Reduction Strategy Papers in 2000) involved policies to promote tobacco and other cash crops to achieve economic growth and ensure that Malawi repays its debts to the World Bank and the International Monetary Fund (International Monetary Fund 2007; Magalasi 2006; World Bank 2006a, 2006b). Malawi derives 70 percent of its foreign earnings from tobacco, making it the most tobacco-dependent economy in the world (International Monetary Fund 2007). Nearly 3 percent of Malawi's arable land (2.8 percent; 301,467 acres) is devoted to growing tobacco (Table 9.1) (Mackay and Eriksen 2006). With about 1.5 million jobs, tobacco is the second largest sector of the economy, after the civil service. Between 1990 and 1995, tobacco accounted for 20 percent of deforestation in Malawi (Geist 1999). Furthermore, pesticide and fertilizer use on the country's tobacco crop depletes nutrients from soils, pollutes water tables, and erodes landscapes.

Tobacco growing thrives alongside poverty in Malawi. Of Malawi's population of 13.2 million, 65.3 percent live at or below the national poverty line ($1.50 U.S. income per day) (United Nations Development Program 2008), life expectancy at birth is 39.8 years, 14 percent are infected with HIV/AIDs (one of the highest rates in the world) (Joint United Nations Programme on HIV/AIDS 2006; World Health Organization 2006b), 64 percent of adults are literate, the per capita GDP is $161 U.S., and 83 percent live in rural areas (United Nations Development Program 2008). Desperate to survive, Malawians sell their labor on tobacco farms but continue to fall deeper into poverty.

Philip Morris and other cigarette manufacturers save $10 million U.S. per year in production costs because the 78,000 children who work growing tobacco are not paid the adult minimum agricultural wage (Mwasikakata 2003; Otañez 2004). Few consumers in the United States and other global markets where Marlboro, Camel, and other American-blend cigarette brands are sold know that men, women, and children in Malawi who earn little or no money and suffer from chronic poverty grow the tobacco contained in many of those cigarettes.

Table 9.1. The Tobacco Business in Malawi

Growing tobacco	
Land devoted to growing tobacco, acres	301,467
Agricultural land devoted to tobacco farming, percentage of total	2.8
Tobacco produced, thousands of metric tons	69.5
Tobacco trade	
Cigarette exports, millions	2
Cigarette imports, millions	269
Tobacco leaf exports, metric tons	107,031
Tobacco leaf imports, metric tons	202
Manufacturing	
Number of cigarette manufacturing workers per 100,000 workers	0.0
Cigarettes manufactured, millions	NA
Price	
Peter Stuyvesant (British American Tobacco) or equivalent international brand, U.S. dollars per pack (Maeresa 2006)	1.40
Local brand	NA
Tax	
Tax as a proportion of cigarette price	NA
Total tax base derived from growing, marketing, and selling tobacco, percent (Jaffe 2003)	23
Cigarette excise taxes as percentage of total excise taxes (Clarke 2006)	60
Tobacco export levy as percentage of total export levy (Clarke 2006)	92
Total tobacco tax as percentage of total tax (Clarke 2006)	8
World Health Organization Framework Convention on Tobacco Control	
Signed	No
Ratified	No

NA = not applicable
Source: Mackay and Eriksen 2006.

While smokers may be unfamiliar with the people who cultivated the tobacco in their cigarettes, consumers are increasingly aware of the health effects of smoking. Tobacco is the most common preventable cause of death worldwide and kills nearly 5 million people each year (Campaign for Tobacco Free Kids 2007). Tobacco farmers and their trade unions in Malawi and other developing countries grow a toxic crop with few allies to help them increase labor rights or make tobacco an economically sustainable crop (Clay 2004). Farmworkers and union organizers with the Tobacco Tenants and Allied Workers Union of Malawi (TOTAWUM), the national union of tobacco farm workers, are inextricably tied to tobacco industry corporate social responsibility programs and campaigns to reduce global tobacco use.

Fieldwork in Malawi

I conducted nineteen months of fieldwork in seven visits to Malawi in the years 1995–2006. The research visits were part of my work as a graduate student at the Institute for Social Studies in The Netherlands (1994–1995), as a doctoral student in anthropology at the University of California at Irvine (1996–2004), and as a postdoctoral researcher in public health at the University of California at San Francisco (2004–2008). Firsthand experience with the social inequity, economic poverty, and political uncertainty in Nigeria, where I earned a master's degree in political science from the University of Ibadan (1991–1992), prepared me for fieldwork in Malawi.

Prior to my extended field research in Malawi (January–September 2000), I worked part-time as a paid labor organizer with the union of academic student employees (teaching assistants, associates, readers, and tutors), an affiliate of the International Union, United Automobile, Aerospace and Agricultural Implement Workers of America (better known as the United Auto Workers [UAW]), Local 2865, at the University of California at Irvine (see Richardson, this volume). The UAW represents a large and growing number of technical, office, and professional workers in manufacturing companies and universities. The position (1997–1999) gave me exposure to different perspectives on union membership, strategies for campaign support at both worker and state legislature levels, and skills gained from negotiating a contract with university authorities that covered 10,000 academic student employees in the University of California. This background made it relatively easy for me to develop trust among Malawian labor organizers and to obtain permission to accompany them to tobacco farms in remote areas of Malawi to interview farmworkers.

In Malawi I asked labor organizers about their views on corporate social responsibility, labor relations on tobacco farms, and child labor, as well as their perspectives on issues specific to their role within Malawi's tobacco sector and policies related to tobacco control. During interviews with tobacco farmworkers I asked their perspectives on the influence of child labor on children's health, education, and futures and on strategies to address the child labor problem within the tobacco sector. Conversations with workers also focused on wages, benefits, grievance procedures, debts to landlords, gender division of labor, occupational health, job history, future plans, union membership, ethnic affiliation, and religious affiliation.

In interviews with officials in the tobacco industry, government, and the donor community, I learned officials' perspectives on corporate social responsibility, child labor, and the health implications of tobacco production in Malawi. I also interviewed representatives in the three key groups funded by tobacco companies to eliminate child labor: the Eliminate Child Labor in Tobacco Growing Foundation (ECLT), Together Ensuring Children's Security, and the Association for the Elimination of Child Labor (AECL). We discussed the roles of officials in these groups involving child labor–free activities, funding sources, and social, economic, and political obstacles to resolving the child labor problem in Malawi.

I cross-checked statements from industry officials, tobacco workers, and other research participants with similar statements from the same individuals and others over time as well as with newspaper stories, published and unpublished reports, archival material, scholarly literature, and corporate literature such as tobacco industry Web sites and international tobacco industry documents. After interviews, I followed up statements and accounts that were central to the research with discussions with key individuals involved in child labor activities or the tobacco sector generally.

The study of trade unions and labor struggles took me to tobacco farms where organizers recruited new members and conducted union meetings, hotel conference rooms where organizers attended training workshops funded by foreign donors, head offices of the Malawi Congress of Trade Unions (MCTU), and to Lilongwe and Blantyre where leaders of the national trade union organization representing nineteen trade unions devised organizing strategies. By accompanying organizers in their routine activities, I witnessed firsthand the day-to-day victories and pressures organizers face in a resource-poor country economically dependent on tobacco cultivation.

From Plant to Cigarette: The Tobacco Commodity Chain

The raw tobacco commodity chain involves multiple steps from tobacco farms to leaf-processing factories in Malawi to cigarette manufacturing plants in the United States and other countries. Independent growers, tenant farmers, and large-scale farmers cultivate tobacco in Malawi. Only licensed farmers can sell raw tobacco at auction. These farmers deliver tobacco from farms to satellite depots in rural areas where the tobacco is stored until the auction authorizes the depots to deliver the tobacco to auction.

The Tobacco Act and other regulations require that tobacco cultivated in and exported from Malawi be sold at auction (Jaffe 2003). Auction

Holdings Limited is a private government-regulated monopoly that has the only license to operate tobacco auction floors in Malawi (Maleta 2004). The Malawi government issued licenses to Limbe Leaf and Alliance One (formerly Dimon and Stancom), a subsidiary of U.S.-based Alliance One International, to buy raw tobacco at auction. These two companies purchase over 90 percent of Malawi's tobacco at three government-run auction floors: Lilongwe, Mzuzu, and Blantyre-Limbe (Food and Agriculture Organization of the United Nations 2003; Matthews and Wilshaw 1992).

Philip Morris and British American Tobacco (BAT) purchase most of Malawi's tobacco from Limbe Leaf and Alliance One. Philip Morris is the top purchaser of Malawi's tobacco, which accounts for 20 percent of the company's burley tobacco supply (Elshof 1998; Opukah 1999; Philip Morris 1999). No corresponding figure is available for BAT, the second largest purchaser of Malawi's tobacco (Elshof 1998), but *The Guardian* newspaper (UK) has reported that Malawi "provides most of the tobacco for Britain's cigarettes" (Vidal 2005).

After auction, tobacco is delivered to Limbe Leaf's and Alliance One's processing factories adjacent to the auction site where threshing machines remove and turn the raw leaf into unmanufactured tobacco. Leaf companies then load the tobacco into shipping containers. Containers of tobacco travel by rail or trucks to ports in Beira, Mozambique, and Durban, South Africa, where they are loaded onto ocean-going ships. Because Malawi is surrounded by Zambia, Mozambique, and Tanzania and is landlocked, its tobacco industry has high transportation costs (Mbekeani 2005). Philip Morris and BAT use the leaf in Marlboro and Camel cigarettes after it arrives in the United States, Europe, or one of over fifty other countries (Otañez 2004; Otañez and Walker 2002). In 2007, Philip Morris posted cigarette revenues of $73.6 billion U.S., and BAT posted cigarette revenues of $48.8 billion U.S. (Table 9.2).

Workers and Their Union

Recognizing the economic disenfranchisement of tobacco farmworkers within the global tobacco industry, farmworkers established TOTAWUM in 1992. TOTAWUM is a member of the MCTU. In August 2008 TOTAWUM had 19,816 members in 245 branches in twenty districts in Malawi. The union is an affiliate of the Switzerland-based International Union of Food, Agricultural, Hotel, Restaurant, Catering, Tobacco, and

Table 9.2. Statistics on Cigarette Manufacturers and Leaf-Buying Companies, 2007

Cigarette Manufacturers	*Revenues (U.S.$ billion)*	*Number of Markets*	*Number of Factories*	*Share of Global Cigarette Market (%)*
Philip Morris	18.5 (domestic)			
	55.1 (international)	160+	50+	18.7
British American Tobacco	48,881	180+	81+	17.1
Japan Tobacco (2008)	31.1 (domestic)			
	9.1 (international)	120+	40+	10.5
Leaf-Buying Companies				
Universal Corporation (2008)	2,145	90+	40+	NA
Alliance One International (2008)	2,011	90+	50+	NA

+, Over; NA = not applicable

Sources: Alliance One International 2008; Altria 2008; British American Tobacco 2008; Japan Tobacco Inc. 2008; Universal Corporation 2008.

Allied Workers' Association (IUF). TOTAWUM has received financial support from Trócaire, a faith-based organization in Ireland; the Norwegian trade union movement; and other global trade unions. Very few members of TOTAWUM can afford or are willing to pay a total of $1.00 U.S. for union entrance fees and annual membership dues.

Malawi has the highest incidence of child labor in southern Africa (Torres 2000), most of which is involved in growing tobacco (Phiri 2004). Since British colonial times, the nation's tobacco industry has relied heavily on different forms of child labor (Chirwa 1993; Nankumba 1990). The majority of children living on tobacco estates have been engaged in part-time or full-time adult work (United Nations Children's Fund 1993). Research has revealed that 45 percent of child workers are ages ten to fourteen and 55 percent are between seven and nine years old. The actual number of children working in Malawi's tobacco sector—78,000—is much higher because the number of child workers there and in other developing economies is commonly underestimated by researchers and the government (Otañez et al. 2006; Torres 2000; World Bank 1995).

Tobacco farmers, tenants, and workers are stuck in a cycle of poverty and indebtedness to landlords. Independent smallholders and tenant farmers cultivate most of the tobacco on 1.25- to 2.5-acre landholdings. Non-Malawians own only a handful of farms, primarily large-scale ones of over 400 acres.

Malawian landlords typically live in urban areas. They hire managers and clerks, often family members, to manage the farms; they themselves visit the farms only periodically during each growing season. Tenants agree to produce tobacco on one acre of the farm and sell it to the landlord. Landlords provide inputs such as seeds, fertilizer, and food and deduct their costs from the tenants' earnings at the end of the growing season. Landlords prefer married tenants with children to ensure enough labor to grow a sufficient amount of tobacco on the allotted land. Many tenants and their family members end up with little or no money at the end of the season because of the landlords' practices. Many landlords overcharge tenants for inputs, rig scales to reduce the weight of tobacco, and pay tobacco prices below what they receive from the tobacco auctions. Tenants in debt to landlords often work additional seasons under the same terms to pay them off.

Many tenants put their children to work in fields instead of sending them to school because they cannot afford clothing and other basic necessities for their children (Otañez 2004; Torres 2000). In 2005 the Center for Social Concern, a Catholic Church–based nongovernmental organization in Malawi, reported that "children spend all their time with the parents helping with tobacco production." Additionally:

> The children are heavily involved in potentially hazardous tasks such as clearing fields, making nursery beds, and watering nurseries; uprooting, transporting and transplanting tobacco seedlings and weeding during the second phase; picking, transporting, tying the leaf, picking the dried tobacco and bundling during the last phase. Some other tasks include child minding, fetching water and firewood. Boys are mostly involved in agricultural related activities while the girls are much [more] into domestic work. (Center for Social Concern 2005:29)

One tenant stated that when her family's landlord discovered her plan to send her children to school instead of to the fields, he threatened to expel them from the farm. Beginning in 1999, when the number of foreign researchers and journalists investigating child labor on tobacco farms in Malawi increased, farm landlords and managers pressured the tobacco families on their farms to conceal their children when visitors came and to inform visitors that any children seen on the farm were eighteen or older.

In Malawi, primary schools are free, but families are unable to send their children to school if they are not within walking distance, as is the case in many tobacco-growing areas (Otañez 2004; Torres 2000). A shortage of teachers also prevents children from attending school (Otañez 2004;

Torres 2000). Each year, HIV/AIDS kills 40 percent of Malawi's teachers (Cammack 2004). Many orphans are being raised by their grandparents, who are unable to provide them with adequate food, clothing, and other basic needs (Center for Social Concern 2006).

Union organizers with TOTAWUM and leaders within the Catholic Church in Malawi recognized child labor and the tenancy system as major problems and, in response, helped create a draft Tenant Bill in 1994 (Center for Social Concern 2006; Greene 1997). The bill would "provide for the regulation of tenancy labour by clarifying the rights and obligations of landlords and tenants with a view to avoid exploitative situations" (Nyirenda 2005:5). Michael Mwasikakata, a representative of the United Nations International Labor Organization (ILO) in Malawi, said the ILO and key stakeholders in Malawi, including the Ministry of Justice, discussed the bill in the summer of 2005 (letter to the author, July 26, 2005). As of October 2009, the bill is in the hands of the Ministry of Justice, which will prepare a draft to send to the Office of the President and the Cabinet for further analysis.

It is doubtful that this process will lead to any enacted law because after the bill was tabled in Parliament and sent to the Ministry of Justice in 1999, the Ministry of Justice held up progress on its passage by doing nothing with it until 2004 (Otañez 2004). In 2003, trade union leaders who were frustrated by the delay asked the Ministry of Justice about the bill's status. The Ministry replied that it had lost the bill. Passage appears to have been delayed indefinitely because several members of Malawi's Parliament and other government officials are tobacco farm landlords (Davies 2003; Shorter 2002).

In 1999, pressure from workers and international groups forced the government of Malawi to publicly recognize for the first time the extremely poor living and working conditions within the tobacco industry. TOTAWUM was a leading force in the movement to publicize the use of extensive child labor and bonded labor in tobacco-growing areas. It continues to push for written labor contracts, higher wages for tobacco workers, and passage of the Tobacco Bill. TOTAWUM's financial and organizational weaknesses played a large part in its decision to partner with global tobacco companies to develop child labor projects in Malawi.

Corporate-Union Relations and Child Labor

In 2000, BAT launched the ECLT, a nongovernmental organization in Geneva, Switzerland, to reduce child labor through projects that included planting trees, building schools, and improving skills such as bookkeeping among tobacco farmers in Malawi. BAT created the scheme to deflect public and media attention away from abusive labor conditions on tobacco farms in Malawi instead of paying better prices for tobacco (Otañez et al. 2006).

In 2001, the Tobacco Association of Malawi (TAMA)—a commercial organization representing farmers responsible for 85 percent of the tobacco cultivated in Malawi (Tobacco Association of Malawi 2007)—established the AECL, the country's first child labor group (BBC World Service 2002). Albert Kamulaga, TAMA's president, said his organization initiated the child labor project "to sensitize local people [to] the evils of child labor" (Kamulaga interview with the author, February 27, 2003). With the appearance of a broadly based social movement such as Sandi Smith-Nonini describes in her chapter in this book or at least a regional group such as Christian Zlolniski describes in his chapter, the AECL board members included representatives from TAMA, TOTAWUM, and traditional chiefs. But they also included members from government ministries, Limbe Leaf, Alliance One, and Save the Children, a nongovernmental organization based in Malawi. Philip Morris, Universal Corporation, Alliance One International, the ILO, and the IUF became members of the ECLT beginning in 2002. In 2002, when BAT and other tobacco companies launched the ECLT in Malawi, the ECLT took control of the AECL (Eliminating Child Labour in Tobacco Growing Foundation 2003). The ECLT takeover of the Association for the Elimination of Child Labor was part of the tobacco industry's effort to increase its control of project funding and decision-making and to consolidate projects funded by leaf companies and cigarette manufacturers.

When tobacco companies, through the ECLT, assumed control of the AECL, companies began to work through TOTAWUM to administer child labor activities. TOTAWUM leaders actively reported child labor in Malawi's tobacco industry at meetings of the ILO in Switzerland and at other global meetings on child labor in Malawi in the late 1990s. Representatives of TOTAWUM and TAMA also participated in the BAT-sponsored child labor conference in Kenya in 2000 at which BAT announced the creation of the ECLT. Nkhotakota District in Malawi, the site of TOTAWUM's headquarters, was the location for ECLT's pilot project under the AECL.

The partnership between TOTAWUM and TAMA within the Association for the Elimination of Child Labor contrasted sharply with the adversarial relations between the two groups prior to the partnership. Since TOTAWUM had registered with the Malawi government as a trade union in 1997, TOTAWUM tried to begin negotiations for a labor contract with TAMA. In 1999 the two groups signed a Memorandum of Understanding to institute collective bargaining, but between 2000 and 2007 TAMA refused TOTAWUM's multiple requests to begin the negotiation process. Revealing TAMA's disregard for its agreement with the union, in 2003 TAMA's Kamulaga said "there is no union" of tobacco workers in Malawi (Kamulaga interview with the author, February 27, 2003). TOTAWUM thus has little or no option except to participate in partnerships with TAMA as well as tobacco companies in hopes of securing a better future for tobacco farmworkers or, at the very least, to access financial resources otherwise unavailable to TOTAWUM leaders.

Through the ECLT, the tobacco companies hired Gibson (a pseudonym), a TOTAWUM organizer and one of my main fieldwork collaborators since 1997, to manage its child labor project. In discussing the mutual dependency between tobacco companies and TOTAWUM, Gibson stated in 2003 that TOTAWUM and union members had received a new primary school, money for administrative costs, and wider public recognition of tobacco workers' struggles through participation in the industry-funded project to end child labor in Malawi (Gibson interview with the author, February 22, 2003).

Such material and financial benefits were valuable in a union campaign that continually battled economic insecurity and neglect by state authorities. In return, the tobacco industry, through its sponsorship of a school construction initiative, has used its relationship with the union and tobacco workers to make claims that it contributes to local economies and generates employment and to threaten that effective tobacco control policies advocated by the World Health Organization (WHO) and other public health groups would reduce domestic demand and threaten farmers' livelihood and government revenue. TOTAWUM organizers who have been able to obtain enforceable labor contracts maintain a tenuous balance among the competing agendas of the tobacco companies, TAMA, and the union in implementing tobacco industry corporate social responsibility projects involving child labor.

Eliminating Child Labor?

At most, a few thousand of the 78,000 children engaged in child labor in Malawi have been affected positively by tobacco industry corporate social responsibility projects, and the overall impact on the number of child laborers in the country has been negligible (Mwasikakata 2003; Otañez 2004). By contrast, in its 2003–2004 annual report (Eliminating Child Labour in Tobacco Growing Foundation 2005:3), the ECLT elaborated the achievements of its Association for the Elimination of Child Labor:

> The school was completed in September 2003 and started to operate in January 2004 after being handed over to the Department of Education [in Malawi]. 328 children were enrolled: 61 percent of them were former child labourers. Teachers' houses, a borehole and latrines were also built. A parent-teacher association was set up; child labour and school committees were formed to consolidate and ensure a long-term impact of the project, beyond its completion.

By associating themselves with child labor achievements, tobacco companies seek to improve their reputations and create distance between child labor and the wealth created through the use of that labor in tobacco growing.

By December 2004, these impacts had been achieved through Together Ensuring Children's Security, ECLT's second group instituted to combat child labor:

- Ngala primary schools (Dowa district): children's enrolment rate was up 45% (630 additional children); dropout and repeat rates were down 33%
- Ngala primary schools (Dowa district): children's enrolment rate was up 45% (630 additional children); dropout and repeat rates were down 33%
- Dwanga primary schools (Kasungu district): children's enrolment rate was up 9% (160 additional children); dropout and repeat rates were down 33% and 30% respectively
- 3 primary schools were rehabilitated; 4 new classrooms were built
- 480 treadle pumps were installed (vs. 150 in the original 4-year project) which provided irrigation to 69 ha. (vs. an initial target of 18). Farmers who benefited from this programme generated an average of USD 350 resulting from the sale of green maize and vegetables. The overall food security situation of the communities thus improved dramatically
- The provision of safe water through the project's shallow wells reduced the incidence of waterborne diseases and death: cholera cases were down 97%
- As a positive and unexpected result of the mobilization campaign, the communities developed their own initiative—outside of the project

> framework—and built kindergartens and one additional primary school. (Eliminating Child Labour in Tobacco Growing Foundation 2005:3)

Since 2001, the model of child labor–free projects developed in Malawi has also been applied to programs in Tanzania, Zambia, Uganda, the Philippines, and Kyrgyzstan and been considered for development in Fiji, Indonesia, and the Dominican Republic (Puckett 2003). In 2005 the ECLT was developing additional programs in Mozambique and Mexico (Eliminating Child Labour in Tobacco Growing Foundation 2005). The content of these programs is similar, involving school construction and rehabilitation projects, reforestation schemes, workshops and training to educate villagers and farmers about child labor, and clean water projects involving shallow boreholes and treadle pumps.

The contradiction between what the tobacco industry says and what it does is evidence that tobacco companies use the ECLT for public relations purposes. ECLT funding of two different, competing child labor groups in Malawi—the Association for the Elimination of Child Labor and Together Ensuring Children's Security—is an example of companies managing partnerships to minimize actual changes in the country's child labor situation. The AECL received $200,000 U.S. for child labor projects from the ECLT in 2003–2004 (Eliminating Child Labour in Tobacco Growing Foundation 2004).

In 2002 Limbe Leaf withdrew its membership in the AECL (Otañez 2004) and, with other processing companies, created Together Ensuring Children's Security, which received $2.1 million from the ECLT (Eliminating Child Labour in Tobacco Growing Foundation 2002). Officials of the leaf-processing companies that operated Together Ensuring Children's Security did not include representatives from TAMA and TOTAWUM and did not contact or consult with union leaders regarding the creation of the group (Otañez 2004). An executive member of TOTAWUM said officials of Together Ensuring Children's Security are "bluffing" about their concern for reducing the amount of child labor and that they have "no constituency" at the farm level (interview with the author, February 22, 2003). Together Ensuring Children's Security is focused more on protecting tobacco companies from negative publicity about their use of child labor than on improving the substandard wages that give rise to child labor in the first place.

An Impossible Situation

TOTAWUM organizers are concerned about global discussions involving the WHO's Framework Convention on Tobacco Control (FCTC). The convention seeks to reduce the global demand for tobacco products and curb tobacco-related mortality through both demand interventions such as marketing, health warnings, and cigarette taxes and supply interventions such as smuggling and tobacco cultivation (World Health Organization 2006a). On May 21, 2003, members of the World Health Assembly (WHA) unanimously adopted the FCTC. On February 27, 2005, the FCTC was enacted after 40 WHA members ratified the convention. As of October 2009, 167 countries had ratified the FCTC. Philip Morris, BAT, and other cigarette manufactures feared the convention would weaken cigarette sales and profits and lobbied government officials and health policy-makers in Malawi, other developing countries, and developed countries to weaken the FCTC (Mamudu and Glantz 2009).

Gibson participated in meetings with officials at Limbe Leaf, Alliance One, and Malawi government ministries to formulate Malawi's position against the FCTC. In August 2000, when the tobacco industry was using Malawi and other tobacco farming countries to lobby for a weak WHO treaty in talks leading up to the writing of the convention in Geneva, Switzerland, Gibson spoke to me about his concerns over the FCTC and global tobacco control policies generally. According to Gibson, the FCTC would threaten job losses and reduced earnings for tobacco farmers. Gibson's view is that relatively wealthy countries that grow tobacco, such as the United States, Brazil, and India, should stop doing so and leave tobacco growing for Malawi. Gibson and TOTAWUM are not opposed to the FCTC. Gibson recognizes Malawi's problems with improving the conditions of work on tobacco farms, protecting farmers from job losses related to the global decrease in tobacco demand, and encouraging the search for resources to assist tobacco farmers who have no other option but to grow tobacco. Gibson stated:

> Yes, this anti-smoking lobby [in support of the WHO treaty] could be there, the convention could be signed, but the government and those who are interested [in seeing] that tobacco [continues to be grown here] should at least find a way to support these workers in the estates. . . . We know at this time that these workers are being mistreated, they are being exploited on these estates, but they get something from these landlords from the beginning [of the growing season] because they agree

> on loans—to take some things on loan on an estate, but at the end [of the season] even though they are being cheated they [get food] from September [when nursery beds for tobacco seedlings are prepared] to May or June [when tobacco harvesting ends in Malawi]. Even though landlords don't take good care of farmworkers, they do something. [Malawians] are growing tobacco not for the sake of liking to grow tobacco; they don't have other means. (Gibson interview with the author, August 6, 2000)

Gibson's view that farmers have no options except to grow tobacco shows the precarious position of both tobacco farmers and TOTAWUM organizers. In addition to problems of chronic poverty for many tobacco families and reliance on foreign donors to fund TOTAWUM, tobacco families and union organizers lack crop substitutes and alternative livelihoods. Since the 1960s, the Malawi government has tried unsuccessfully to implement crop diversification schemes to reduce the country's economic reliance on tobacco (Food and Agriculture Organization of the United Nations 2003).

In addition to TOTAWUM, TAMA has participated in lobbying for a treaty that would not harm tobacco farming in Malawi. Kamulaga, TAMA's president, advised the Malawi government and other tobacco-growing countries during negotiations for the FCTC to refuse to sign the convention. According to Kamulaga, "Malawi should not ratify that convention because we depend on tobacco. If we sign it what message will we be sending to the buyers? . . . Ratifying the treaty will mean banning advertisements and smoking in all public places[,] among several issues that have been highlighted in the FCTC" (newswire article from *Xinhau News* 2000). Kamulaga later explained to me that TAMA's main concern regarding the FCTC is that Malawians

> have no alternative to tobacco at the moment and if we are given financial assistance to diversify . . . until we find an alternative to tobacco we will comply fully [with the FCTC]. But at the moment we can't. We are happy to see that it is left up to countries. [The World Health Organization] is not a world body now ruling for everybody. [Treaty adoption] would [vary] from country to country. The countries that want to adopt that ban can adopt it, those who can't can take their own law. We are happier that way. And I believe some countries have rejected [the treaty] because they feel that smoking is a human right.
>
> If someone wants to smoke you can't stop him. You can sensitize him but it is up to him to make a choice. So, a breach of human rights

> should be avoided so people are left free to decide what they want. You can sensitize them but not ban it outright. That way we can go along with [the FCTC]. [The WHO] wanted to force countries to adopt certain restrictive measures. But now it depends from country to country. Whichever country wants to adopt those restrictive measures they can adopt it. Those that feel they can't are not forced to do it. (Kamulaga interview with the author, March 10, 2003)

TAMA's position on the FCTC is little different from TOTAWUM's position. However, Gibson suggested that TOTAWUM and tobacco farmworkers felt betrayed by TAMA for partnering with the union on tobacco industry–funded child labor activities while TAMA, Limbe Leaf, and Alliance One used TOTAWUM to argue that the WHO treaty will destroy jobs and hurt tobacco workers in Malawi. Tobacco companies took up Gibson's concern about the livelihoods of tobacco farmworkers in negotiations with members of the World Health Assembly over the drafting of the FCTC beginning in October 2000. Tobacco companies used the livelihoods of tobacco farmers and potential threats to them posed by the FCTC to lobby Malawi officials to argue for a treaty that was weak from the standpoint of tobacco industry interests in Malawi and other tobacco-farming countries (Otañez et al. 2006; World Health Organization 2000).

Conclusion

As the only substantial organization in Malawi asserting the rights of tobacco workers, TOTAWUM remains stuck in a tobacco commodity trap. Tobacco workers produce a product that harms human health. Tobacco companies use tobacco workers and their trade union in public relations campaigns to counter criticism of the tobacco industry's reliance on child labor, and tobacco control campaigners prioritize public health at the expense of tobacco labor issues. These apparently unresolvable problems for union organizers in Malawi impede the rights of tobacco farmworkers as tobacco companies' reputations grow and health policy-makers' victories spread.

References Cited

Alliance One International

2008 2008 Annual Report. http://media.corporate-ir.net/media_files/IROL/96/96341/Reports/AOI2008AR.pdf, accessed August 18, 2008.

Altria

2008 2007 Annual Report. ww.altria.com/download/pdf/investors_AltriaGroupInc_2007_AnnualRpt.pdf, accessed August 17, 2008.

BBC World Service

2002 Malawi: Non-smokers Hooked on Tobacco. www.bbc.co.uk/worldservice/sci_tech/features/health/tobaccotrial/malawi.htm, accessed August 5, 2005.

British American Tobacco

2008 Annual Reports and Accounts 2007. http://www.bat.com/group/sites/uk__3mnfen.nsf/vwPagesWebLive/DO52AK34/$FILE/medMD-7D9KKN.pdf?openelement, accessed August 17, 2008.

Cammack, D.

2004 Poorly Performing Countries: Malawi, 1980–2002. www.odi.org.uk/pppg/activities/concepts_analysis/poorperformers/BackgroundPaper3-Malawi.pdf, accessed February 23, 2006.

Campaign for Tobacco Free Kids

2007 Campaign for Tobacco Free Kids. http://tobaccofreekids.org, accessed March 25, 2007.

Center for Social Concern

2005 Working and Living Conditions of Tobacco Tenants. *The Lamp* [Malawi] (May-June): 23.

Chirwa, W.

1993 Child and Youth Labour on the Nyasaland Plantations, 1890–1953. *Journal of Southern African Studies* 19(4): 662–680.

Clarke, J.

2006 Country Study: Malawi. www.wti.org/conf/documents/Clarketobaccoin-Malawi.doc, accessed March 3, 2006.

Clay, J.

2004 *World Agriculture and the Environment: A Commodity-by-Commodity Guide to the Impacts and Practices.* Washington, DC: Island Press.

Davies, P.

2003 Malawi: Addicted to the Leaf. *Tobacco Control* 12(1): 91–93.

Eliminating Child Labour in Tobacco Growing Foundation

2002 ECLT Foundation Program in Malawi with "Together Ensuring Children's Security" (TECS) 2002–2006. www.eclt.org/filestore/TECSProgramme.pdf, accessed March 21, 2007.

2003 Annual Report 2001 and 2002. www.eclt.org/filestore/ECLTAnnualReport.pdf, accessed November 22, 2004.

2004 ECLT brochure. www.eclt.org, accessed August 12, 2004.

2005 Annual Report 2003–2004. www.eclt.org/filestore/Annual%20report%202003–2004.pdf, accessed May 1, 2006.

Elshof, P.
1998 Malawi Tobacco and Child Labour: The Involvement of Tobacco Companies. October 13, British American Tobacco. http://bat.library.ucsf.edu//tid/tzt63a99, accessed September 14, 2006.

Food and Agriculture Organization of the United Nations
2003 Issues in the Global Tobacco Economy: Selected Case Studies. ftp://ftp.fao.org/docrep/fao/006/y4997E/y4997e01.pdf, accessed January 3, 2007.

Geist, H. J.
1999 Global Assessment of Deforestation Related to Tobacco Farming. *Tobacco Control* 8(1): 18–28.

Greene, J.
1997 Tobacco Tenants: Justice and Peace. www.thewhitefathers.org.uk/336ml.pdf, accessed January 26, 2006.

International Monetary Fund
2007 Malawi: Poverty Reduction Strategy Paper—Growth and Development Strategy. www.imf.org/external/pubs/ft/scr/2007/cr0755.pdf, accessed March 1, 2007.

Jaffe, S.
2003 Malawi's Tobacco Sector: Standing on One Strong Leg Is Better Than on None. www.worldbank.org/afr/wps/wp55.pdf, accessed January 25, 2006.

Japan Tobacco Inc.
2008 Annual Report 2008. www.jti.co.jp/JTI_E/IR/08/annual2008/annual2008_E_all.pdf, accessed August 17, 2008.

Joint United Nations Programme on HIV/AIDS
2006 2006 Report on the Global AIDS Epidemic. www.unaids.org/en/HIV_data/2006GlobalReport/default.asp, accessed September 5, 2006.

Mackay, J., and M. Eriksen
2006 The Tobacco Atlas, 2nd ed. http://62.193.232.43:8080/statmap, accessed March 14, 2007.

Maeresa, A.
2006 Fate of Country's Tobacco Farmers Goes under the Hammer. www.panos.org.uk/global/featuredetails.asp?featureid=1257&ID=1023, accessed February 13, 2007.

Magalasi, C.
2006 Little to Celebrate as IMF, World Bank Clock 60. *Business Evolution* [Malawi]: 17.

Maleta, M.
2004 Malawi Tobacco Sector Performance Audit. http://lnweb18.worldbank.org/ESSD/sdvext.nsf/81ByDocName/MalawiTobaccoReformInstitutionalAssessmentNov2004/$FILE/MW+Tobacco+Study+-+institutional+component+-+121404.pdf, accessed September 21, 2006.

Mamudu, H., and S. Glantz
2009 Civil Society and the Negotiations of the Framework Convention on Tobacco Control (FCTC). *Global Public Health* 4(2): 150–168.

Matthews, A., and C. Wilshaw
1992 *Fodya: The Tobacco Handbook.* Blantyre: Central Africana Limited.

Mbekeani, K.
2005 Malawi: Studies on Past Industrial Trade Reforms; Experience and Economic Implications. In *Coping with Trade Reforms: A Developing Country Perspective on the WTO Industrial Tariff Negotiations,* ed. S. de Cordoba and S. Laird, pp. 158–170. New York: United Nations Conference on Trade and Development.

Mwasikakata, M.
2003 Tobacco: An Economic Lifeline? The Case of Tobacco Farming in the Kasungu Agricultural Development Division, Malawi. www-ilo-mirror.cornell.edu/public/english/dialogue/sector/papers/tobacco/wp184.pdf, accessed January 22, 2003.

Nankumba, J. S.
1990 *A Case Study of Tenancy Arrangements on Private Burley Tobacco Estates in Malawi.* Report no. 4. Zomba: University of Malawi.

Nyirenda, K.
2005 Tenancy Labor Bill [draft]. Lilongwe.

Opukah, S.
1999 Unofficial Minutes—CECCM Board Mfg & Argumentation Group 3rd June Brussels. June 7, British American Tobacco. http://bat.library.ucsf.edu//tid/bzw92a99, accessed March 26, 2007.

Otañez, M.
2004 "Thank You for Smoking": Corporate Power and Tobacco Worker Struggles in Malawi. PhD dissertation, University of California, Irvine.

Otañez, M., M. E. Muggli, R. D. Hurt, and S. A. Glantz
2006 Eliminating Child Labour in Malawi: A British American Tobacco Corporate Responsibility Project to Sidestep Tobacco Labour Exploitation. *Tobacco Control* 15(3): 224–230.

Otañez M., and C. Walker, dirs.
2002 Up in Smoke. 26 min. Television Trust for the Environment, London. www.tve.org/lifeonline/index.cfm?aid=1228, accessed January 9, 2007.

Philip Morris.
1999 RE GMT. Philip Morris. http://legacy.library.ucsf.edu/tid/hzx04c00, accessed March 26, 2007.

Phiri, M.
2004 Assessment of the Potential Impact of the Abolition of the Tenancy Labour System in Malawi: International Labor Organization. ILO Report. Lilongwe: Malawi Commercial Agriculture Program.

Puckett, A.
2003 Unacceptable: Supported by the Tobacco Industry, a New Foundation Is Fighting Child Labour in Leaf-Producing Countries. *Tobacco Reporter*: 182–184.

Shorter, D.
2002 Up in Smoke: Tobacco, Health, and Hunger in Africa. www.abc.net.au/science/slab/tobacco/default.htm, accessed August 10, 2006.

Tobacco Association of Malawi
2007 Agricultural Diversification and Crop Alternatives to Tobacco—A Perspective of the Tobacco Association of Malawi. www.who.int/tobacco/framework/cop/events/tobacco_association_malawi.pdf, accessed February 27, 2007.

Torres, L.
2000 The Smoking Business: Tobacco Workers in Malawi. www.fafo.no/pub/rapp/339/339-web.pdf, accessed June 3, 2007.

United Nations Children's Fund
1993 *Situation Analysis of Poverty in Malawi*. Lilongwe: Association with the Government of Malawi.

United Nations Development Program
2008 Human Development Report 2007/2008: Fighting Climate Change: Human Solidarity in a Divided World. http://hdr.undp.org/en/media/HDR_20072008_EN_Complete.pdf, accessed August 17, 2008.

Universal Corporation
2008 Annual Report. http://library.corporate-ir.net/library/89/890/89047/items/298788/2008AnnualReport.pdf, accessed August 17, 2008.

Vidal, J.
2005 How Malawi's Livelihood Went up in Smoke. www.guardian.co.uk/international/story/0,1501416,00.html, accessed August 26, 2006.

World Bank
1995 *Labor and the Growth Crisis in Sub-Saharan Africa.* Washington, DC: World Bank.
2006a Malawi: Country Assistance Evaluation. http://lnweb18.worldbank.org/oed/oeddoclib.nsf/DocUNIDViewForJavaSearch/B82C98258A9044B9852571BE007892E4/$file/malawi_cae.pdf, accessed January 26, 2007.
2006b Malawi: Country Assistance Evaluation. http://lnweb18.worldbank.org/oed/oeddoclib.nsf/DocUNIDViewForJavaSearch/F62810BF345B232B852571BF007240A1/$file/malawi_reach.pdf, accessed October 31, 2006.

World Health Organization
2000 Tobacco Company Strategies to Undermine Tobacco Control Activities. http://repositories.cdlib.org/context/tc/article/1107/type/pdf/viewcontent, accessed January 11, 2007.
2006a WHO Framework Convention on Tobacco Control. www.who.int/tobacco/framework/en/, accessed September 12, 2007.
2006b Working Together for Health: The World Health Report 2006. www.who.int/whr/2006/whr06_en.pdf, accessed March 24, 2007.

Xinhau News
2000 Malawi to Ratify WHO Convention on Tobacco Control. www.eastday.com, accessed October 12, 2006.

TEN

Concluding Thoughts

Karen Brodkin

The chapters in this book offer a valuable repertoire of ground-level portraits of the changing nature of the working class and its discontent, as well as some of the many disconnects between unions and workers in today's era of neo-liberal and global capitalism. But that is not all they do. Some chapters also speak to promising and innovative forms of worker organizing and organization that are coming from some of the lowest-paid, marginalized sectors of the working class. These and less optimistic analyses also suggest arenas of working-class activism that have shown potential for creating working-class social movements. In this conclusion I read both the bad news and the good news in the assembled case studies and link their insights to wider themes in labor and working-class studies. This may serve as a way of thinking about what a specifically anthropological and ethnographic study of labor and working-class activism might contribute to work by other activists and scholars wrestling with the state of the working class in the age of globalization.

Lydia Savage's chapter was not part of the session and thus is not considered in these comments. EPD

Bad News

Tolstoy tells us that "[h]appy families are all alike, but every unhappy family is unhappy in its own way" (Tolstoy, *Anna Karenina*). The varieties of discontent and disconnect chronicled in these case studies and in the editors' Introduction resonate with Tolstoy's sentiment.

The chapters by Marty Otañez and Christian Zlolniski illustrate the uneven impacts of capitalism's neo-liberal globalization and some of the consequences of those impacts. Otañez takes on big tobacco's outsourcing of tobacco growing to Malawi, where an alliance of government, big landowners, and global tobacco has benefited handsomely but the tenant farmer families who grow the tobacco can barely make ends meet. He describes a global public relations campaign against child labor that big tobacco companies orchestrated—largely to block anti-smoking efforts by the World Health Organization—which brought together the Malawi government, landlords, international unions, and nongovernmental organizations. Long-standing efforts by the Malawi tobacco workers' union to improve working conditions and to end the conditions that force their children to work were systematically stymied thanks to many of these same forces. Although the union felt forced to join big tobacco's anti-child labor campaign, it did nothing to improve tenant farmers' livelihoods or end the conditions that make child labor a necessary part of tobacco growing.

Zlolniski describes how the North America Free Trade Agreement (NAFTA) has helped intensify the internationalization of big agribusiness control over the growing of fresh fruits and vegetables. In northern Mexico, this situation has supported the permanent settlement of agricultural workers and waged agricultural work for women, on the one hand. On the other, women's wages are lower than men's had been for agricultural work, an amount insufficient to support their families. This economic reality has forced men to migrate to the United States for work, where they in turn are simultaneously politically stigmatized and economically exploited, as Sandy Smith-Nonini shows in her chapter. Like Otañez, Zlolniski also describes how government policies and practices cripple workers' unionization. In Mexico the particular capital-state nexus operates in the ruling party's control of official unions, so they serve business instead of workers; further, the state regularly takes aggressive action against workers' efforts to build independent unions.

State hostility toward unions combined with International Monetary Fund–backed free-market policies have made it difficult for workers in newly industrializing countries to organize and have weakened even the strongest unions in the West. In the United States, where unions today represent approximately 12 percent of the labor force (perhaps 9 percent of the private sector), down from a high of 35 percent in the early 1950s, simply "servicing" a shrinking and aging membership constitutes institutional suicide. Paul Durrenberger and Suzan Erem found that a union leadership that focuses exclusively on "servicing" may be short-lived as well. The five chapters that focus on workers and unions in the United States do so against this background, in which capital's global reach makes it able to seek out highly exploitable workers anywhere in the world but where capital and government policies deny workers the corresponding freedom (and the means) to seek better pay or working conditions.

Four of these five chapters describe varieties of unhappiness within union families as they struggle to survive in this hostile climate. Ethnographic chapters by Durrenberger and Erem and by Pete Richardson take on structural divides between union leadership and rank-and-file members. Durrenberger and Erem's well-told tale of the pitfalls and potential of ethnography focuses on a union election to indicate lines of fissure, in part along job lines but also between the leadership and membership of a Teamster local. Richardson also looks at the ways leadership in a union local can become separated from rank-and-file interests, but with much greater consequences. He asks why the once strong United Auto Workers (UAW) cannot rebuild the solidarity and collective action that once gave it strength. His answer is that its demise is the result of a long pattern of union response to government and corporate policies designed to break the union softly. From UAW acceptance of a two-tier workforce that gives older workers different wages and benefits than newer ones to buyouts that have transformed individual jobs into private cash payouts, leadership of the union local has colluded with management (in exchange for union leaders gaining control over hiring workers to fill scarce jobs) to dispossess the union of the collective entitlements, union jobs, and benefits that make it a union. As a result, union jobs first became the family property of union leadership and then were sold off as cash buyouts until no collective stake or spirit was left.

Jessica Smith's chapter attributes some of the strong anti-union sentiment among workers in the relatively new Powder River Basin (Wyoming) coalfields to such legacies of business unionism but also to good wages, benefits, and management's recognition of worker skills and independence. Much of that sentiment is also a result of the real convergences between the ways the big oil companies that own these mines construct jobs and the ways workers see themselves. Both convergences evoke idealized images of hardworking, skilled, independent ranchers and cowboys. Miners identify as workers but not as working class. They associate the latter term "with poorer and more exploited workers who needed unions to represent their interests" (Smith, p. 116). Although Smith seems to argue that women miners are accepted by their male colleagues, I read the data as showing that they are tolerated more than accepted as full peers.

Karaleah Reichart's chapter on eastern coal miners also deals with gender differences, here between the class interests of women and men in a mining town. She shows how women of mine worker families created coalitions across both class and local lines that helped male miners gain concessions during the Pittston coal strike—almost in spite of themselves—but also how women sometimes weighed in by withholding financial support, thereby cutting short strikes they saw as contrary to their needs. The focus on women's cross-class coalitions within this one-industry coal town illuminates the fact that working-class issues go beyond the workplace, sometimes dividing and sometimes uniting the women and men of this working-class mining community.

These very different case studies describe varieties of what is ultimately a defensive posture. They show unions as restricting representation or practicing forms of exclusion that convey the notion that some members of the working class are more entitled than others. Teamster officers feel entitled to hold office because they service grievances, but they seem also to exclude feeder drivers from union entitlement, even if the precise ways they do so are not clear. By representing only the workplace and male miners, the United Mine Workers has de facto made men of this working-class mining community more entitled than its women; when working-class gender interests sometimes conflict, the union does not consider women's interests. This results in women acting sometimes for and sometimes against the union. By a slow process of death by a thousand cuts, UAW officer families have acted as if they are the union, that union patrimony is private, alienable, and ultimately nothing more. And Wyoming miners have no union or working class, only independent workers skilled and smart enough—in explicit contrast to the less well-endowed working class—to negotiate successfully with big oil and coal corporations on their own behalf. Such self-constructed distinctions may be understandable as defensive responses to the growing power of global capital, but they mainly reinforce a downward spiral in unionization.

Marx was wrong in believing that a global working class shared fundamental class interests, even if its members did not yet know it. Workers, capitalists, and states have been co-constructing invidious distinctions and ideas of differential worth that have been part of capitalism's organization since its birth. These distinctions are real in the sense that they structure who gets what kinds of job, where and under what circumstances one lives, and therefore the life chances, priorities, and interests of different groups of workers—not unlike the differences and agreements between the women and men of the mining community Reichart describes.

Most contemporary social movements recognize this, and many also recognize that to build coalitions around agreed-upon issues requires negotiating points of conflict as well. But labor unions all too often still tend to act as if socially structured racial, religious, gender, and other differences are "merely" false consciousness. In the history of labor union practice, this belief has resulted in representations of the interests and priorities of some sectors and groups within the labor force, usually white and male, as those of the entire working class and those of other sectors and groups as special interests. This strategy is particularly problematic in today's global economy, when who is at the top of any given working-class pyramid is amenable to local variation and rapid change while the *fact* of occupational segmentation and inequality along lines of citizenship, nation, religion, ethnicity, race, and gender maintains a global working class whose interests and priorities remain variegated and as often in conflict as in concert. (I return to this theme in the last section of this chapter.)

Good News: New Directions in Organizing

Smith-Nonini's and Zlolniski's chapters explore some of the new kinds of worker organizing and the coalitions workers are building in response to capital's global reorganization and repression. Smith-Nonini speaks to a coalition built around social justice for farmworkers. She focuses on a specific event organized by the Farm Labor Organizing Committee (FLOC) in Toledo, Ohio, one of many innovative forms of workers' groups springing up across the United States. FLOC works in coalition with the National Farm Worker Ministry. Social justice is the basis of this coalition among unionists, clergy, and people of faith. It is representative of the bigger social justice visions many other new forms of workers' groups are generating. Smith-Nonini was both participant in and analyst of an anti-union church conference farmworkers attended. Their presence and insistence on speaking deeply unsettled the intended agenda by confronting attendees with workers' claims for social justice on moral grounds, deploying shared concerns to disrupt an adversarial relationship.

Zlolniski directs us to think broadly about the disparate impacts of globalization on workers and the kinds of organizations they may or may not be able to organize in different places. The NAFTA-stimulated rise of export-oriented agribusiness brought stable jobs and new, year-round populations to parts of Northern Mexico, but it also greatly strengthened the power of growers—who are now organized across national lines—and weakened that of the largely indigenous agricultural workers. Zlolniski analyzes workers' ongoing and diverse efforts to organize and the ways the state represses class-based organizing while encouraging ethnic-based and local organizing—in which class issues, in part for reasons of organizational survival, play a minor role. He offers insightful and realistic analyses of the strengths and weaknesses of the different organizational forms workers create. Yet, he also shows that class and ethnic issues within a largely indigenous populace are tightly braided, and he suggests that what is needed are new kinds of unionism that speak to citizenship, work, and political issues and that also organize across borders. One way to read these chapters is that they suggest that deeply felt class issues go far beyond both workplace issues and borders and that when workers' groups foreground the moral and social justice dimensions of their issues, they can garner strong cross-class participation and neutralize some of their opponents' support base.

These principles were borne out on a larger scale in Los Angeles and other cities in the 1990s. In Los Angeles immigrant workers built a grassroots-fueled social movement that garnered widespread support from the middle class and from both traditional and innovative unions within the Los Angeles County AFL-CIO. The movement revitalized labor unions in the city. Starting with Justice for Janitors' creative organizing and success among Mexican and Central American janitors, the largely new immigrant workforce organized most commercial building centers in Los Angeles. Immigrant workers from Mexico organized their own drywallers' union covering virtually all wallboard installation from Los Angeles to San Diego; Latino immigrants also ran a ground-up campaign to organize an auto wheel plant. Immigrant workers in hotels and restaurants backed a massive change in leadership of the Hotel and Restaurant Employees Union (HERE). From a moribund local, HERE has become a major force in organizing hotel workers across California and Nevada and in creating innovative, participatory practices among its membership. The Service Employees Union has undertaken several large, successful campaigns to unionize the largely African American and new immigrant workers in California's largest hospital chains as well as home healthcare workers in Los Angeles County (Milkman 2000; Milkman and Milkman 2004; Waldinger et al. 1997).

Much of the labor movement vitality in Los Angles in the 1990s came from unions that listened to and worked closely with new immigrant workers and in synergy with community groups, including several that created new forms of independent worker organizations; labor unions thus helped create an organizational landscape in which unions were one of several forms of workers' organization. Such innovative worker centers and organizations expanded the envelope of issues considered labor issues. Under new leadership, the Los Angeles County Federation of Labor took the lead in turning around the anti-immigration position of the national AFL-CIO. It challenged both immigration policy and racism, demanded amnesty, and built broad coalitions to put in place city and county living wage ordinances. Cultural citizenship—the sense of being part of a social collectivity with social entitlements by virtue of being a contributing part of multiple societies—underpinned the huge demonstrations for immigrant rights and legalization of undocumented immigrants in 2005 and is one of those ideas that may have a potentially subversive and perhaps a reconstitutive force among the heterogeneously dispossessed and the subordinated. Although Los Angles was a center of labor innovation, this synergy took place in other cities and some rural areas across the United States as well. There is an emerging literature on the new working-class social justice organizations and movements that bring together new immigrants, people of color, and poor working-class whites (Brodkin 2007; Clawson 2003; Lichtenstein 2002; Tait 2005).

Labor historians point out three things this movement shares with the vibrant labor movement of the 1930s that led to the formation and organizing success of the CIO: (1) the CIO was created and led by sectors of the working class that had been largely excluded from unions on the basis of race and ethnicity; (2) it had a clear social justice message and mission that generated widespread support within and beyond the working class; and (3) it created new forms of organization and strategies for organizing. New immigrants—then Southern and Eastern European, Mexican American, and African American workers—were at the heart of these efforts and created the innovative strategies that shifted the labor movement's center of gravity from insular and exclusionary guilds of largely white, male workers to organizing massive numbers of workers in the Fordist industries then at the heart of the American industrial economy. Active anti-racist platforms, political engagement, community-focused issues, coalition building, and grassroots tactics were critical to success then, as they seem to be today (Frank 1985; Lichtenstein 2002).

These parallels have led some analysts, such as Lichtenstein, to argue that unions need to transform themselves into social movement organizations—like labor in the 1930s and the civil rights movement in the 1950s and 1960s—if they are going to survive. They argue that it is difficult to get more than a few people at a time excited about a dollar-an-hour raise. What is needed, and what the new groups and union coalitions led by recent immigrants and workers of color in the lowest-paid jobs are creating, is a bigger vision and an agenda for social justice that brings a wide coalition of people together and that may be able to shift the public view of what a just and democratic social order could look like.

More unions are responding to these new worker movements. Some are rethinking standard operating practices and defensive responses to a hostile political climate. In the United States the Change to Win coalition, a group of unions that left the AFL-CIO, took as its mission the organization of massive numbers of new workers—largely workers of color and recent immigrants—in service industries not represented by unions in the past. Unions are also rethinking what the working class and a working-class movement look like. The movement's traditional constituency of white men in heavy industries had its first public death in the 1980s, with deindustrialization. Women's labor groups such as 9 to 5, a proto-union of office workers, began to point out that the prototypical worker in the U.S. labor force at the time was a female office worker. At the same time, unions began to recognize the importance of public-sector unionization to the labor movement. More recently, as new immigrants from Latin America and Asia have entered the U.S. labor force, unions have begun to see that issues of culture, citizenship, and immigrants' rights are also central working-class issues.

Toward an Anthropology of Progressive Working-Class Activism

As E. P. Thompson demonstrated clearly for the English proletariat in his classic *The Making of the English Working Class*, turning human beings into abstract laborers may have been capital's project, but it surely was not the workers' goal (Thompson 1963). If we were to translate Thompson's historical framework into the ecological anthropology framework the editors of this book evoke in their Introduction, capitalism might be akin to the natural and political environment—the context—within and against which Thompson's nineteenth-century English workers forged a class-based view of the world; its attendant beliefs, values, and vision of justice, truth, and virtue; and ways of organizing social life: in short, a working-class culture. It is not unreasonable to think that political ideas, from revolutionary visions of international socialism to trade unionism, appealed to workers to the extent that they resonated with existing working-class experience, cultural values, and organizational principles. If working-class activism is rooted in working-class cultures, then we need to focus on the connections between culture and political activism—and to remember that unions are but one among many forms of working-class activism.

How should an anthropology of labor and working-class activism think about working-class culture today, as one (national, international) working class with its own culture or as many working classes with many cultures? This is not an academic question because the question of why more working-class unity does not exist is one of the big questions within labor and working-class history. With reason: if the way forward is to build wider, not smaller, alliances, more inclusive coalitions around bigger goals, and social justice visions that go beyond bread-and-butter priorities for specific campaigns, we need to analyze the institutions, beliefs, and values that separate and divide working-class cultures as well as what a working-class social justice agenda that could generate a broad social movement might look like.

In the United States that means giving a central place to analyzing the ways race, gender, and citizenship operate to constitute work, workers, and varieties of working-class cultures and experience. Anthropology can contribute some answers to this big project, but we need to be in conversation with the enormous body of work already done by historians and other scholars. In what follows, I focus on the United States because that is what I know best.

It is no secret that occupational segregation is pervasive and persistent within the U.S. labor market and that people of color and women receive preferential treatment for the worst jobs. Understanding the historical persistence of job segregation and the political and economic policies and practices that have continued to produce it is foundational to understanding the culture-making processes and repertoires available to working-class cultures to make themselves. By the beginning of the twentieth century, the U.S. labor force was marked by broad, regionally specific patterns of occupational and residential segregation based on race and ethnicity. Not-quite-white Southern and Eastern European immigrants produced America's industrial wealth largely in factories of the East and the Midwest.

The labor force of American agribusiness has been as racially segregated as that of industry. In the West and in Hawaii agribusiness grew rapidly, depending on labor forces made up of Asian immigrants as well as resident and in-migrating Mexicans. In the Southeast, the post-Reconstruction white plantocracy continued to hold its African American agricultural labor force in various forms of debt peonage. A new pattern of segregation that has striking similarities with its early–twentieth-century counterpart has developed largely as a result of changes to immigration policies in 1965. New immigrants have become the backbone of the postindustrial growth sectors of the working class—farmworkers and mean processing, personal services, and construction. Since around 1980, Central American and Asian men and women have become concentrated within rapidly growing personal service industries such as hotels and restaurants, healthcare, and cleaning, as well as in the manufacture and processing of food, clothing, and, increasingly, shelter (in the form of nonunion construction). Within these patterns, women's and men's jobs are differently segregated from one another, so that women of color work in far fewer gender-segregated environments than white women do (Brodkin 1998; Glenn 1985; Kessler-Harris 1982).

The United States has a widely understood cultural repertoire of constructing work and ways of talking about jobs and their entitlements in racially and gender coded ways. It is like a history of jazz variations on the distinction between free and servile workers in the colonial period. For example, in the first textile factories, employers and the free, white New England farm daughters who comprised their labor force cooperated in constructing these workers as respectable women. They did so by organizing their work to offer at least a modicum of dignity, in implied or explicit contrast to constructions and treatment of women of color. Venus Green offers one of the most dramatic demonstration of the racial coding of respectability as a specific entitlement of white women. She showed how as the workforce at a telephone company shifted from white to nonwhite women, the jobs and those who held them became redefined as unskilled and unworthy of autonomy and self-supervision. A corporate culture of respect through amenities and chivalrous paternalism shifted to one of intense supervision, speedup, and institutionalized high turnover (Green 1995). When management begins hiring those socially constructed as inferior and reorganizes the work and treatment of workers to reflect those stereotypes, formerly privileged workers find their work and wages deteriorating. Such politically and socially constructed inequalities along race or gender lines give the relatively privileged a real stake in the invidious distinctions they make, to the extent that white women have a history of refusing to work alongside African American women and white men refusing to work with men of color (Kessler-Harris 1982, 1990; Montgomery 1979).

Historical discourses on skilled and unskilled labor are one way gender and racial coding about worker worthiness has been expressed. I have argued elsewhere that the reorganization of U.S. industrial production from that of relatively autonomous skilled craftspeople to intensely supervised and driven assembly lines staffed by "unskilled" labor (regardless of the actual skills workers had or were required to use) came about as new "off-white" immigrants (many of whom had a high level of craft skill) became available to displace older generations of white immigrants. Since then, wages have continued to be lowered and work has continued to be reorganized in degrading ways as new, vulnerable groups seek work and are hired in the industries currently in America's economic core. The new labor force finds itself in turn segregated, stigmatized regarding its ability, and economically exploited (Brodkin 1998, 2000).

In this context, it is worth revisiting the independent cowboy masculinity embraced by Wyoming miners to explain their anti-union sentiment. Smith's description resonated with the sentiments I heard from white male maintenance workers—and statements by anti-union consultants to and about those workers—when I studied efforts to unionize at Duke Medical Center in Durham, North Carolina, in the 1970s (Brodkin and Strathmann 2004; Sacks 1988). We do not know the racial and ethnic makeup of the Wyoming miners. In the Duke case, however, the distinction was overtly racial: white maintenance workers, unlike African American health service workers, saw (and were encouraged to see) themselves as smart enough and good enough not to need a union. Indeed, labor historians have noted that the particular construction of masculinity Smith encountered has a long history as part of the culture by which skilled white male workers have constructed themselves as more entitled than nonwhite and women workers (Montgomery 1979). Alexander Saxton (1990) has suggested that this perspective is at the heart of a particularly working-class form of right-wing ideology, which he terms Herrenvolk (master race) democracy.

Given that gender, race, citizenship, and other politically constructed invidious distinctions divide workers throughout the global economy, the assumption that there is one working class with identical interests (even if we and they do not yet know what they are) is probably not the best assumption on which to build an anthropology of labor and working-class activism. Anthropology's strengths in close-grained study and rethinking the taken-for-granted make it a valuable resource for rethinking approaches to class and culture in a world that has what is arguably a single mode of production and a multiplicity of cultures, all of which are strongly—but very differently—shaped by capitalism. The heterogeneity of the landscape of the world's global political economy underpins enormous diversity in local environments and responses to it, even among the dispossessed who have to sell their labor to live. All of this is bound to real differences and conflicts of interest.

As a working hypothesis, perhaps we should think of the working class as less an already existing class with known shared interests than a potential coalition beginning the process of discovery of its shared interests and negotiations around the issues that divide it. A research agenda with more open assumptions would parallel the openness to new possibilities that seems to be emerging among activists. They are aided by the force fields exerted by global capital on working people across the globe, which bring workers with a variety of political and cultural experiences into proximity with one another. Labor unions and some of the new worker centers and working-class–centered social justice groups springing up across the United States create social spaces for workers to come together away from elite surveillance. From these contacts, new political organizations and ideologies are developing that have at least the potential to deeply trouble their neo-liberal troubles. An anthropology of labor and working-class activism can make a valuable contribution to such efforts by analyzing the promises, potentials, and limitations of these varied approaches.

References Cited

Brodkin, K.
1998 *How Jews Became White Folks and What That Says about Race in America.* New Brunswick, NJ: Rutgers University Press.

2000 Global Capitalism: What's Race Got to Do with It? *American Ethnologist* 27(2): 237–256.

2007 *Making Democracy Matter: Identity and Activism in Los Angeles.* New Brunswick, NJ: Rutgers University Press.

Brodkin, K., and C. Strathmann

2004 The Struggle for Hearts and Minds: Organization, Ideology and Emotion. *Labor Studies* 29(3): 1–25.

Clawson, D.

2003 *The Next Upsurge: Labor and the New Social Movements.* Ithaca: ILR Press.

Frank, D.

1985 Housewives, Socialists, and the Politics of Food: The 1917 Cost of Living Protests. *Feminist Studies* 11 (Summer 1985): 255–285.

Glenn, E. N.

1985 Racial Ethnic Women's Labor. *Review of Radical Political Economics* 17(3): 86–108.

Green, V.

1995 Race and Technology: African American Women in the Bell System, 1945–1980. *Technology and Culture, Supplement to* 36(2): S101–S143.

Kessler-Harris, A.

1982 *Out to Work.* New York: Oxford University Press.

1990 *A Woman's Wage: Historical Meanings and Social Consequences.* Lexington: University Press of Kentucky.

Lichtenstein, N.

2002 *State of the Union: A Century of American Labor.* Princeton: Princeton University Press.

Milkman, R., editor

2000 *Organizing Immigrants: The Challenge for Unions in Contemporary California.* Ithaca: ILR Press.

Milkman, R., and K. V. Milkman, editors

2004 *Rebuilding Labor: Organizing and Organizers in the New Union Movement.* Ithaca: ILR/Cornell University Press.

Montgomery, D.

1979 *Workers' Control in America.* Cambridge: Cambridge University Press.

Sacks, K. B.

1988 *Caring by the Hour.* Urbana: University of Illinois Press.

Saxton, A.

1990 *The Rise and Fall of the White Republic: Class Politics and Mass Culture in Nineteenth Century America.* London: Verso.

Tait, V.
2005 *Poor Workers' Unions: Rebuilding Labor from Below*. Cambridge: South End.

Thompson, E. P.
1963 *The Making of the English Working Class*. New York: Pantheon Books.

Waldinger, R., C. Erickson, R. Milkman, D.J.B. Mitchell, A. Valenzuela, K. Wong, and M. Zeitlin
1997 Justice for Janitors: Organizing in Difficult Times. *Dissent* (Winter): 37–44.

ELEVEN

Afterword

E. Paul Durrenberger and Karaleah Reichart

While the ethnographic studies collected here are not sufficiently broad or inclusive to comprise a comprehensive report on global labor or labor unions in general, there are sufficient similarities to draw some conclusions. All of the contributors recognize the importance of the global context of labor. Sandi Smith-Nonini, Christian Zlolniski, and Marty Otañez show how relations among corporations, national polities, global markets, and national and local organizations affect possibilities for local unions. Lydia Savage and Peter Richardson describe the importance of the export of manufacturing jobs from the United States. All the chapters show the significance of national policies in shaping the environment for unions, from the way unions have been established in Malawi and Mexico to the importance of the Taft-Hartley amendments to the Wagner Act in the United States. Further, they suggest that local cultural differences such as the strength of religious dominations in the southeastern United States, the ideology of individualism in and about the American West, and the history of unions in the coalfields of the southeastern United States may be significant.

Thus the anti-union miners of Wyoming whom Jessica Smith discusses are basically correct when they characterize unions as large, ineffective bureaucracies led by ineffective, self-interested, and self-important leaders. The changes to U.S. law starting in 1947 urged such development, and sociologist C. Wright Mills foresaw it in the middle of the twentieth century. There was little difference in outlook, Mills suggested, between a United Auto Workers member and a white-collar union member. They were both chiefly interested in unions as a means to the individual goal of increasing their remuneration rather than as a "collective means of collective ascent" (1951:309). Little ethnographic evidence suggests any difference today when ethnographic and quantitative work shows that union members see securing wages and benefits as their organizations' most important objectives (Durrenberger and Erem 2005).

Richardson shows how this shift from "collective means to collective ascent" became translated first into practices of treating access to jobs with full benefits as prerogatives of families to pass on as hereditary privileges and finally to individually owned private property the owners could sell to the corporation in return for sufficiently attractive severance packages. This is analogous to the shift from collective fishing rights to private property in Iceland by means of individual transferrable quotas; although the process was longer and move convoluted, it came to the same end.

While Reichart and Smith-Nonini point out explicitly the importance of community outreach, participation, and inclusiveness that characterize social movements, other contributors suggest similar relationships. The Service Employees International Union explicitly modeled its Justice for Janitors drive on these lessons from social movements (Brodkin 2007; Zlolniski 2006). Such approaches move beyond the labor movement into various communities to mobilize people beyond the narrow confines of unions (Brodkin 2007). Zlolniski's chapter in this book, however, points out the dangers of identity politics and the limits of social movements based on ethnicity.

Sometimes this brings union organizers face to face with their own moribund leadership (Erem 2001). Events forced such an activist approach on the International Longshoremen's Association (ILA) Local 1422 in Charleston, South Carolina, when an ambitious state's attorney tried to ride the prosecution of a handful of members for a labor protest into the governor's office. The president of the local knew that if he lost the fight, he would never again be able to mobilize his members to express their solidarity as a union; the potential for losing their jobs on the waterfront would be too intimidating. A parallel civil suit would have ravaged the local's treasury. But his own international was arrayed in opposition to him because of his activism within the union to reduce the influence of the mob in the ILA. To that end he had participated in the organization of the Longshore Workers' Coalition, for which the ILA leadership wanted to punish him (Erem and Durrenberger 2008).

This is a familiar story in the labor movement (Benson 2005). Reformers of a similarly corrupt International Brotherhood of Teamsters met similar resistance and formed the Teamsters for a Democratic Union as a response in the form of a social movement (Parker and Gruelle 1999; Durrenberger and Erem, this volume).

Thus, when Mills (1951:323) suggested that the business of labor unions "may well become the regulation of insurgent tendencies among those groups and strata that might reorganize American society," he was prophetic. In short, even a few years after the Taft-Hartley amendments, he was not sanguine about the labor movement becoming a social movement favoring social justice or even defending working-class interests in class warfare.

Still, such movement-like new approaches are proving successful or at least promising (Brodkin 2007). As we will suggest, it is not appropriate for anthropologists to preach to the labor movement, but a unifying theme and implicit message in all the contributions to this volume is about *solidarity*—among workers, among their families, in their communities, and across international borders. Sometimes, labor can exhibit such solidarity. A shining example is the organization of the International Dockworkers Council in 2000, a group of longshoremen's locals in more than a dozen countries that exercises solidarity with other dockers by organizing horizontally with each other under, rather than through, their own national and international federations of labor (Erem and Durrenberger 2008).

The ethnographic works in this book document other obstacles to solidarity closer to home. They include the paternalism and racism Smith-Nonini documents, the politics of obligation within unions Durrenberger and Erem discuss, the patriarchy and sexism of union leaders Reichart documents, the familism Richardson indicates, and the usual opposition by the capitalist class we see here in the works of Durrenberger and Erem, Otañez, Reichart, Savage, Smith, Smith-Nonini, and Zlolniski—in short, in all ethnographies of labor organizing and acting in the collective interests of a segment of the working class. Zlolniski shows how ethnic identity politics can be turned against the working class to undermine solidarity. Otañez provides stark evidence that movements to "do good" are all too easily co-opted by governments and corporations alike. These are some of the limitations on social movements and identity politics organized around any segment smaller than the entire global working class.

As institutions, labor unions can only arise in industrial states in which production is centralized in a few hands that have privileged class access to the means of production. Labor unions build strength in numbers and combined wills to constitute a counter to the potentially overweening economic power of these industrial elites. That is why they are a threat. But as a worldwide economic meltdown in 2008 suggests, without such a counter-power industrial labor is virtually enserfed, as the Mexican and Malawian studies in this volume illustrate well.

Bill Fletcher Jr. and Fernando Gapasin (2008) have suggested that until and unless U.S. labor can see itself asserting the interests of the working class as opposed to simply representing employees in contract negotiations, there is little likelihood that U.S. unions will be capable of internal, much less national or global, solidarity. The U.S. labor movement, insofar as it can be called a movement as opposed to a crumbling bureaucracy, exhibits a similar tendency. One may be aware of and sympathetic to the impossible organizing tasks facing labor, but when any critical voice is shunned rather than incorporated it seems to be a defensive response rather than a creative one. Criticizing the labor movement is easy sport, and working with it can be difficult, if only because a personalistic and hierarchic leadership seeks to contain dissent as Mills suggested. But this kind of response is one reason the labor movement is a self-defeating set of hierarchic and personalistic bureaucracies rather than a progressive movement.

The organizing task is so immense as to be almost unimaginable. It requires linking low-wage factory workers in Sri Lanka, China, Latin America, Indonesia, and other slave labor emporia with highly paid labor such as the unionized longshoremen of the First World into a group that understands and acts upon its common interests as a class within the global economy.

In short, it requires a rebirth of the vision of organizations such as the International Workers of the World (IWW) and a replacement of the current corrupt and unimaginative leadership with those who share such a vision. It will only result from a rebirth of the spirit the IWW displayed at its founding meeting in Chicago in 1905 when Eugene V. Debs said, "The Industrial Workers is organized not to conciliate but to fight the capitalist class. . . . The capitalists own the tools they do not use, and the workers use the tools they do not own" (quoted in Kornbluh 1964:1). Bill Haywood was even more blunt in saying that the IWW's goal was to establish an organization to overthrow, rather than negotiate within, the capitalist system and to replace capitalist-class with working-class control of the political economy (quoted in Kornbluh 1964:1). This kind of rebirth will not result from more self-congratulatory conferences, nostalgia for days of yore.

Anthropologists can contribute continued ethnographic observation to try to understand empirically and concretely whether the labor movement is capable of halting its self-destructive infighting to unite in a meaningful social movement that can transcend the personal interests of its leadership.

Unfortunately, anthropologists cannot speak from a position of experience of supporting social justice. Anthropologists who favor economic democracy can become part of the process by supporting the union movement through their professional organizations such as the American Anthropological Association (AAA) and the Society for Applied Anthropology. At the very least, they can use the power of those organizations as purchasers of commodities such as hotel space for meetings to support unions such as UNITE-HERE, as AAA members did in 2004 by canceling their contract with a Hilton hotel in San Francisco because the hotel refused to negotiate with the union.

That was constructive and concerted action. Yet many members feel, like the miners Smith describes, that this action has nothing to do with them, that they are expert workers who cannot be replaced, that they are secure behind their shields of tenure and do not require the support of fellow workers. Many feel they have nothing to do with a class structure or an ideology they perpetuate and re-create with each class they teach.

Archaeologist Dean J. Saitta uses archaeology to restore the memory of the capitalist's appropriation of the state apparatus to massacre workers at Ludlow, Colorado: "The coal mining West is not the West that people want to see or hear about" (2007:91). It is the West the capitalist class would like historians to continue to shroud in the mythologies of individualism, boundless freedom, and wide-open spaces Smith discusses in this volume in place of the realities of a rapacious war on the working class in which, as robber baron Jay Gould boasted, a capitalist could "hire one half of the working class to kill the other." Saitta points out that these processes of capitalism were exacerbated under the Bush administration's assault on labor, knowledge, and memory.

The majority of visitors to the Ludlow monument at the massacre site who expect to learn about an Indian massacre (Saitta 2007:45) are testament to the expurgation of class and class warfare from popular history.

How many of those tourists know that the United States is virtually the only country that does not celebrate Labor Day on May 1 in commemoration of the violence against workers at Chicago's Haymarket that was emblematic of the Progressive Era?

A steel mill executive faced with hard bargaining in contract negotiations complained that workers were still angry about the Ludlow Massacre (Saitta 2007:94). The whole world is still angry about the Haymarket Massacre. It is time Americans caught up and believed what we see in front of our eyes in our daily lives—a long and protracted class war that we are losing whenever we accept the corporate ideology that neo-liberal ideologies, markets, and corporate depravations are natural, inevitable, and necessary. Saitta persuasively argues that it is time academics stopped purveying this ideology in our research, writing, and teaching; that we stop making class and class warfare invisible in our work and teaching and engage the politics of the living.

It is time that we as anthropologists become aware of, and put our collective strength behind, the goals of social justice and stop tolerating our own organizations' decline into triviality and meaningless gestures. In the years since the San Francisco event, the AAA has moved with greater hesitation, has changed a requirement that it meet only in union hotels to a preference for union hotels. The AAA founded a Labor Relations Commission that was immediately pushed to the periphery and out of any decision-making processes. That commission soon became a committee; from the vantage of the fall of 2008, it appears that it is doomed to continuing marginality as it moves toward being moribund.

And so as the labor movement pulls its house down on its head and anthropologists seek privilege and individualist goals, little seems to suggest the possibility of the kind of global social movement that would meaningfully address the significant issues.

While well warranted, this conclusion may be premature. There are gleams of hope, and we think anthropologists can be part of the process of fostering that hope and translating it into collective action.

Longtime labor activists Bill Fletcher and Fernando Gapasin (2008) have argued that besides replacing the corrupt with the incorruptible, the labor movement must move to reclaim a relevant understanding of political economy. Anthropologists can help with our ethnographic and theoretical work. Fletcher and Gapasin further argue that the labor movement should reclaim its role as champion of the working class and of the broader cause of social justice in the United States and around the world. To have this kind of voice, anthropologists would need to stop being timid, carping, and evasive.

The heirs of the IWW, the International Longshore Warehouse Union, and, in Europe, of the anarcho-syndaclists, the Spanish dockworkers, the Norwegians and British, and other dockers who formed the International Dockworkers Council have successfully resisted the neo-liberal revolution. They are maintaining this tradition with due vigilance, waiting for the day when the rest of their countries join them in a worldwide social movement focused on liberty and justice for all. Suzan Erem and Paul Durrenberger tell that story in *On the Global Waterfront: The Fight to Free the Charleston 5* (2008). They see their analysis and their writing as part of the process, as Saitta's is. We invite other anthropologists to join us in these efforts.

The chapters collected in this book are a start.

References Cited

Benson, Herman

2005 *Rebels, Reformers, & Racketeers: How Insurgents Transformed the Labor Movement.* Amherst: Association for Union Democracy.

Brodkin, Karen

2007 *Making Democracy Matter: Identity and Activism in Los Angeles.* New Brunswick, NJ: Rutgers University Press.

Durrenberger, E. Paul, and Suzan Erem

2005 *Class Acts: An Anthropology of Urban Service Workers and Their Union.* Boulder: Paradigm.

Erem, Suzan

2001 *Labor Pains: Inside America's New Union Movement.* New York: Monthly Review Press.

Erem, Suzan, and E. Paul Durrenberger

2008 *On the Global Waterfront: The Fight to Free the Charleston 5.* New York: Monthly Review Press.

Fletcher, Bill, and Fernando Gapasin

2008 *Solidarity Divided: The Crisis in Organized Labor and a New Path toward Social Justice.* Berkeley: University of California Press.

Kornbluh, Joyce L.

1964 *Rebel Voices: An I.W.W. Anthology.* Ann Arbor: University of Michigan Press.

Mills, C. Wright
1951 *White Collar: The American Middle Classes*. New York: Oxford University Press.

Parker, Mike, and Martha Gruelle
1999 *Democracy Is Power: Rebuilding Unions from the Bottom Up*. Detroit: Labor Notes.

Saitta, Dean J.
2007 *The Archaeology of Collective Action*. Gainesville: University Press of Florida.

Zlolniski, Christian
2006 *Janitors, Street Vendors, and Activists: The Lives of Mexican Immigrants in Silicon Valley*. Berkeley: University of California Press.

Contributors

KAREN BRODKIN teaches anthropology and women's studies at UCLA. She writes about race, gender, and social movements in the United States. Her latest book is *Making Democracy Matter: Identity and Activism in Los Angeles* (Rutgers, 2007). She is finishing a book on an environmental justice struggle in southeast Los Angeles.

E. PAUL DURRENBERGER is a professor of anthropology at Penn State University. He has written numerous academic papers and books in the last decade, mainly on labor issues. With Suzan Erem, he wrote an introductory text, *Anthropology Unbound: A Field Guide to the 21st Century* (Paradigm, 2007) and *Class Acts: An Anthropology of Service Workers and Their Union* (Paradigm, 2005). He is married to Suzan Erem.

SUZAN EREM is a free-lance writer. She has worked as a union organizer in Iowa, New Jersey, and Chicago, Illinois. She was director of communications for one of Chicago's largest SEIU locals. She is the author of *Labor Pains: Inside America's New Union Movement* (Monthly Review Press, 2001) and, with Paul Durrenberger, of *On the Global Waterfront: The Fight to Save the Charleston 5* (Monthly Review Press, 2008).

MARTY OTAÑEZ is an assistant professor in the Anthropology Department at the University of Colorado at Denver. He produced the videos *Up in Smoke* (2003), about tobacco farmers and global tobacco companies in Malawi, and *120,000 Lives* (2005; co-produced with Stanton Glantz), about smoking in youth-rated movies. He operates the blog sidewalkradio.net.

KARALEAH REICHART received her PhD in anthropology from Northwestern University in 2000. She is an adjunct assistant professor of anthropology at the University of North Carolina, Chapel Hill. She was a Rockefeller Fellow at the Center for the Study of Ethnicity and Gender in Appalachia in 2001 and continues to conduct research on women's community activism, social justice, and class consciousness.

PETER RICHARDSON has a PhD from the University of Michigan and lives outside Seattle.

LYDIA SAVAGE is an associate professor of geography and chair of the Department of Geography-Anthropology at the University of Southern Maine. She earned her BA in geography from the University of California, Berkeley, and her MA and PhD in geography from Clark University. A former member of the International Association of Machinists, she is currently a member of the Associated Faculties of the University of Maine System, MEA/NEA.

JESSICA SMITH is a PhD candidate in socio-cultural anthropology at the University of Michigan and a former pre-doctoral fellow at the Alfred P. Sloan Center for the Ethnography of Everyday Life. Her dissertation investigates gender, kinship, and labor in northeastern Wyoming coal mining communities. In particular, she studies the ways analytic divisions between home and workplaces, affective and instrumental action, and feminine and masculine persons have been mapped onto ethnographies of mining communities, anthropological theories of kinship and work, and the emerging field of feminist technology studies.

SANDY SMITH-NONINI is a research assistant professor of anthropology at the University of North Carolina, Chapel Hill. She has conducted engaged research on immigrant labor in North Carolina since 1998 and helped found a Unitarian-Universalist community education project on farm labor. She just completed *Healing the Body Politic*, a book on struggles over health rights in El Salvador (Rutgers University Press, forthcoming). Prior to attending graduate school, she worked as a journalist based in Central America.

CHRISTIAN ZLOLNISKI is an assistant professor of anthropology at the University of Texas at Arlington. He is the author of *Janitors, Street Vendors, and Activists: The Lives of Mexican Immigrants in Silicon Valley* (University of California Press, 2006). His research interests revolve around issues of economic globalization, transnational labor migration, and forms of collective resistance.

Index